GEMS O

The Tales of the Ningbobang Told Through Historical Artifacts

F TIME

拾珍

藏品里的宁波帮

宁波博物院（宁波帮博物馆）编

宁波出版社
NINGBO PUBLISHING HOUSE

《拾珍：藏品里的宁波帮》编辑委员会

主　　编　张　亮

副 主 编　施小蓓　李忠学

执　　笔　陈　茹　康京京　丁悠初　徐克天

藏品摄影　丁悠初

序 Introduction

宁波帮是有着深厚家国情怀和不懈奋斗精神的地域人文群体，在不同时代不同领域，做出了不凡建树，与时代同行，与社会共进。

2009年10月22日，作为宁波市“十一五”重点文化建设项目的宁波帮博物馆建成开馆。宁波帮博物馆通过系统展示明末至今宁波帮艰苦奋斗、玉汝于成的发展史诗，弘扬宁波帮的财智文化、桑梓情怀，营造“情感地标、精神家园”，倡导寻根谒祖、慎终追远的人文主题。在城市发展层面，宁波帮博物馆通过打造宁波城市的“金名片”、城市地缘的“情感源”、广大民众认可的“城市客厅”，借由弘扬宁波帮人文精神，传承城市文脉，坚定城市文化自信，助推宁波文化软实力提升。

藏品征集是博物馆的一项基本业务，为多项工作提供实物来源和支撑。作为抢救、挖掘、整理、保护、展示宁波帮珍贵史料、实物的有效平台，宁波帮博物馆自筹建伊始，就于全球范围开启了宁波帮史料、实物的征集工作，不仅实现了藏品的从无到有，更感召和吸引了诸多乡贤和家族多次捐赠珍贵史料、实物，并亲临博物馆参观。目前，宁波帮博物馆藏品来源90%以上为社会各界无偿捐赠，涉及各历史时期宁波帮人士、家族、优势发展领域、重点发展区域、代表社团组织等，这些

Ningbo has always had a knack for good business. It's something the city has given to the world via the Ningbobang, the city's community of business people living abroad. The group embodies a deeply rooted sense of patriotism, as well as an unyielding spirit of perseverance. Over the course of several centuries, they have made noteworthy contributions to society, propelling positive progress.

Inaugurated on October 22, 2009, Ningbobang Museum stands as a cultural cornerstone of Ningbo's 11th Five-Year Plan. Far beyond a mere repository, the museum weaves a compelling narrative of the Ningbobang's arduous journey and triumphant evolution from the late Ming Dynasty to the present. Going beyond a conventional display, it aspires to serve as a significant emotional touchstone for people of Ningbo origin worldwide, inspiring them to celebrate their history and ancestors. The museum also contributes to elevating Ningbo's cultural influence by serving as an emotionally charged urban hub and a universally embraced communal space.

At the heart of the museum's essence lies careful curation, a fundamental practice that provides tangible sources and sustenance for diverse initiatives. Since its inception, Ningbobang Museum has embarked on a global quest to collect meaningful historical artifacts. The collection has notably grown, with 90% contributed by the Ningbobang members through generous donations. These items represent various

藏品不仅凝聚着宁波帮艰苦奋斗、诚信务实、情系家国、回馈桑梓的历史记忆，也彰显着他们在促进宁波发展、国家富强、民族复兴等方面做出的努力与贡献。

经过十余年的发展，宁波帮博物馆实现了藏品征集在广度和深度上的跨越式发展，构建起独具特色的藏品征集工作模式，形成了具有一定规模的藏品体系。来自海内外宁波帮的捐赠，寄寓了这一群体“回乡”“叶落归根”的情感，从这个意义上讲，宁波帮博物馆的藏品具有超过物品本身价值的情感价值，是维系地域传统和家国情怀的重要纽带；社会层面的捐赠，亦见证着各界人士对“宁波帮”这一地域人文主题、对宁波文化事业发展的关注与支持。

多年来，宁波帮博物馆深耕学术研究，立足博物馆主题的特殊性，依托藏品资源和大量史料，针对性地开展研究、展示、教育等相关工作。这本《拾珍——藏品里的宁波帮》，便是基于馆藏资源所开展的专门研究。全书分为“发展史迹”和“人文传承”两大篇章，通过挖掘藏品背后的故事，从宁波帮历史和人文特质两个层面，为读者提供走近、了解宁波帮的生动路径。而在博物馆发展层面，这本书凝聚了当下对于“宁波帮”这一概念的思考和探索，同时，也借由结集成册的形式，向海内外宁波帮及社会各界的关注与支持致以诚挚谢意。因体例及容量所限，本书无法涵盖所有藏品，请各界捐赠人见谅。希冀以此为契机，在海内外宁波帮及社会各界的支持下，进一步丰富馆藏资源，让宁波帮博物馆这座全世界宁波人的“情感地标、精神家园”能够更深入、更广泛地去讲述宁波帮历史，阐释宁波帮精神，加深宁波人文底蕴。

historical eras, significant Ningbo families, sectors involving Ningbo businesspeople, and organizations representing Ningbo people. They encapsulate not only the historical saga of the Ningbobang's perseverance, integrity, and patriotic endeavors but also underscore the community's pivotal role in propelling Ningbo's development, fortifying China's prosperity, and fueling the rejuvenation of the Chinese nation.

Over the past decade, Ningbobang Museum has undergone a transformative journey, expanding both in breadth and depth. It has forged a distinctive model for artifact acquisition, giving rise to a vast collection. Donations from the Ningbobang members worldwide symbolize a form of "homecoming" for those residing overseas, carrying a distinctive sentimental value that surpasses the material worth of the objects themselves. These donations serve as a vital conduit in preserving regional traditions and nurturing patriotic sentiments. They also attest to broad societal support for the Ningbobang and the growing cultural sector of Ningbo.

Throughout the years, Ningbobang Museum has been a crucible for academic inquiry, leveraging its vast collection and historical archives. Rooted in its distinctive thematic focus, the museum conducts research, orchestrates exhibitions, and delivers public learning programs. *Gems of Time: The Tales of the Ningbobang Told Through Historical Artifacts*, a catalog of the museum's collection in two chapters (*History* and *Legacy*), unveils the narratives behind each artifact, providing readers with a vivid and insightful journey into the Ningbobang history. Additionally, it artfully captures the museum's reflections on the significance of the Ningbobang identity, while serving as an expression of gratitude to the community and all those who have supported our endeavors. Owing to the inherent restrictions in structure and size, this volume cannot accommodate all of the items we wish to showcase. We extend our sincerest apologies to our supporters. It is our earnest hope that this endeavor might pave the way, through the unwavering support of the Ningbobang and kindred spirits from across the globe, for a more substantial augmentation of our collection.

目 CONTENTS 录

发展史迹

HISTORY

003 / Origins in Ningbo

027 / Expansion in Shanghai

人文传承

LEGACY

文化类

Culture

发展史迹

HISTORY

宁波地域

Origins in Ningbo

甬江入海口明信片

Postcard Depicting the Yong River's Estuary

19 世纪末

27.0 cm × 20.0 cm

郑介初捐赠 Acquired from Zheng Jiechu through donation

这张明信片描绘了 19 世纪末镇海甬江入海口商船往来、贸易繁盛的景象。

甬江，古称大浃江，是中国浙江省宁波市境内的一条入海河流，浙江省八大水系之一，被誉为宁波的“母亲河”。通常所说的甬江，指的是姚江和奉化江在宁波市中心三江口汇合直至镇海口入海的下游河段。甬江是浙东运河入海前的最后一段河道，历史上曾在漕粮海运中起到重要作用，也曾沟通内陆和海上丝绸之路。甬江口曾发生的一系列战事给宁波带来动荡，但同时，宁波的近代化也从甬江畔开始。

This postcard depicts a bustling trade port at the estuary of Yong River, present day Zhenhai district, Ningbo, at the end of the 19th century.

The Yong River, formerly known as Dajia River, flows into the East China Sea through the city of Ningbo in eastern China's Zhejiang Province. It is one of the eight major waterways in the province, and is often referred to as Ningbo's "mother river".

The river has seen peace, connecting grain and cargo to sea trading routes; and violence, with many armed conflicts having taken place in the waters of the estuary throughout history.

“鄞县”五两银锞

Five-Tael Silver Ingot With “Yin Xian” Inscription

清代

直径 4.7 cm × 2.7 cm

储建国捐赠 Acquired from Chu Jianguo through donation

宁波本土金融业从钱庄起步，宁波钱庄业大约兴起于 16 世纪中叶至 17 世纪初叶。到了清乾嘉年间（1736—1820），宁波商业繁荣所带来的货币大流通使江厦街成为以经营钱业为主的“钱行街”。宁波钱庄业创造的过账制度，使得各行各业与钱庄的交往不用现金，而以过账方式进行，方便了手续，推动了信贷的发展，也翻开了中国近代金融史的扉页。

到了清末和民国，宁波钱庄业迎来黄金时代，通过形成巨大的存、放、汇一体的业务网，有力地支持了宁波帮群体在外埠的发展。同时，宁波帮率先把近代银行、保险、信托、证券等新型金融模式引入中国，相继创办了国内首家商业银行、上海首家证券交易所及首家保险公司，对近代上海金融中心的形成起到了巨大的推动作用。

这枚清代圆形五两银锞上刻有“鄞县”“玖年”和“徐璋”三个戳记，表明了银锞的出处、制造时间以及工匠的姓名。

Ningbo's financial sector had its origins in *qianzhuang*, “money shops” run by private owners that provided banking services from the mid-16th century to the early 17th century. In the 18th century, Ningbo's bustling commerce led to a significant increase of currency circulation and the establishment of numerous *qianzhuang* along Jiangxia Road. The innovative accounting system introduced by Ningbo's *qianzhuang* made their dealings with local businesses more convenient, as it eliminated the need for physical coins and allowed for transactions through bookkeeping. This system furthered the development of lending services and marked the beginning of modern finance in China.

In the early 1900s, the final years of the Qing Dynasty and the early Republican era, Ningbo's *qianzhuang* thrived, creating an extensive network for deposits, loans, and currency exchange. This network proved invaluable as the Ningbo business community expanded its presence throughout China.

This circular five-tael silver ingot from the Qing Dynasty bears three inscriptions on its surface: “Yin Xian”, “Jiu Nian”, and “Xu Zhang”, signifying its origin, production year, and the craftsman's name.

严信厚芦雁团扇扇面

Fan Painted with Wild Goose and Reeds by Yan Xinhou

清代

33.5 cm × 28.0 cm

严国荣捐赠 Acquired from Yan Guorong through donation

该芦雁图是严信厚为上海籍画家沈锡龄所作，绢本淡设色。题有“迢递关山计客程，湘云湘水动离情。夜深都傍芦花宿，三十六湾夜月明”一诗。款识：“仿边颐公并缮其诗。介眉尊兄大人方家正之。小舫弟严经邦作于甬上。”钤“经邦”白文印。

严信厚（1838—1906），原名严经邦，字筱（小）舫，号石泉居士，宁波慈溪人。清末著名实业家、书法家、画家。严信厚善作芦汀雁渚图，画面大多简约岑寂，落纸有风。

1902 年，严信厚创立上海商业会议公所（即后来有“天下第一商会”之称的上海总商会的前身）并任总理，成为中国近代商会组织的开创者。该会成立后多方参与上海乃至全国的内政、外交事务，颇有执全国商界牛耳之势。作为上海总商会的首任经理，严信厚在沪期间，通过数十年的金融及工商业活动，把一大批宁波商人吸引到自己周围，并使得宁波帮在金融及工商界的势力声名远播，被誉为宁波帮先驱。

This painting was created by Yan Xinhou for the Shanghai-based artist Shen Xiling.

Yan Xinhou (1838-1906), originally named Yan Jingbang, courtesy name Xiaofang, literary name Shiquan Jushi, was a prominent industrialist, calligrapher, and painter from Cixi, Ningbo. He was known for his skilled paintings of reeds and wild geese, characterized by their simplicity and subdued beauty.

镇海柤墅方家红丝砚

"Red Silk" Inkstone Owned by Zhenhai's Jiushu Fang Family

清代

10.0 cm × 8.0 cm × 3.0 cm

钱维多捐赠 Acquired from Qian Weiduo through donation

该砚台采用红丝石制作而成，质地温润，配以木盒，上刻“镇海柤墅方　甲戌夏”字样，为清代柤墅方家专用。根据“甲戌夏”推测为1874年，当时正值柤墅方家第二代在钱庄业发展的鼎盛时期。从砚台的尺寸来看，该砚便于随身携带，需签字和填数时取出，作为笔舔使用。

镇海柤墅方家是宁波帮中最负盛名的家族之一。清末民初，柤墅方家除主营钱庄业务外，还经营多种商业，包括糖业、沙船、银楼、丝绸、药材等，活动范围以上海为中心，覆盖天津、南京、汉口、重庆以及浙江的宁波、绍兴、杭州、湖州等地，是当时名闻江南的家族工商集团。从这款砚台中，也可一窥柤墅方家叱咤商界的峥嵘岁月。

This inkstone comes with a wooden box bearing the inscription "Zhenhai Jiushu Fang, Jia Xu Xia" (Jiushu Fang family of Zhenhai, Summer of the Jiaxu Year).

The Jiushu Fang family of Zhenhai were an industrious bunch, active in sugar production, sand shipping, silk production, selling of medicinal herbs, and, of course, banking. Their business activities were centered in Shanghai and extended to cities like Tianjin, Nanjing, Hankou, Chongqing, Ningbo, Shaoxing, and Hangzhou. They were a prominent business conglomerate in the Jiangnan region during the Qing Dynasty.

“镇海点梅主人自制”瓷碗、瓷盘

Bowl and Plate Customized for the Owner of Zhenhai Dianmei

晚清

①直径 15.0 cm × 6.0 cm ②直径 19.0 cm × 3.0 cm

李名章捐赠 Acquired from Li Mingzhang through donation

① 瓷碗

② 瓷盘

碗、盘底皆铭款“镇海点梅主人自制”，为小港李氏坤房李梅塘家用定制瓷器。李梅塘（1841—1900），为小港李家基业创始人李也亭的独子。民国《镇海县志》载：“李容子嘉，字梅塘，袭先人遗业，操奇制胜，家资至数百万。与从兄弟源、濂等合资建成养正义庄，规模之宏，为一郡冠。好义勇为，凡沪甬及本邑公益事务，暨输饷、赈灾、浚河、平道等费，前后至十余万金。晚岁构园家中，亭台花木，曲折有致，卒赠荣禄大夫。”

该碗、盘由李梅塘重孙、李征五孙李名章捐赠。李名章，燕京大学毕业，曾任兰州高压阀门厂总工程师，中国通用机械工业协会阀门分会副秘书长兼技术发展部主任，高级工程师。

Bowl and plate both bear the inscription “Customized for the owner of Zhenhai Dianmei”. They were custom-made porcelainware for the family of Li Meitang of Xiaogang. Li Meitang (1841–1900) was the only son of Li Yeting, the *Zhenhai County Annals* describe Li Meitang as a successful businessman who was active in philanthropy and funding public infrastructure.

The bowl and plate were donated by Li Meitang’s great-grandson, Li Mingzhang.

烧炭铁熨斗

Clothing Iron

民国时期

21.0 cm × 9.5 cm × 21.0 cm

金维明捐赠 Acquired from Jin Weiming through donation

明清之际，包袱裁缝在北京成立了成衣会馆，红帮裁缝即起源于此。清乾隆年间，鄞县茅山张家漕人张尚义在日本港口帮助海员缝补救生衣和水手服时学到了制作西装的方法，并在横滨开办了自己的成衣店。回乡后，他从奉化江两岸的鄞南和奉北带去了数批青壮年。孙家漕的孙通江也在日本神户创办了“益泰昌”呢绒洋装店，最早的红帮裁缝队伍就这样形成了。1905 年，根据孙中山等人的意见，鄞县人张方诚设计出最早的一款中山装。1913 年 2 月，南京路上六大家之一的“荣昌祥”创办者奉化人王才运据此改进缝制出中国第一套中山装。可以说，红帮裁缝在历史上掀起了一场服装革命。

During the Ming and Qing dynasties, a number of traveling tailors from Ningbo opened successful clothing shops in Beijing. They were the forerunners of the *Hongbang* tailors, Ningbo tailors renowned for their Western-style suits. In the 18th century, during the reign of Qing Emperor Qianlong (1736-1795), a tailor named Zhang Shangyi, who hailed from Maoshan Village in Yin County, Ningbo, learned how to make Western-style suits while helping sailors mend life jackets and sailor uniforms in a Japanese harbor.

Zhang went on to establish his own garment business in Yokohama. At the same time, the contemporaneous Sun Tongjiang, also from Ningbo, founded the “Yi Tai Chang” woolen suit shop in Kobe, Japan. In 1905, following suggestions from Sun Yat-sen, Yin County-born tailor Zhang Fangcheng designed the earliest version of the Zhongshan suit. In February 1913, Wang Caiyun, a Fenghua native and founder of “Rong Chang Xiang”, one of the six most prominent establishments on Shanghai’s Nanjing Road, improved upon Zhang Fangcheng’s design, producing the first Zhongshan suit as we know it today.

《乾仲房录乾坤房分书稿》

Qianzhongfang Lu Qiankunfang Fenshugao Manuscript

1907 年

18.5 cm × 13.0 cm

李名陆、李维统捐赠 Acquired from Li Minglu and Li Weitong through donation

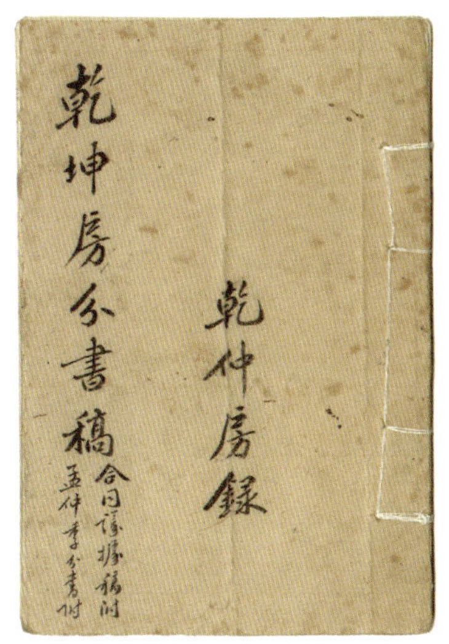

小港李家乾仲房析产书

Xiaogang Li Family Property Division Document

1909 年

26 cm × 15.3 cm × 0.5 cm

李锦捐赠 Acquired from Li Jin through donation

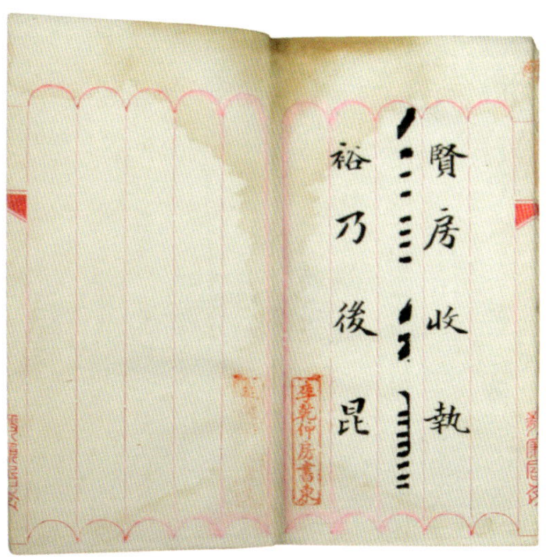

小港李家是宁波帮代表性家族之一。1823 年，时年 15 岁的李也亭（1808—1868）前往上海谋生，后依托沙船贸易起家，创立久大沙船号，开辟久大码头，后建立钱庄，成就家族基业，被誉为家族“发财太公”。其兄长李承辅（弼庵）与李也亭（容）分乾、坤两房，始终伯埙仲篪，同力协契，并建立了家族“不论子侄，只能以能者为劳”“传能不传长”的继承制度，家族产业不断扩大，涉及领域与时偕行。

宁波帮博物馆收藏有李氏家族分书 2 本，一为 1907 年乾坤房分书稿（乾仲房录），一为 1909 年乾仲房析产书。其中乾坤房分书为清光绪二十八年（1902）乾坤二房对家产的析分，分书内包含合同议据、乾坤房分书、孟仲季三部分。乾仲房分书为李濂水为其七子分家立。

The Li family of Xiaogang is one of the most prominent Ningbobang families. In 1823, Li Yeting (1808–1868), who was only 15 years old at the time, went to Shanghai to seek his fortune. He founded the Jiudashachuan Sand Shipping Company, established the Jiuda Wharf, and later started a banking business. All this allowed him to achieve great success in building the family's wealth.

His elder brother Li Chengfu and Li Yeting divided the family into two branches, the Qian line and Kun line. They maintained a harmonious relationship, working together and establishing a family tradition of “reward based on ability, not age”, ensuring that inheritors were chosen for their abilities rather than order of succession. This approach contributed to the continuous expansion of the family's business interests. Ningbobang Museum holds two important documents related to the Li family.

陈宝琛题赠李祖基对联
Calligraphy Work Gifted by Chen Baochen to Li Zuji

1923年

131.6 cm × 30.3 cm

李维绥、李维统、李维绪捐赠 Acquired from Li Weisui, Li Weitong, and Li Weixu through donation

这副楷书七言联曰："满庭诗景飘红叶，旧馆秋阴生绿苔。"题识："癸亥十月陈宝琛。"钤印："陈宝琛印""太傅之章"。上联集自唐代诗人雍陶的《韦处士郊居》，下联集自唐代诗人贾至的《答严大夫》，为一副集句联。

对联的书者陈宝琛（1848—1935），字伯潜，号弢庵，福建闽县（今福州市）人，官至正红旗汉军副都统、弼德院顾问大臣，为宣统帝老师。对联受赠者李祖基（1891—1956），镇海小港李氏坤房李如山（厚祺）之子，历任吉林中国银行经理，张家口、北京、天津等处中国银行副经理，南京、汉口金城银行经理，中国通商银行经理，东南银行总经理等职，终身从事银行金融工作。

该藏品系小港李氏家族后人捐赠。对联落款"癸亥"应为1923年。陈宝琛1922年撰成《德宗实录》，被赏以"太傅"衔，与该联钤有"太傅之章"相吻合。

This pair of couplets reads "The courtyard is adorned with red leaves; the old mansion is covered in autumn moss." The inscription states "Chen Baochen, October of the year Guihai". The seal imprints read "Seal of Chen Baochen" and "Seal of the Grand Tutor".

The calligrapher who wrote the couplets, Chen Baochen (1848-1935, courtesy name Boqian, art name Tao'an) was a native of Min county (now part of Fuzhou), Fujian. He held official positions as Deputy Commander of the Han Army under the Red Banner and Counselor to the Bide Council. He was best known as a private tutor of Emperor Xuantong, or Puyi, the last emperor of China.

The recipient of these couplets, Li Zuji (1891-1956), was the son of Li Rushan (courtesy name Houqi) of Xiaogang, Zhenhai. He dedicated his entire career to banking and finance, holding managerial positions at various local branches of the Bank of China: Jilin, Zhangjiakou, Beijing, and Tianjin. He had also been the manager of the Kincheng Bank in Nanjing and Hankou, manager of the Imperial Bank of China, and general manager at Southeast Bank.

祖基仁兄雅屬

滿庭詩景飄紅葉

舊館秋陰生綠苔

癸亥十月 陳寶琛

《宁波钱业规则》

Regulations for the Banking Industry in Ningbo

1930 年

50.0 cm × 39.0 cm

储建国捐赠 Acquired from Chu Jianguo through donation

金融为百业之首。宁波帮靠着沙船起家，积累资本后创办钱庄。清乾嘉年间，宁波的江厦街形成了以经营钱业为主的“钱行街”，其盛时，资金在六万元以上的大同行有 42 家，一万元以上的小同行有 31 家。

《宁波钱业规则》中明确了钱业经营中的基本规则和违规的相关惩处措施。值得一提的是，钱业规则中明文规定小同行和大同行的处罚措施和力度一视同仁，如若违背或者不遵守规则将会面临全体同行绝交的处罚。宁波钱业注重诚信、规范操作的经营理念可见一斑。

Finance is the pillar of any economy. Several centuries ago, the merchants of Ningbo, using the capital they had accumulated from the sand shipping business, opened a number of highly successful *qianzhuang*, privately-run “money shops” offering banking services.

The *Regulations for the Banking Industry in Ningbo* served as a code of ethics for banks operating in the city. It clearly outlined the consequences for violations, with penalties applied uniformly to both small and large banks. One of the most severe penalties was the possibility of being ostracized by the entire guild. This is one example the strong emphasis Ningbo’s banking community placed on integrity and adherence to rules.

寧波錢業規則

一議規元進出壹千兩以上每百兩加手續費起碼壹分未滿壹千兩者每百兩加手續費起碼貳分

一議小同行公所拆進單銀歸同行轉賬欠息加貳分計算

一議凡主客進出現洋照市升減每百元取手續費五分

一議客帮收解無利不能補期有利補拆不補期如遇風雨局班延期則挨期補理之

一議如遇主客臨時計款放款家必須半月內報告本公會委員常會追認如認爲有違背莊規者得令其取消之倘低價私放隱瞞不報察出公議處分

一議姚帮收解以壹百元起碼

一議規元評盤如遇照前一日上落離半率之巨報告司年後再評

一議規元進出落地照匯

一議同業逐日申銀匯賬彼此抑有錯匯等情不得作還賬論銀拆照補

一議同業論派司年一莊凡遇公共事務由司年承值之

一議本埠及外埠各主客往來票貼最少以貳錢起碼

一議往來欠息每千元每天照洋拆加壹角貳分半算欠銀每千兩每月照申甬轉加四兩五錢算惟欠銀如遇甬市特別情形另行酌議提加違者照公議罰則處分之

一議各種押款利息至少每月每千元照日拆加叁元七角半算如係長期不得少於本期洋盤議價違者照公議罰則處分之

一議蘇杭紹同行欠息每千元每天照洋拆加五分算違者照公議罰則處分之

一議小同行上內牌入會館者欠息照拆起碼加四分算上外牌現兌莊欠息甲組照拆起碼加七分半算乙組照拆起碼加九分算丙組照拆起碼加壹角算違者照公議罰則處分之

一議長期盤價每期於起期前兩天由本公會召集會員會議決行之未議之前不得預放既議之後不得亂盤並不得陽奉陰違照欠息私放過年欠戶除擱戶呆戶外其欠數滿千元者須照雙對計實不得浮欠過年違者照公議罰則處分之

一議洋盤除公共議放外不得再有長期名目違者照公議罰則處分之

一議中途如有新開同業開放紅盤應定盤價由該莊酌定報告本公會召集會員會議決後照放各莊新用朋友所放紅盤其盤價不得低於公共議放之大盤議價違者照公議罰則處分之

一議凡客埠及各鄉鎮託解外項之款或解同行入外項之賬付賬須追前一天惟本轉本劃不在此例此乃客路對客路而言若客路對本街外項本轉本劃仍須追前一天如在洋拆寄棧期間免除早付但每千元取手續費壹角五分違者照公議罰則處分之

一議各主客代收票款班遲一天收賬如遇上即即過之票須早付一天如在洋拆寄棧期間免除遲收早付但每千元取手續費一角五分違者照公議罰則處分之

一議各客帮及鄉鎮主客上票十二月一日起年終止概歸見票付賬違者照公議罰則處分之

一議一月間未開市之前各主客如計規元務須按日記賬違者照公議罰則處分之

一議十月份起同業如放本街外項銀盤應先期召集會員會議定盤價在未議定以前不得私放議定之後不得亂盤違者照公議罰則處分之

一議小同行對客帮各鄉鎮及本街主客議規罰款一切照大同行辦理如有違背照議處罰或有不遵全體同行絕交

一議自己巳年爲始新立同業行公會章程規則坐簿两本一存公會一存司年以資備查

民國十九年　訂

俞明仿陈洪绶麻姑献寿图轴

Yu Ming's Imitation of Chen Hongshou's *Goddess Ma Gu Offering Longevity Peaches*

1930 年

143.0 cm × 39.7 cm

李名陆捐赠 Acquired from Li Minglu through donation

此图轴为俞明（1884—1935）贺李詠裳六十寿作。释文：“詠裳先生六旬双庆属画寿意，为仿陈章侯笔意，率成麻姑献寿一图奉乞，大雅正之。老莲画法取唐宋之精华，参于己意而化之，自成一格。布局恢奇，参差有序，其用笔也圆而劲，赋色也古而艳，有明以来无出其右者。余深嗜也。奈学力腕力相去万万，神似愧难耳。”款识：“庚午端阳前二日归安俞明。”

李詠裳（1871—1953），字厚垣，李濂水之子。按照家族产业开创者李也亭“能者为继”的遗训，在其伯父李听涛手中接管家业。李詠裳顺应时局，创办了许多新兴产业，例如，将李家赖以发迹的久大沙船号注册登记为“新记营运股份有限公司”，实行新式的股份制管理模式，使李家跻身上海钱庄业九大家族之列，同时创办或参与了现代性金融机构——正华商业银行、恒利银行和中华劝业银行，成立了天丰、地丰、元丰、黄丰 4 家地产公司，兴办电气公司、机器榨油厂、薄荷提炼厂等现代工业。

This scroll was created by Yu Ming (1884-1935) to celebrate the 60th birthday of Li Yongshang. The inscription states "By Yu Ming of Gui'an County, painted two days before Dragon Boat Festival in the Gengwu year."

Li Yongshang (1871-1953), courtesy name Houyuan, was the son of Li Lianshui, a successful businessman. He was one of the pioneers of modern industry in China, having founding numerous firms and companies, including shipping companies, real estate companies, banks, and chemical refineries.

贝时璋和程亦明的订婚凭证、结婚请帖

Engagement Certificate and Wedding Invitation of Bei Shizhang and Cheng Yiming

1931 年

① 17.4 cm × 13.3 cm ② 14.1 cm × 8.9 cm

袁兴光捐赠 Acquired from Yuan Xingguang through donation

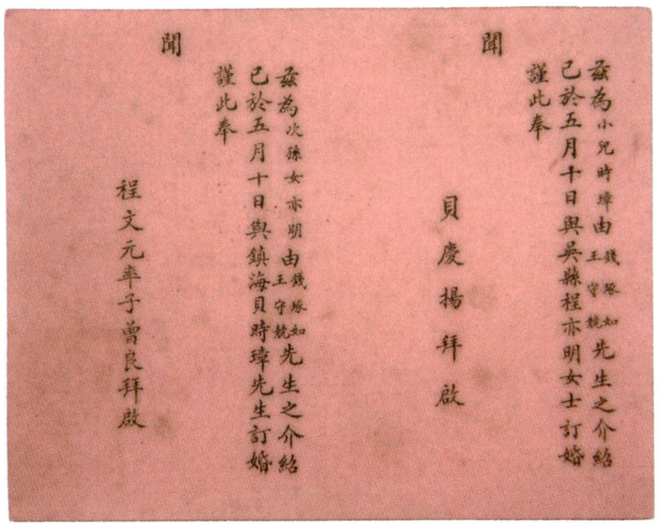

茲為小兒時璋由錢琢如王守競先生之介紹
已於五月十日與吳縣程亦明女士訂婚
謹此奉
聞
貝慶揚拜啟

茲為次孫女亦明由錢琢如王守競先生之介紹
已於五月十日與鎮海貝時璋先生訂婚
謹此奉
聞
程文元率子曾良拜啟

① 订婚凭证

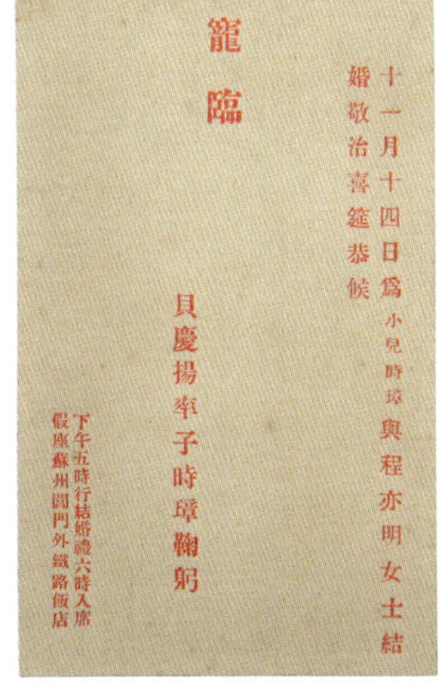

十一月十四日為小兒時璋與程亦明女士結
婚敬治喜筵恭候
寵臨
貝慶揚率子時璋鞠躬
下午五時行結婚禮六時入席
假座蘇州閶門外鐵路飯店

② 结婚请帖

贝时璋（1903.10—2009.10），生物学家，中国科学院院士，中国生物物理学奠基人和开拓者。毕生热爱科学，致力于祖国科学事业发展，捐资设立贝时璋奖、贝时璋青年生物物理学家奖。国际编号 36015 号的小行星被命名为“贝时璋星”。

1903 年 10 月 10 日，贝时璋出生于宁波镇海憩桥镇，祖辈靠打鱼为生，父亲是德商洋行的一位职员。贝时璋 12 岁随父亲外出求学，先在汉口的德华学校学习，后到上海的同济医工专门学校德文科读中学。1921 年至 1929 年，贝时璋留学德国，于 1929 年秋回国。1931 年 11 月，贝时璋与苏州振华女中教师程亦明女士结婚。

该订婚凭证、结婚请帖系在贝时璋祖居发现，是其人生的重要见证物。

Bei Shizhang (1903.10-2009.10) was a biologist, a member of the Chinese Academy of Sciences, and a pioneer in the field of biophysics in China. He devoted his entire life to promoting scientific development in China, and even established the Bei Shizhang Award and the Bei Shizhang Young Biophysicist Award. An asteroid with the international designation number 36015 was named in his honor.

Born in 1903, Bei Shizhang came from a family of fishermen. At the age of 12, he began his educational journey, initially studying at the German School in Hankou and later attending the German-language section of Tongji Medical and Engineering School in Shanghai.

Between 1921 and 1929, Bei Shizhang pursued his studies in Germany, returning to China in the autumn of 1929. In November 1931, he married Cheng Yiming, a teacher at Suzhou Zhenhua Girls' School.

The engagement certificate and wedding invitation were discovered in Bei Shizhang's ancestral home.

乌统旸的浙东中学修业证明书

Wu Tongyang's Certificate of Completion from East Zhejiang Middle School

1941 年

26.3 cm × 18.8 cm

乌蔚庭捐赠 Acquired from Wu Weiting through donation

修業證明書

學生烏統暘係浙江省鄞縣人現年

拾叁歲在本校初中秋壹年級第貳

學期肄業期滿持此證明

浙江省鄞縣私立浙東中學校長

中華民國三十年六月 日

该证明书为 1941 年 6 月，鄞县人乌统旸在浙江省鄞县私立浙东中学初中秋一年级第二学期的肄业期满证明书。

1941 年 4 月 20 日，日军占领宁波，宁波沦陷。当时，乌统旸正在私立浙东中学读初中一年级的第二学期。在日军侵袭的情况下，学校暂时解散，除给学生退回学费和食宿费外，还给每名学生发了一张修业证明书。乌统旸一生辗转多地，却一直将该证件带在身边妥善保存，直至耄耋之年回乡，将它与见证其求学、助学的一系列珍贵史料一并捐赠给宁波帮博物馆。

乌统旸（1928—2014），后改名乌蔚庭，生于宁波。乌蔚庭年少时辗转求学，曾就读于宁波星荫小学、浙东中学、明州中学、鄞县县立中学等，后于台湾大学求学。1955 年，他前往美国攻读研究员，完成硕士、博士学位，并一直在美国生活。乌蔚庭虽身居海外，但始终关注祖国、家乡教育事业的发展，以并不丰厚的收入慷慨捐资助学，设立多个奖助学金。曾在宁波大学成立帮助贫困大学生的助学基金，建立实验室。得知贵州少数民族地区教育事业的困难后，他又在贵州兴义捐资建校。

This certificate, dated June 1941, belongs to Wu Tongyang, a resident of Yin County. It certifies his completion of the second semester of the first year of junior high at the private East Zhejiang Middle School in Yin County, Zhejiang Province.

Wu Tongyang (1928-2014), later known as Wu Weiting, was born in Ningbo. In 1955, he went to the United States for advanced studies, earning his master's and doctoral degrees, and lived the rest of his life in the US. Despite living abroad, Wu was a generous donor to China's education sector. He established multiple scholarships and financial aid programs with his modest income, including one at Ningbo University. Wu even sponsored a laboratory at the same university. Upon learning about the lack of educational access in Guizhou's ethnic minority communities, he funded a new school in Xingyi, Guizhou.

“鹤范堂胡”甬式食篮

Ningbo-Style Food Basket

民国时期

直径 33.0 cm × 43.0 cm

胡运熹、胡运焕捐赠 Acquired from Hu Yunxi and Hu Yunhuan through donation

该食篮为两格，篮身髹以朱红漆，提篮刻有各式花纹。食篮，在宁波又称冰盆篮，采用篾青劈细锉光手艺精工编制而成，一般为宁波殷实人家所用。平日赠送附近亲友一两盘小菜或面点之类，常用此篮，利于手提而行。

篮盖上写有“鹤范堂胡”字样，“鹤”“范”两字指胡氏家族胡访鹤、胡立范父子二人。胡立范曾任上海华记洋行经理，是一名非常出色的宁波籍买办。1843 年上海开埠后，早期的宁波帮商人凭借着敏锐的商业嗅觉，迅速投身于对外贸易领域，取得了巨大的成功，从而确立了其产业在近代中国经济中心上海的重要地位。

This is a dual-compartment food basket coated in vibrant red lacquer, its handle adorned with intricately engraved patterns. The basket was expertly crafted using finely cut and polished bamboo bark strips. Its lid bears an inscription “He Fan Tang Hu.” “He” and “Fan” denote two members of the Hu family, specifically Hu Fanghe and his son Hu Lifan. Hu Lifan had been a manager at the Shanghai Hua Ji Foreign Trading Company and was a successful comprador from Ningbo.

宁波《市情日刊》

Ningbo *Market Daily* Newspaper

民国时期

27.5 cm × 26.0 cm

王天杨捐赠 Acquired from Wang Tianyang through donation

民国时期，宁波《市情日刊》每日印发钱业相关市场行情和各类商业广告，集中反映了宁波与上海以及全国各地之间的一些汇兑信息。

贸易催生金融，素以贸易著称的宁波是中国钱庄最早出现的地区。到清代，钱庄业的发展使宁波成为中国东南地区的金融中心。清乾隆五年（1740）以后的 100 多年中宁波钱庄业集中开设在江厦一带，故有宁波谚语“走遍天下，不及宁波江厦”。宁波钱庄业实行“大同行、小同行、现兑店”分类制度，成立了最早的钱业公会组织，目前位于宁波战船街 10 号的宁波钱业会馆是现存最为完好的会馆建筑之一，也是全国唯一保存完整的钱庄业历史文化遗迹。

近代开埠后，宁波钱庄与时偕行，不断进行以过账制度为代表的变革与创新，努力推动钱庄业近代化进程，从而在各地社会经济生活，特别是近代上海发展成为全国金融中心中发挥了重要作用，同时也为宁波商帮的发展壮大乃至称雄商界提供了强有力的金融支持。

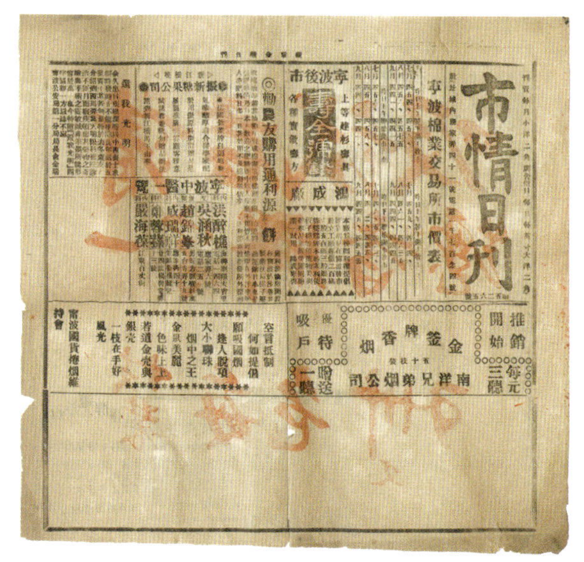
市情日刊

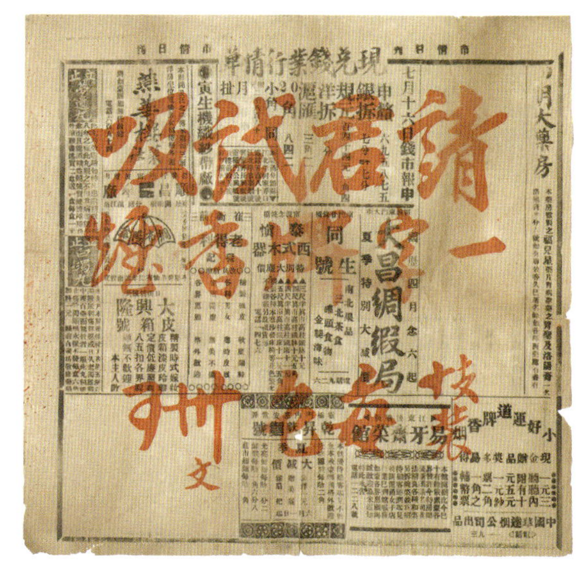

During China's Republican era, Ninbgo's *Market Daily* newspaper published daily updates on the city's banking scene, alongside commercial advertisements. It provided valuable financial insights covering not only Ningbo but also Shanghai and various cities across China.

As Ningbo had become a treaty port in the 1800s, the city's *qianzhuang* continued to adapt and transform, notably by adopting the practice of posting in accounting. This evolution played a pivotal role in modernizing banking in Ningbo. Ultimately, Ningbo's banking success contributed the expansion of the city's far reaching business community. It also played a crucial part in the socioeconomic growth of the city's surrounding regions, particularly Shanghai, which went on to become a national financial center.

宁波恒丰染织厂广告画

Advertisement Flyers for Ningbo Hengfeng Printing and Dyeing Mill

民国时期

① 24.0 cm × 21.0 cm　② 23.0 cm × 17.0 cm　③ 23.0 cm × 17.5 cm

刘方川捐赠 Acquired from Liu Fangchuan through donation

五四运动后，国人反帝爱国热情高涨，喊出了“外争国权”的口号，提倡国货，抵制洋货。在这一形势下，宁波的早期民族工业得到了发展良机。

开设于 1928 年的恒丰印染织厂，由裕成棉布号经理王稼瑞等人经营。建厂伊始，以生产有线呢、条子漂白布等低档棉布为主。随着设备的更新和技术的进步，推出高档印染花布，畅销沪甬等地。20 世纪 30 年代，王稼瑞在上海法租界马当路开设分厂，出产“金榜乐”士林兰布，“九恒”毛蓝、元色哔叽、“恒丰塔”与“五子夺魁”等花色布，以宁波为中心转销内陆地区，产品风行一时。1953 年底，恒丰印染织厂实行公私合营。1966 年，改名为宁波印染织厂。

Founded in 1928, the Hengfeng Printing and Dyeing Mill was managed by Wang Jiarui, a business manager at the Yucheng Cotton Company. Initially, the mill primarily produced basic cotton fabrics such as plain clothes and bleached cloth. However, as the company upgraded its equipment and technology, it began producing high-quality printed and dyed fabrics that gained popularity in Ningbo and even Shanghai.

During the 1930s, Wang Jiarui established a production facility in Shanghai's French Concession on Madang Road, producing a range of sought-after textiles, including Indanthrene-dyed, woolen, serge, and patterned fabrics. These products gained immense popularity and were distributed from Ningbo to customers all across China. By the end of 1953, Hengfeng Printing and Dyeing Mill had transitioned into a publicly and privately owned joint enterprise. In 1966, it was renamed the Ningbo Printing and Dyeing Mill.

①

②

③

镇宁商轮公司“对客联票”木印章

Zhenning Merchant Shipping Company's Wooden Stamp for Tickets

民国时期

5.0 cm × 2.0 cm × 4.2 cm

沈天祥捐赠 Acquired from Shen Tianxiang through donation

该印章为镇宁商轮公司所用，馆藏若干，分木、牛角两种质地，印鉴内容有“对客联票”“镇宁商轮信缄”“镇宁商轮回单”“统舱”“认捐”“乙丑”。

20世纪20年代，航行于宁波至舟山群岛主要岛屿之间的轮船公司有两家，分别是东海轮船公司和镇宁商轮公司，两家各有一艘200余吨的轮船。镇宁商轮公司于民国十二年（1923）通航，航线为宁波—沈家门—岱山—衢山—象山—黄岩。

In the 1920s, there were two shipping companies operating between Ningbo and the main islands of the Zhoushan Archipelago: the Donghai Shipping Company and the Zhenning Merchant Shipping Company. Each had a 200-ton ship. The Zhenning Merchant Shipping Company started its operations in 1923 with a route that included Ningbo, Shenjiamen, Daishan, Qushan, Xiangshan, and Huangyan.

楼茂记牌匾

Lou Mao Ji Storefront Sign

民国时期

194.0 cm × 83.0 cm × 8.0 cm

楼茂记集团捐赠 Acquired from Lou Mao Ji Group through donation

楼茂记，全称“楼恒盛茂记酱园”，始创于清乾隆八年（1743），以经营具有江南风味特色的各档花色酱菜，以及醋、酱油、香干、鲜麸、黄酒等产品为主。其秘制的楼茂记香干，因色香味俱佳而尤为出名。楼茂记距今已有近 300 年历史，不仅代表了宁波帮历久弥新的商道传承，也蕴含着宁波人柴房灶间的温馨回忆。

Founded in the 8th year of the Qianlong Emperor's reign (1743), Lou Mao Ji specializes in producing pickled vegetables, pressed tofu, vinegar, soy sauce, and yellow wine. One of their most renowned products is Lou Mao Ji pressed tofu, which is made from a secret recipe. With its nearly 300 years of history, Lou Mao Ji represents the enduring traditions of the Ningbo merchants.

宁波大昌祥“真不二价”广告纸

Flyer for Ningbo Da Chang Xiang General Store

民国时期

89.0 cm × 60.0 cm

金国铭捐赠 Acquired from Jin Guoming through donation

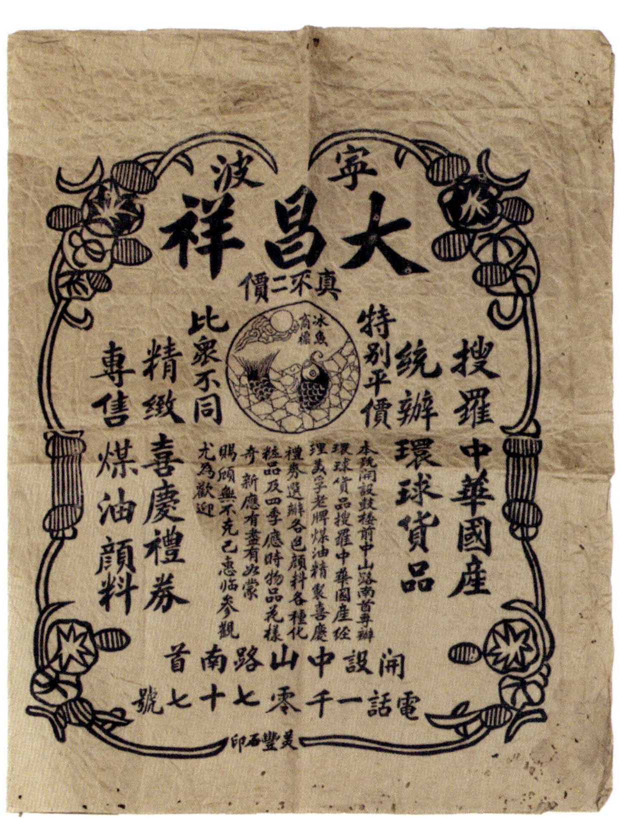

民国时期，宁波大昌祥以“搜罗中华国产，统办环球货品”为宗旨，经营美孚牌煤油、喜庆礼券、各色颜料、化妆品等物品，品种繁多，应有尽有。同时大昌祥还打出“真不二价”的宣传口号，保证所有商品货真价实，明码标价，童叟无欺。

During China's Republican era, Ningbo's Da Chang Xiang sold a wide range of items, ranging from pigments and cosmetics to Mobil kerosene and more. Da Chang Xiang stuck to the slogan "Truly Unbeatable Prices," and went to lengths to ensure all their products were genuine, fairly priced, and transparently labeled, providing honest and reliable service to their customers.

“乾坤亭”纪念簿《宁波小港乾坤亭记》

Commemorative Book of the Xiaogang Li Family’s Qiankun Pavilion

36.0 cm × 29.5 cm

李名信捐赠 Acquired from Li Mingxin through donation

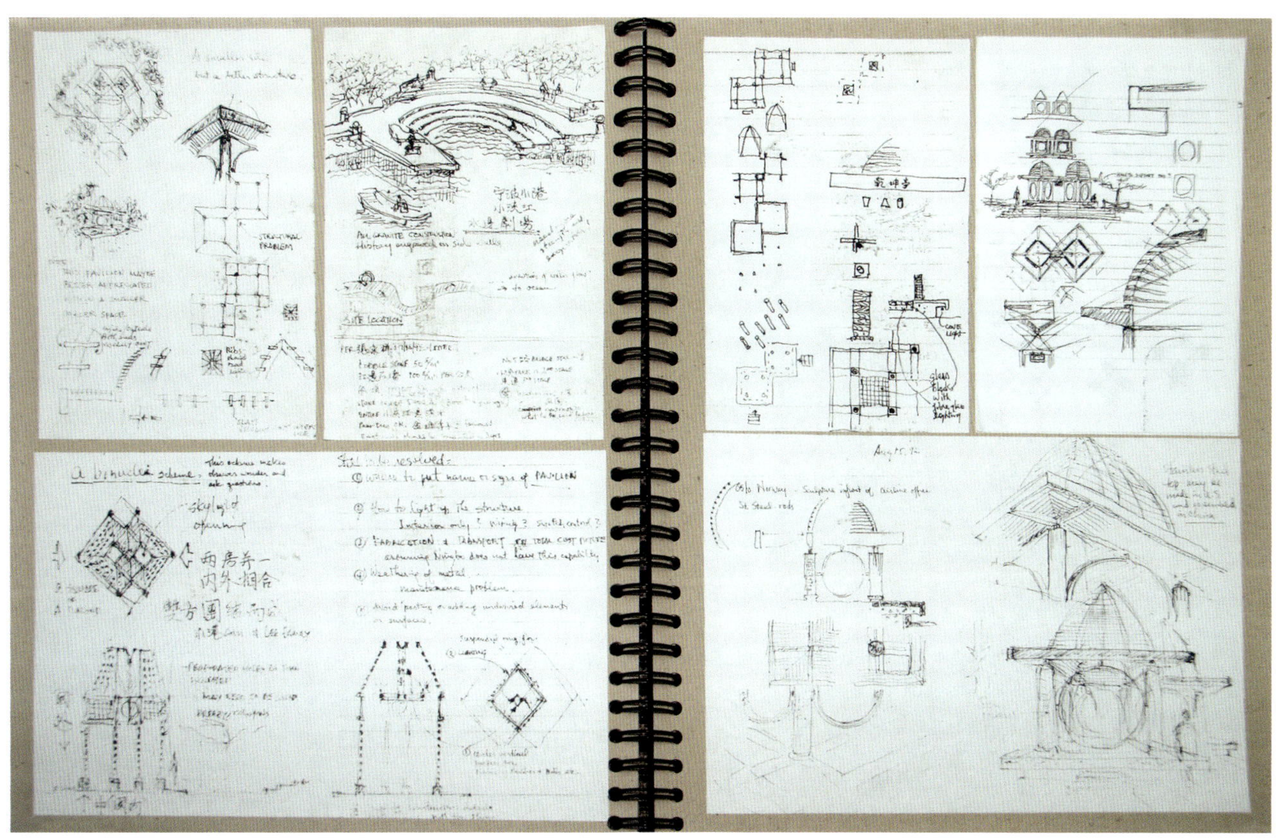

《宁波小港乾坤亭记》为宁波帮望族小港李家族人所作，内容主要为乾坤亭的设计图纸、来往信函、相关照片等。小港李家分为乾、坤两房。1996 年 4 月，海内外小港李氏后人共同倡议建造“乾坤亭”，寓意两房子孙将永远相互携手，为国尽力。后有多位从事艺术、建筑事业的李氏后人一道参与设计。其中，设计图由世界知名设计师、小港李氏家族后人李名仪先生完成。

In this volume are the design blueprints for the Qiankun Pavilion, along with correspondence and photographs associated with the project. In April 1996, descendants of the Xiaogang Li family proposed the construction of the pavilion, symbolizing unity between the family’s Qian and Kun branches. Several members of the Li family were personally involved in the pavilion’s design and construction, with Li Mingyi, a world-renowned architect, being the most notable.

享誉沪上

Expansion in Shanghai

俞庆堂的信成银行有限公司正股票

Sin Chun Bank Stock Certificate, Owned by Yu Qingtang

1907 年

30.0 cm × 24.0 cm

俞昌铭捐赠 Acquired from Yu Changming through donation

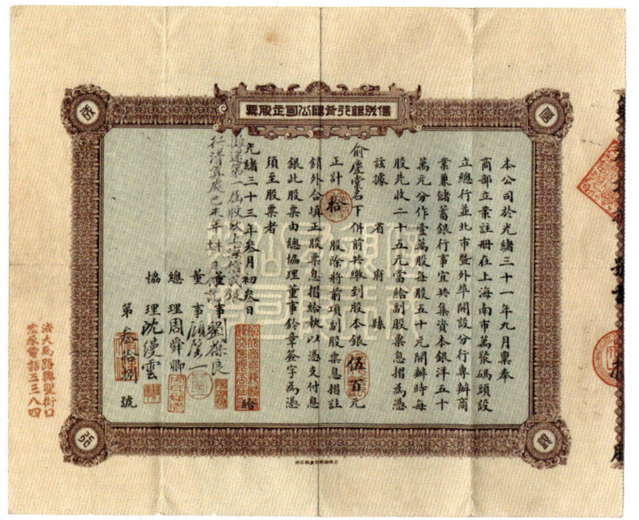

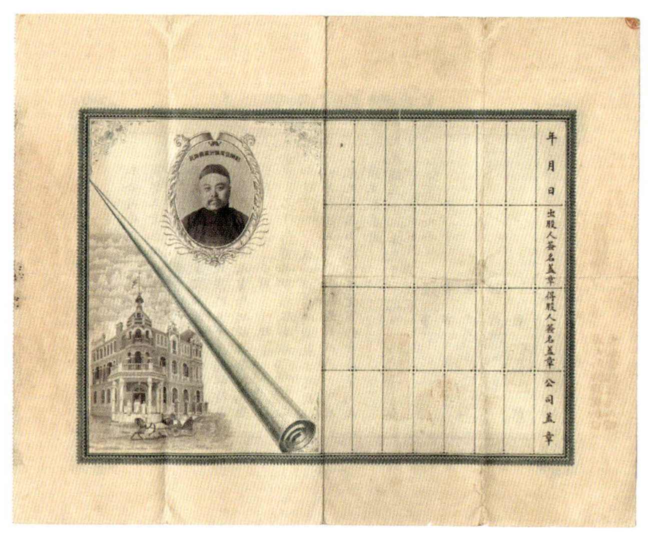

2023 年 5 月，加拿大宁波同乡会顾问俞昌铭在回乡寻根之际，向宁波帮博物馆捐赠了一张其祖父俞庆堂的信成银行股票。信成银行于 1906 年（清光绪三十二年）在上海成立，是中国第一家商业储蓄银行。

该股票为信成银行第叁拾捌号股票，股本五百元银洋，共计十股，有总理周舜卿、协理沈缦云签名，为股东俞庆堂所持有。俞庆堂，宁波姜山人，名义庆，字庆堂，国学生，钦加同知衔，赏戴蓝翎并赏换花翎二品衔。

In May 2023, during a journey to reconnect with family roots in Ningbo, Yu Changming, an advisor to the Canadian Ningbo Association, generously presented the Museum with a stock certificate from his grandfather, Yu Qingtang. This certificate pertained to the Sin Chun Bank, China's first commercial savings bank, founded in Shanghai in 1906. Specifically, it was the thirty-eighth stock issued by Sin Chun Bank, with a capital of 500 silver dollars, divided into ten shares. This stock certificate bore the signatures of Chairman Zhou Shunqing and Deputy Manager Shen Manyun, and was registered in the name of shareholder Yu Qingtang.

周宗良的谦信洋行颜料木桶

Qian Xin Foreign Trading Company's Paint Barrels, Owned by Zhou Zongliang

民国时期

直径 45.0 cm × 59.0 cm

丁铁俊捐赠 Acquired from Ding Tiejun through donation

周宗良（1875—1957），宁波鄞县人。1910 年，周宗良出任谦信洋行买办，由此开始了其长达 35 年的买办生涯。

1914 年第一次世界大战爆发，在华经商的德国人纷纷回国。当时的谦信洋行已是在华最大的德国洋行，不仅在沪置有大量房地产，而且贮存的染料也数量巨大。该行老板轧罗门深恐大战中谦信遭受损失，就与周宗良密商，将谦信在沪的不动产的户名全部改为周宗良，托其隐匿保管，而谦信所有的染料，全部折价以很低的价格卖给周氏，周氏接受了这一计划。不久，亚欧之间运输阻断，进口染料由于货源断绝一下子成了紧俏商品，而周宗良手里掌握了谦信全部的仓储，因而一跃成为颜料业的巨擘。

Zhou Zongliang (1875-1957) was a native of Yin County, Ningbo. When WWI broke out in 1914, the owner of a German trading house in Shanghai sold his inventory of dyes to Zhou at a significantly discounted price, after which the owner left China with the exodus of German merchants fleeing conflict. Shortly thereafter, due to the wartime interruption of dye shipments between Asia and Europe, imported dyes became a scarce commodity. Zhou thus quickly became a dominant force in China's dye industry.

经纪人公会敦请上海交易所职所员在大市场行团拜礼合影

Group Photo of Shanghai Stock Exchange Staff, Organized by the Shanghai Brokerage Association

民国十一年（1922）

108.3 cm×21.0 cm

毛浮海捐赠 Acquired from Mao Fuhai through donation

1920 年，宁波人虞洽卿、盛丕华等创办华商物品证券交易所。它是上海第一家华商证券交易所，开设证券、棉花、棉纱、布匹、金银、粮油、皮毛等 7 部，兼作定期、约期、现期买卖。

In 1920, a group of merchants from Ningbo, including Yu Qiaqing and Sheng Pihua, founded the Huashang Commodity Stock Exchange, the first Chinese-owned securities exchange in Shanghai. It operated various departments for trading in securities, cotton, cotton yarn, fabric, precious metals, grains, oils, fur, and other goods, encompassing both spot and futures transactions.

上海澄衷学校商科第一届毕业纪念明信片

Commemorative Postcard of the First Graduation of Business Program, Shanghai Chengzhong School

民国时期

13.7 cm × 9.2 cm

郑介初捐赠 Acquired from Zheng Jiechu through donation

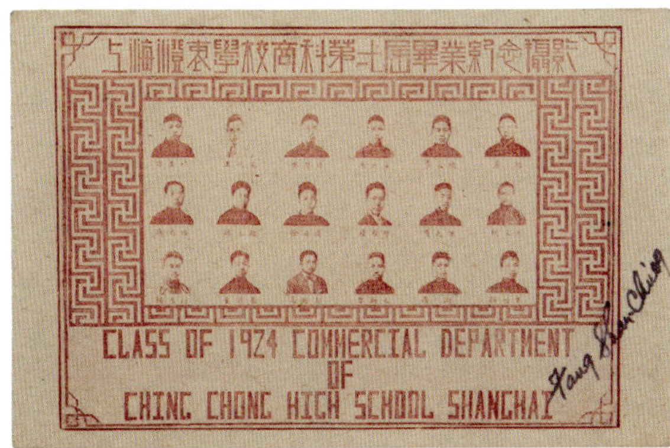

叶澄衷（1840—1899），字成忠，镇海庄市人。1862 年在虹口独资开设顺记五金洋杂货店（英文名澄衷公司），并经销美孚火油，不数年获利甚巨，并先后在长江中下游及天津等商埠遍设分号，人称“五金大王”。继后他又投资金融业，在上海、杭州、镇江、芜湖、湖州等地广设票号、钱庄；创办近代早期民族企业纶华缫丝厂和燮昌火柴厂，从而成为横跨商业、地产、工业、金融业和航运业等几大领域的巨贾。

1899 年，叶澄衷以“兴天下之利，莫大于兴学”的远见卓识，决意在上海创办中国第一所新式学校——澄衷蒙学堂，为我国教育制度进步做出了独特的贡献。蔡元培曾任代理校长，丰子恺、钱君匋曾在此任教，胡适、竺可桢等曾就读于此。

Ye Chengzhong (1840-1899), also known as Chengzhong, hailed from Zhuangshi, Zhenhai. In 1862, he independently founded the Shunji Hardware and Foreign Grocery Store in Hongkou, Shanghai. The store dealt in Mobil kerosene and quickly became highly profitable. Within a short span, he expanded his business by establishing branches along the middle and lower reaches of the Yangtze River and in Tianjin. This earned him the moniker “King of Hardware”.

Ye subsequently ventured into finance, establishing pawnshops and money exchanges in Shanghai, and other cities including Hangzhou, Zhenjiang, Wuhu, and Huzhou. He also played a pivotal role in early modern Chinese enterprises, founding the Lunhua Silk Reeling Factory and Xiechang Match Factory. This diversified his business interests across commerce, real estate, industry, finance, and shipping.

In 1899, Ye Chengzhong made a significant contribution to China’s education system by founding the first modern school in Shanghai, known as the Chengzhong School. This institution had notable figures such as Cai Yuanpei serving as acting principals, renowned teachers like Feng Zikai and Qian Juntao, and notable alumni like Hu Shi and Zhu Kezhen.

胡访鹤使用过的四轮铁保险箱

Four-Wheeled Iron Safe used by Hu Fanghe

民国时期

57.0 cm × 36.0 cm × 44.0 cm

胡运熹、胡运焕捐赠 Acquired from Hu Yunxi and Hu Yunhuan through donation

该保险箱的主人是宁波籍商人胡访鹤。保险箱由两部分组成：一个金属制的外壳和一个内部的保险箱。保险箱采用了当时较为先进的安全技术，只有本人拥有的密钥才能打开，这种特殊设计的保险箱是民国时期较为常见的款式，保证了商人的财产安全。

胡访鹤（1866—？），浙江慈溪人，其先祖系明初慈溪田湖胡氏胡富钊。据唐熊为胡访鹤七秩寿八条屏所载，胡访鹤早年失怙，赖有贤母，克成大器，十五岁来沪，入启成玉号学习布业，年少多才，受历任经理所器重。自从业至擢升经理，和蔼待人、俭约自奉，五十年来如同一日。胡访鹤热心社会事业和地方公益，不辞劳瘁，曾出任绮藻堂布业公所会董、县商会会董、上海市议会议员、十五铺商团会计董事、救火联合会北区会董、邑庙整理会委员等职，在任期间曾提议豫园路改建、修牌谱、请免捐税等事务，深受同业尊重和赞誉。

The owner of this safe was Hu Fanghe, a businessman from Ningbo. It features a robust metal outer shell and can be locked or unlocked using a key. This design style was commonly seen during China's Republican period, ensuring the security of the merchant's assets.

Hu Fanghe (b.1866) was born in Cixi, Zhejiang. His ancestry could be traced back to the Hu Fuzhao family of Cixi's Tianhu in the early years of the Ming Dynasty. According to Eight-Panel Calligraphy Work for the 70th Birthday of Hu Fanghe by Tang Xiong, Hu Fanghe lost his father at a young age and was raised by his mother. At the age of 15, he moved to Shanghai to work as an apprentice in a textile shop. With his business acumen, he soon gained the trust of the senior managers and eventually ascend to a managerial role. For the five decades that he was active in business, Hu remained a kind and frugal man. He was committed to philanthropy and was well regarded by his peers.

《新时代国语教科书》

New Era Chinese Language Textbook

1923 年

19.5 cm × 13.5 cm × 0.7 cm

金国铭捐赠 Acquired from Jin Guoming through donation

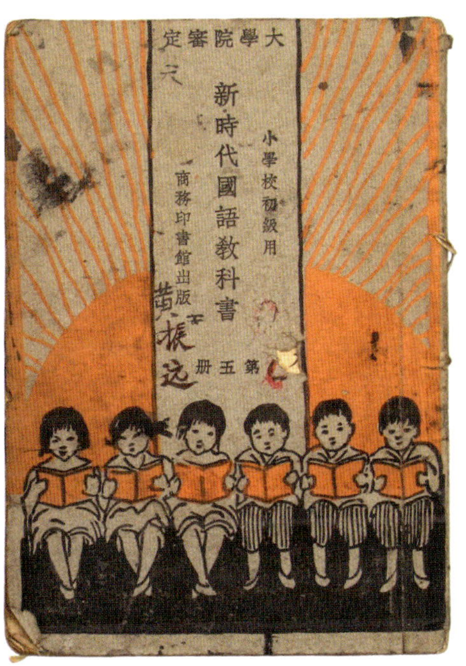

该书是商务印书馆早期发行的教科书。清末取消科举，兴办学堂，新式教科书应运而生，上海商务印书馆于 1904 年编撰出版了初等小学《最新国文教科书》10 册。这套教科书由蒋维乔等编写，张元济、高凤谦校订。

商务印书馆是近代中国历史最悠久的现代出版机构。1897 年，印书馆由鄞县人鲍咸昌等创办，初始以印制教科书为主业，后陆续出版《辞源》等大型工具书。

This book is an early textbook published by the Commercial Press. New textbooks like this one emerged following the abolition of the imperial examination system in the late Qing Dynasty and the establishment of modern schools. In 1904, the Commercial Press compiled and published a series of ten volumes titled *The Latest National Language Textbook for Elementary Schools*.

The Commercial Press is one of the first publishing houses in modern Chinese history, having been founded in 1897. Its founders included Bao Xianchang from Ningbo's Yin County. The Press initially concentrated on printing textbooks. Yet, as time advanced, it diversified its offerings to encompass reference works and a wide array of publications.

笑舞台账册

Ledger from the Xiao Wu Tai Theatre

1927 年

24.5 cm × 19.5 cm

郭达生捐赠 Acquired from Guo Dasheng through donation

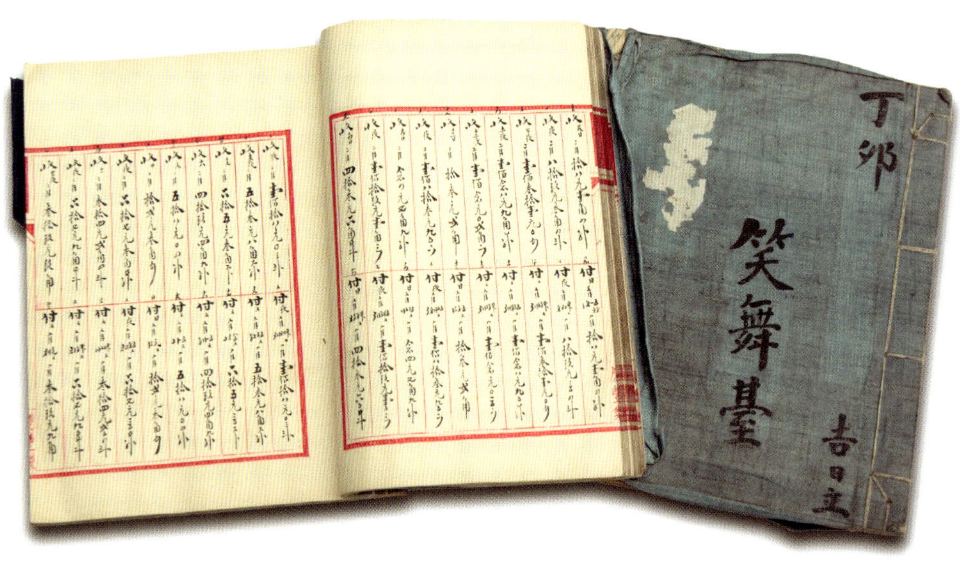

1920 年，上海“笑舞台”剧院被邵逸夫的父亲邵玉轩收购，后交由邵氏兄弟经营。1925 年，邵氏兄弟以笑舞台为基础成立了天一影片公司，后辗转南洋创业。由于没有固定的戏院，他们发明流动电影放映机露天放映电影。流动车的名字为“RUN RUN SHAW”，意思为跑来跑去放映，这个流动车的名字也成了邵逸夫的英文名。

这两本账册是 1927 年“笑舞台”所记的对外营收账目，内容涉及当年上海一些团体、个人来看戏购票时赊欠、归还钱钞等情况。

In 1920, the Shanghai based Xiao Wu Tai Theater was purchased by Shaw Yuh Hsuen, the father of Run Run Shaw, and later managed by the Shaw Brothers. In 1925, the Shaw Brothers established the Tianyi Film Company and later ventured into Southeast Asia. Before the brothers owned their own movie theatre, they had a self-made mobile movie projector for outdoor film screenings. The name of this mobile unit was “RUN RUN SHAW”, signifying their constant movement for film projection. This mobile unit’s name also became Run Run Shaw’s English name.

These two ledgers date back to 1927 and contain ticket transactions and tabs from the Xiao Wu Tai Theater.

竺梅记奉化电气有限公司股票

Zhu Mei Ji Fenghua Electric Company Stock Certificate

1929 年

37.5 cm × 31.0 cm

竺士性捐赠 Acquired from Zhu Shixing through donation

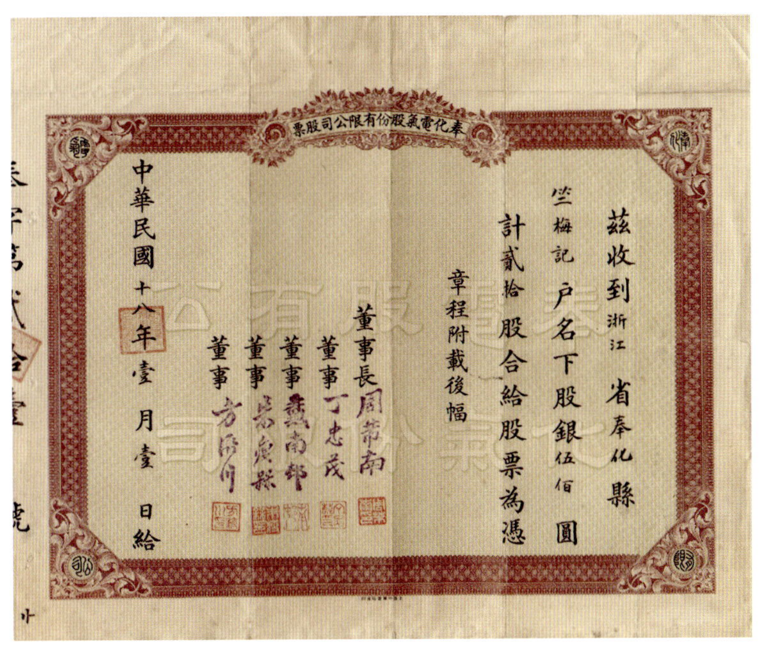

奉化電氣股份有限公司股票

茲收到浙江省奉化縣
竺梅記戶名下股銀伍佰圓
計貳拾股合給股票為憑
章程附載後幅

董事長
董事
董事
董事
董事

中華民國十八年壹月壹日給

竺梅先（1889—1942），字佑庭，学名炽潮，宁波奉化人。13 岁到上海，在何源通五金杂货号当学徒，辛亥革命时加入同盟会，参加了 1911 年上海光复起义。1914 年奉命去长春，秘密组织救国团体，图谋倒倾军阀。后秉承“生产救国”的理念，弃政从商。1929 年起，先后创办或接办大来银行、嘉兴民丰造纸厂、杭州华丰造纸厂、宁绍轮船公司及上海丰裕公行、宁波大新军服厂等企业，出任经理、总经理等职务。在国内首创薄白纸板和卷烟纸，获制造专利权，是中国近代民族造纸工业及烟草业的先驱人物。1938 年，和夫人徐锦华在奉化后琅泰清寺创办国际灾童教养院，接收流浪孤儿 600 余人，免费食宿，并进行小学、初中教育。灾童中有 30 多名毕业生参加新四军浙东游击纵队三五支队，为抗日战争的胜利做出贡献。

该股票为奉化电气有限公司颁发给股东竺梅记（竺梅记即竺梅先）的二十股股票凭证，是竺梅先大力支持电力事业发展、积极投身家乡建设的实证。

Zhu Meixian, a native of Fenghua, Ningbo, was a pioneer in China's modern papermaking and tobacco industries.

This stock certificate, issued by Fenghua Electric Company to shareholder Zhu Meiji (Zhu Meixian's alternative name), reflects Zhu's strong support for the development of the electric power industry and his active involvement in the development of his hometown.

《钱业月报》第 11 卷第 1 号

Volume 11, Issue 1 of *Qianye Yuebao* (*The Native Bankers' Monthly*)

1931 年

26.0 cm × 18.5 cm

储建国捐赠 Acquired from Chu Jianguo through donation

1921 年，旅沪宁波帮钱业巨擘秦润卿倡议创办月刊《钱业月报》，每年汇集一卷。该刊不囿于旧习，博采众长，被誉为上海钱庄业的喉舌。主要栏目有传略栏、论说栏、调查栏、选论栏、新闻摘要栏、外部金融及商情栏、本埠金融及商情栏、表类栏、小说栏等。主要撰稿人有王渭耕（笔名楚声）、魏友棐、施督辉等人。该刊每遇重大金融事件、当局重大经济决策，无不及时做出反应；对于钱业营业方针、经营方式也时有评议；又一反过去对各庄资力保密的旧规，首先公布各庄股东、经理姓名以及资本金额，并于 1924 年第 4 卷 4 月号起连续刊载银洋进出、公单划解的统计表，为钱业刊物金融统计之滥觞。

In 1921, Qin Runqing, a prominent figure in the Ningbo business community in Shanghai, began publishing *The Native Bankers' Monthly*. Its main content was finance and business news. The magazine always promptly covered significant events in the financial world and the government's economic decisions. It also provided commentary on banking business policies and practices. The *Monthly* was the first publication to disclose the names of shareholders, managers, and capital amounts for various banks, marking a break from the tradition of keeping such information confidential. Starting from the April 1924 issue of Volume 4, the *Monthly* consistently published statistical tables on foreign exchange transactions and public fund allocations, marking the beginning of financial statistics in Chinese banking publications.

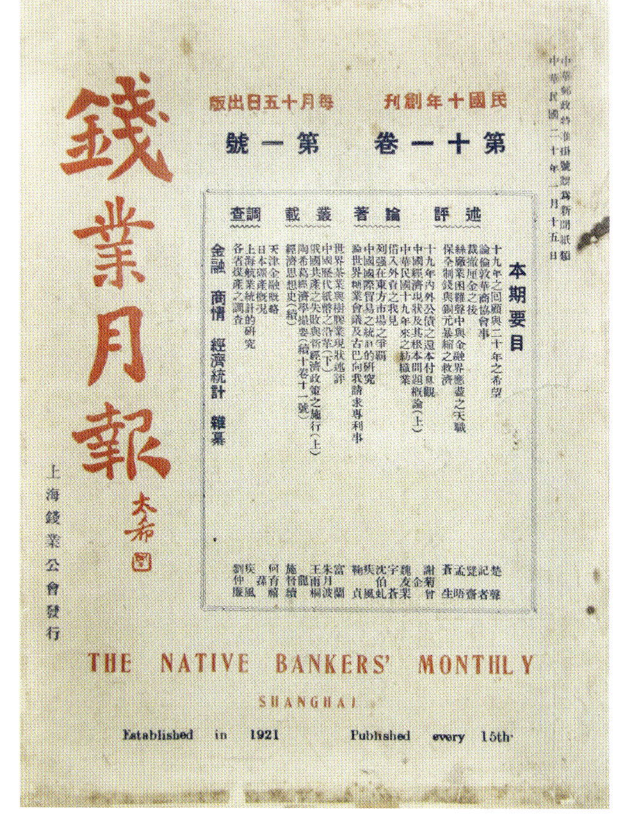
中華郵政特准掛號認為新聞紙類
中華民國二十年一月十五日

錢業月報

民國十年創刊 每月十五日出版

第十一卷 第一號

本期要目

述評

十九年之回顧與二十年之希望 楚聲
論倫敦華商協會事 記者
裁撤厘金之後 覺齋
絲廠業困難聲中與金融界應盡之天職 孟晤
保全制錢與銅元暴縮之救濟 蒼生

論著

十九年內外公債之還本付息觀 謝菊曾
中國經濟現狀及其根本問題概論（上） 金
中華民國十九年來之紡織業 魏友棐
借入外債之我見 宇蒼
列強在東方市場之爭霸 沈伯虬
中國國際貿易之統計的研究 疾風
論世界煙業會議及古巴向我請求專利事 鞠貞

叢載

世界蠶業與樹膠業現狀述評 富闐
中國歷代紙幣之沿革（下） 朱月波
我國共產之失敗與新經濟政策之施行（上） 王雨桐
陶希葛經濟學撮要（續十卷十一號） 龍
經濟思想史（續） 施督績

調查

天津金融概略 何育觸
日本礦產概況 森
上海航業統計的研究 疾風
各省煤產之調查 劉仲服

金融 商情 經濟統計 雜纂

上海錢業公會發行

大希

THE NATIVE BANKERS' MONTHLY
SHANGHAI
Established in 1921 Published every 15th

四明银行壹圆纸币

Siming Bank One Yuan Banknote

1933 年

14.3 cm × 7.4 cm

沈天祥捐赠 Acquired from Shen Tianxiang through donation

该纸币面值一元，由四明商业储蓄银行（简称四明银行）发行。清光绪三十四年（1908），宁波帮人士袁鎏、朱葆三、周晋镳、虞洽卿等在上海发起成立四明银行（位于宁波路江西路口），该行是中国近代最早的华资商业银行之一，被誉为宁波人自己的银行。

四明银行的纸币甫一发行，就遭到企图独霸中国金融市场的外商银行的夹击，他们将四明银行印发的纸币攒到一定程度就来挤兑现洋，给四明银行造成极大的冲击。在这样的情况下，宁波同乡会发动宁波同乡施以援手，各大商店、钱庄、银号争相代兑四明银行的纸币，挤兑风潮才得以很快平息。由此，四明银行得到了人们的信任。

This banknote has a face value of one yuan and was issued by the Siming Commercial and Savings Bank. In 1908, a group of prominent Ningbo businesspeople including Yuan Liu, Zhu Baosan, Zhou Jinbiao, and Yu Qiaqing, founded the bank in Shanghai. It was one of the earliest Chinese-funded commercial banks in modern China and was located at the intersection of Ningbo Road and Jiangxi Road.

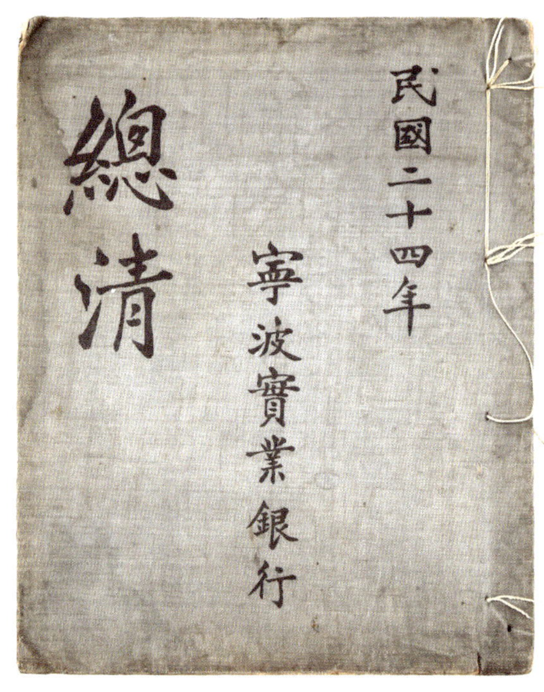

宁波实业银行总清册

Ningbo Industrial Bank General Ledger

1935 年

24.0 cm × 19.0 cm × 2.2 cm

储建国捐赠 Acquired from Chu Jianguo through donation

宁波实业银行成立于 1931 年 6 月，由项松茂、王才运、邬志豪等联合宁波金融、实业两界人士共同创建，资本总额 50 万元，由邬志豪任董事长兼总经理，总行设在上海南京路。该行以“面向实业，支援工商，帮助农、渔，服务平民和同乡”为宗旨。

1933 年，在宁波、沈家门设分行，在上海南市提篮桥和霞飞路（现淮海中路）设办事处。后又在苏州、昆山、青浦等地设立分行。在昆山设有堆栈，办理农民质押放款。宁波分行设于 1933 年 9 月 12 日，地址在小缸桥。除经营一般存、放、汇业务外，还办理米、麦、耕牛贷款，国货流动押汇，沪甬汇款则免收汇费。1935 年，全国性金融风暴时，上海总行于 6 月停业，1937 年 1 月 9 日正式复业，总行改设沈家门，宁波分行改为办事处，其他各地分支行均行裁并。1941 年，宁波沦陷，办事处迁上海总行，同年 11 月裁撤。

The Ningbo Industrial Bank was founded in June 1931 by a group of individuals from the financial and industrial sectors in Ningbo, including Xiang Songmao, Wang Caiyun, and Wu Zhihao. The bank had a total capital of 500,000 yuan, and Wu Zhihao served as the bank's Chairman and General Manager. Its headquarters were located on Shanghai's Nanjing Road.

In 1933, the bank established branches in Ningbo and Shenjiamen, as well as offices in Shanghai at Tilanqiao and Xiafei Road (now Huaihai Middle Road). It later opened branches in Suzhou, Kunshan, Qingpu, and other cities across China. In Kunshan, the bank operated warehouses and provided loans to farmers.

The Ningbo branch was established on September 12, 1933 at Xiaogang Bridge. In addition to handling general deposits, it provided loans for the purchase of rice, wheat, and draft animals. The bank also offered services related to domestic exchange of goods without charging exchange fees.

During a nationwide financial crisis in 1935, the Shanghai headquarters temporarily closed in June but resumed operations on January 9, 1937. The headquarters relocated to Shenjiamen, and the Ningbo branch became an office. Branches in other cities were consolidated. In 1941, during the occupation of Ningbo, the office moved to the Shanghai headquarters and was eventually closed in November of the same year.

上海虞洽卿路命名纪念明信片

Commemorative Postcard of the Naming of Shanghai's Yu Ya-Ching Road

1936 年

14.5 cm × 9.0 cm

郑介初捐赠 Acquired from Zheng Jiechu through donation

1936 年，为表彰虞洽卿对上海各项事业所做的贡献，并庆祝其七十虚岁华诞和旅沪五十五周年，上海公共租界工部局决定将租界内最繁华的道路西藏路命名为“虞洽卿路”。同年 10 月 1 日，“虞洽卿路”命名仪式举行，社会各界纷纷前来参加庆祝典礼，规模之盛大，轰动当时的上海。此明信片即为纪念这一盛典而发行。

在近代上海租界内以华人名字命名的马路屈指可数，而以旅沪宁波帮人士命名的道路就有两条——虞洽卿路和朱葆三路。宁波帮在近代上海地位突出，贡献巨大，以其雄厚的工商实业能力、广泛的社交能力以及乐善好施的品德，赢得了上海各界的普遍认可和推崇。

In 1936, as a tribute to Yu Qiaqing's (also romanized as Yu Ya-Ching) remarkable contributions to various aspects of Shanghai's development and in celebration of his 70th birthday and 55th year in the city, the Shanghai Public Concessionary Administration made the decision to rename the bustling West Tibet Road to "Yu Ya-Ching Road". A naming ceremony was held on October 1, 1936. This event garnered widespread attention and participation from all kinds of people, leaving a lasting impression on Shanghai residents. This postcard serves as a commemoration of this significant occasion.

上海市呢绒工厂业同业公会主席《征募寒衣捐启》附募捐名录

Shanghai Woolen Mills Industry Guild Chairman's *Winter Clothing Fundraising Initiative* Attached with Donor List

1940 年
34.0 cm × 26.0 cm
陈贤本家族捐赠 Acquired from the Chen Xianben family through donation

陈贤本（1899—1975），时任中国统一呢绒厂总经理、上海市呢绒工厂业同业公会主席。日军占领上海期间，陈贤本在上海公共租界冒险主办难民收容所，救济难民，并为抗日游击队募捐御冬寒衣，支援抗战前线。根据他的子女回忆，当时家里也住满了逃难的亲戚朋友。

1940 年上海市呢绒工厂业同业公会主席《征募寒衣捐启》附募捐名录记录的即为征募寒衣时的认捐情况，为陈贤本后人捐赠。

Chen Xianben (1899-1975) served as the General Manager of the China United Woolen Mill and Chairman of the Shanghai Woolen Mills Industry Guild. Amidst the Japanese occupation of Shanghai, Chen courageously operated refugee shelters within the Shanghai International Settlement. He provided refuge and relief to those displaced by the conflict, actively raised funds for winter clothing for anti-Japanese guerrilla forces, and supported the resistance's front lines. His children recall that their home was a sanctuary for relatives and friends seeking escape from the chaos.

Shanghai Woolen Mills Industry Guild Chairman's *Winter Clothing Fundraising Initiative* Attached with Donor List chronicles the commitments made during the winter clothing fundraising campaign. It was donated to the Museum's collection by the descendants of Chen Xianben.

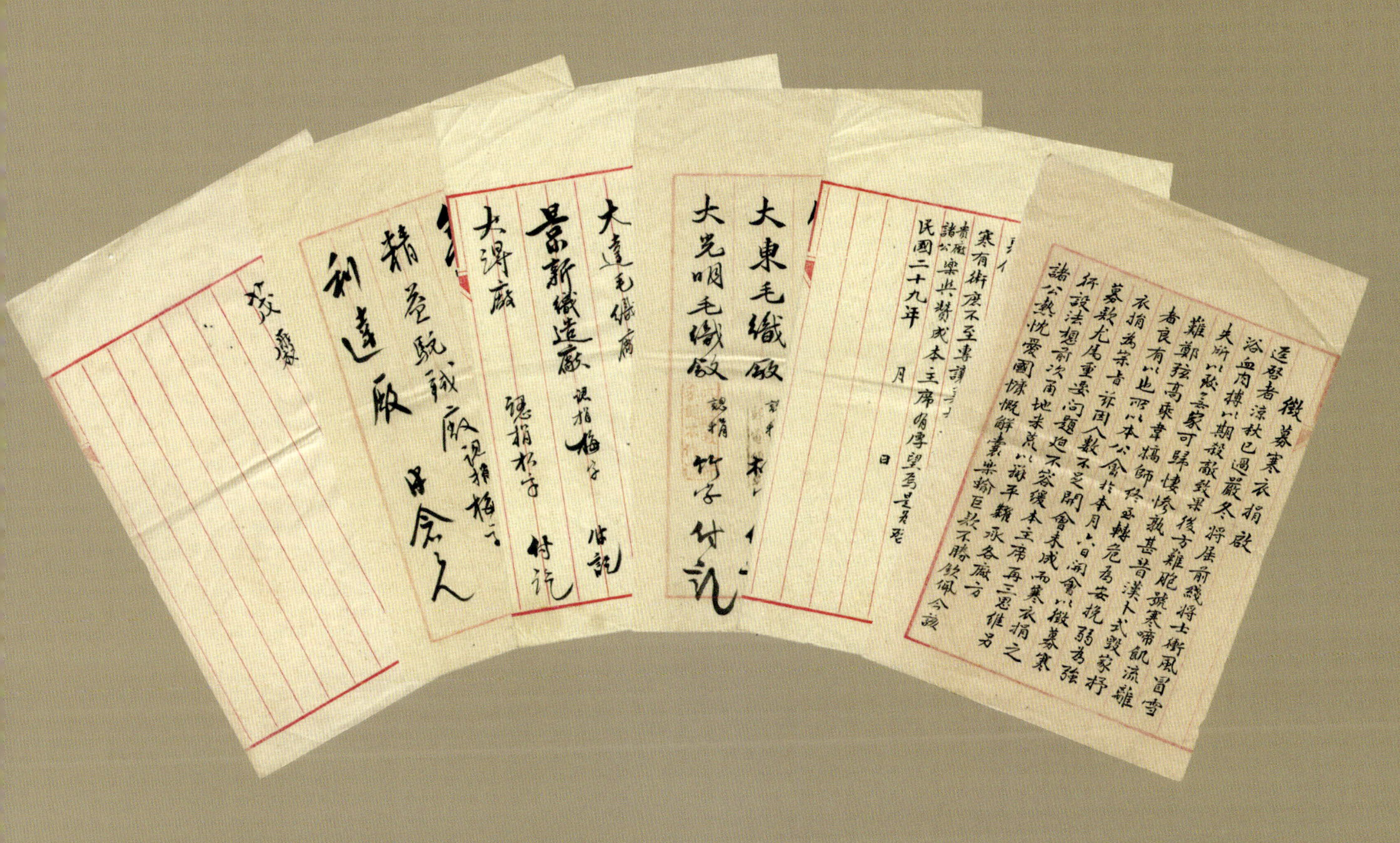

徵募寒衣捐啟

逕啓者涼秋已過嚴冬將屆前綫將士衝風冒雪浴血肉搏以期殺敵致果後方難胞號寒啼飢流離失所以致無家可歸悽慘孰甚昔漢卜式毀家紓難鄭弦高乘韋犒師終于轉危為安挽弱為強者良有以也爰以本公會於本月六日開會以徵募寒衣捐為宗旨祗因人數不足開會未成而寒衣捐之募款尤屬重要問題迫不容緩本主席再三思維另行設法想前次兩地米荒以籌平糶承各廠方諸公熱忱愛國慷慨解囊集輸巨款不勝欽佩今該

寒有衛度不至專請[illegible]
貴廠諸公樂與贊成本主席有厚望焉[illegible]
民國二十九年　月　日

大東毛織廠　認捐[illegible]
大光明毛織廠　認捐竹字　付訖

大達毛織廠
景新織造廠　認捐梅字　付訖
大渭廠　認捐松字　付訖

精益駝絨廠　認捐梅字
利達廠　[illegible]

五和织造厂股份有限公司票存

Deposit Receipt of Wuhe Weaving Factory Co., Ltd.

1942 年 5 月 25 日

25.5 cm × 11.0 cm

收购 Acquired through purchase

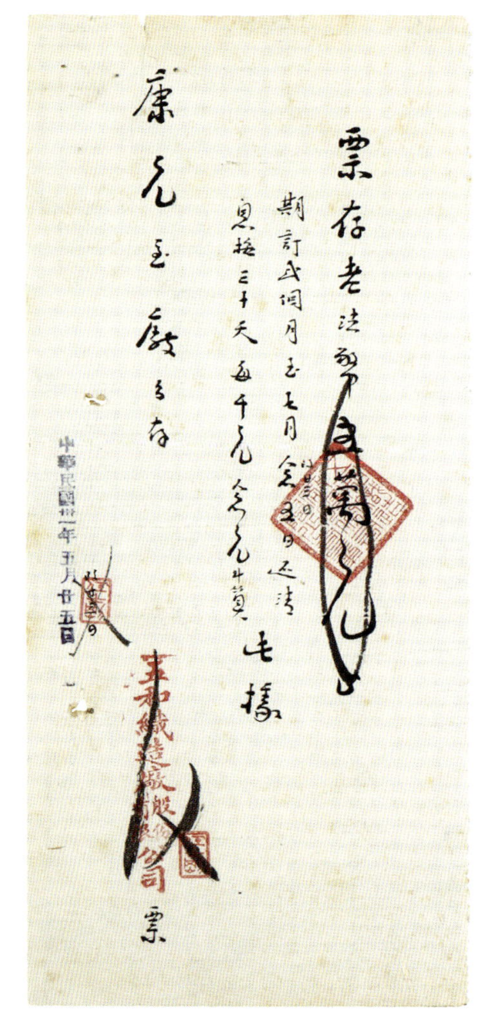

票存老法幣壹萬元整

期訂貳個月至七月念五日還清

息按三十天每千元念元計算

屯據

康元五廠存

中華民國卅一年五月廿五日

五和織造廠股份有限公司票

任士刚（1896—1946），宁波慈城人，近代纺织业先驱之一，也是红极一时的“鹅牌”汗衫商标创立人和大师级广告宣传家，被时人誉为“汗衫大王”。他发现上海针织品市场被法、日等国洋货长期占领，受“抵制洋货，挽回利权”爱国思潮影响，遂力邀罗庆藩、杨光启、钱箕传、梁悟庵 4 位同学、老乡，集资创办五和织造厂。1928 年，改组为五和织造厂股份有限公司，创立自己的品牌“鹅牌”，主要生产卫生衫裤、汗衫背心等。

1932 年九一八事件一周年时，任士刚在上海《申报》发表《外感与外侮》一文，文中写道：“鹅牌卫生衫可防止外感，吾人从人身的外感，便想到国家的外侮。国人应精诚团结，共御外侮。”1937 年 7 月抗战全面爆发，上海沦陷，日军放火烧毁五和针织厂厂房。任士刚刚正不阿，决不与日本人妥协，呕心沥血维持厂务，导致积劳成疾。1945 年，抗战胜利后，任士刚又带病重建厂房，终因劳累过度，于 1946 年在上海寓所逝世。

Ren Shigang (1896-1946), a native of Cicheng, Ningbo, was a prominent figure in the textile industry. He earned the moniker “Sweater King” in China, and is the creative mind behind the famous “Goose Brand” sweater trademark. Influenced by the patriotic movement to boycott foreign goods, he took notice of the long-standing dominance of foreign knitwear in the Shanghai market, particularly those of countries like France and Japan. In response, he joined forces with several fellow students and associates from Ningbo, and together, they raised funds to establish the Wuhe Weaving Factory, which produced shirts, sweaters, and undershirts.

泰康罐头食品有限公司礼券

Tai Kong Canned Food Co., Ltd. Voucher

1942 年

23.0 cm × 12.5 cm

沈天祥捐赠 Acquired from Shen Tianxiang through donation

中国泰康罐头食品股份有限公司前身为“泰康食品厂”“济南泰康罐头食品有限公司”，1929 年改为现名并迁至上海，宁波人乐汝成任总经理。1931 年，该公司出产了第一批饼干和福字牌罐头，远销新加坡、菲律宾及南洋各埠。

泰康罐头食品有限公司铁饼干箱

Tai Kong Canned Food Co., Ltd. Iron Biscuit Box

民国时期

13.5 cm × 13.5 cm × 17.0 cm

沈天祥捐赠 Acquired from Shen Tianxiang through donation

Tai Kong Canned Food Co., Ltd. was initially known as “Tai Kong Food Factory” and “Jinan Tai Kong Canned Food Co., Ltd.” In 1929, it adopted a new name and relocated to Shanghai, with Le Rucheng, a native of Ningbo, serving as the company’s general manager. The company produced its first batch of biscuits and canned goods in 1931, which were then exported to Singapore, the Philippines, and across Southeast Asia.

华通牌电风扇
Huatong Electric Fan

民国时期

44.0 cm × 22.0 cm × 53.0 cm

姚久龙捐赠 Acquired from Yao Jiulong through donation

华通牌电风扇由宁波帮人士姚德甫所创办的华通电业机器厂所生产。1919 年 1 月，宁波镇海人姚德甫与友人在上海创办了华通电业机器厂（今华通开关厂前身），初期租借两间厢房，雇用 10 余名工人，制造熔断器和从事电器修理业务。1931 年和 1940 年，工厂先后进行了扩建，职工增至 900 人左右。1934 年，华通牌电风扇和自冻器（即电冰箱）在全国国货展览会上荣获实业部颁发的优质产品奖。1941 年改名为华通电业机器厂股份有限公司。1950 年元旦，经上海市政府批准，实行公私合营，成为上海市第一批公私合营的电工企业。1953 年改名为华通开关厂。

华通电业机器厂股份有限公司股票

Huatong Electric Machine Factory Co., Ltd. Stock Certificate

1944 年

32.0 cm × 24.0 cm

姚久龙捐赠 Acquired from Yao Jiulong through donation

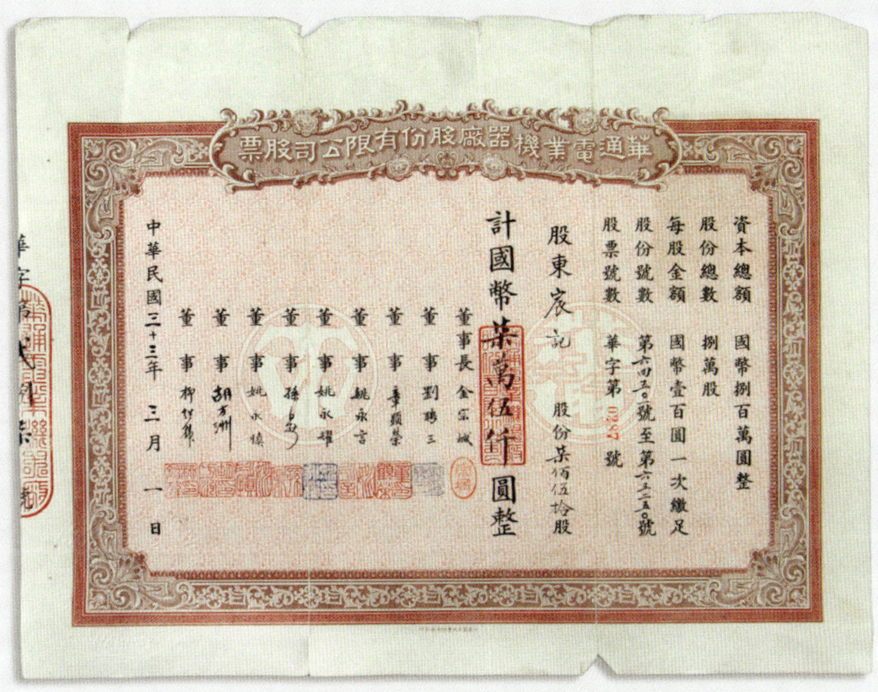

Huatong Electric Fans were produced by the Huatong Electric Machine Factory, established by Yao Defu, a prominent figure of the Ningbobang. In January 1919, Yao and his associates founded the machinery factory in Shanghai. Initially, they operated out of two rented rooms with less than 20 workers, manufacturing fuses and offering electrical repair services. The factory underwent expansions in 1931 and 1940, increasing the workforce to about 900 employees. In 1941, it was renamed Huatong Electric Machine Factory Co., Ltd. On January 1, 1950, with approval from the Shanghai Municipal Government, it transitioned to a public-private partnership, becoming one of the pioneering enterprises in Shanghai to do so. Finally, in 1953, it was renamed Huatong Switch Factory.

上海达丰染织厂广告纸

Shanghai Dafeng Dyeing and Weaving Factory Advertisement

民国时期

16.5 cm × 11.0 cm

收购 Acquired through purchase

王启宇（1883—1965），浙江定海人。20世纪初，在“实业救国”的影响下，王启宇辞去洋行工作，创办达丰染织工厂，生产国货染织品。后又扩建新厂，开始生产中国第一代机器印染棉布。王启宇首创中国机器印染，是我国机器印染业的先驱。

王启宇十分重视企业品牌和影响，在产品的商标广告上狠下功夫。达丰厂生产销售的布匹都夹有宣传标签，最上方印有醒目的“中国首创”，中间是“永不退色”四字。这些广告宣传标签是达丰的品质保证。

Wang Qiyu (1883-1965), who hailed from Dinghai, Zhejiang, was deeply influenced by the early 20th century movement advocating industrial development for China's national restoration. In response, he left his position in a foreign trading company and established the Shanghai Dafeng Dyeing and Weaving Factory, producing dyed and woven goods. Later, he expanded his operations and became a pioneer in China's machine printed and dyed cotton fabric industry, introducing the first generation of such textiles.

Wang was highly committed to building a strong brand and influence for his business, and he devoted significant efforts to trademark and advertising. Every fabric produced and sold by the Dafeng Factory came with a distinctive label. At the top, it proudly bore the inscription "China's First", and in the center, it carried the assurance of "Everlasting Dye". These promotional labels served as a testament to Dafeng's commitment to quality.

福源钱庄支票

Foo Yuan Bank Cheque

1949 年

19.3 cm × 9.2 cm

沈天祥捐赠 Acquired from Shen Tianxiang through donation

福源钱庄，初名协源钱庄，经宁波慈城人秦润卿经营后，成为上海钱业中资本最雄厚的一家。秦润卿也据此长期任上海钱业公会会长、上海总商会副会长等职，在整个上海金融界享有很高的声誉。

支票由上海信和纱厂股份有限公司总经理黄首民签发。该公司创办于 1937 年 12 月，宁波帮知名人士厉树雄就是该厂董事之一。支票票面价值国币十亿元整，这与当时物资匮乏、通货膨胀、货币大幅贬值有关。

Foo Yuan Bank became one of the wealthiest banks in Shanghai after coming under the management of Qin Runqing, a native of Cicheng, Ningbo. Qin Runqing held various prestigious positions in the Shanghai financial sector, serving as the long-standing president of the Shanghai Banking Association and vice-president of the Shanghai Chamber of Commerce.

The cheque was issued by Huang Shoumin, general manager of Shanghai Xinhe yarn Factory Co., Ltd. Li Shuxiong, a well-known figure in the Ningbo business community, was one of the directors of the company. The face value of the cheque was a staggering 1 billion yuan of the national currency of the Republican era, reflecting the rampant inflation and significant currency devaluation of the time.

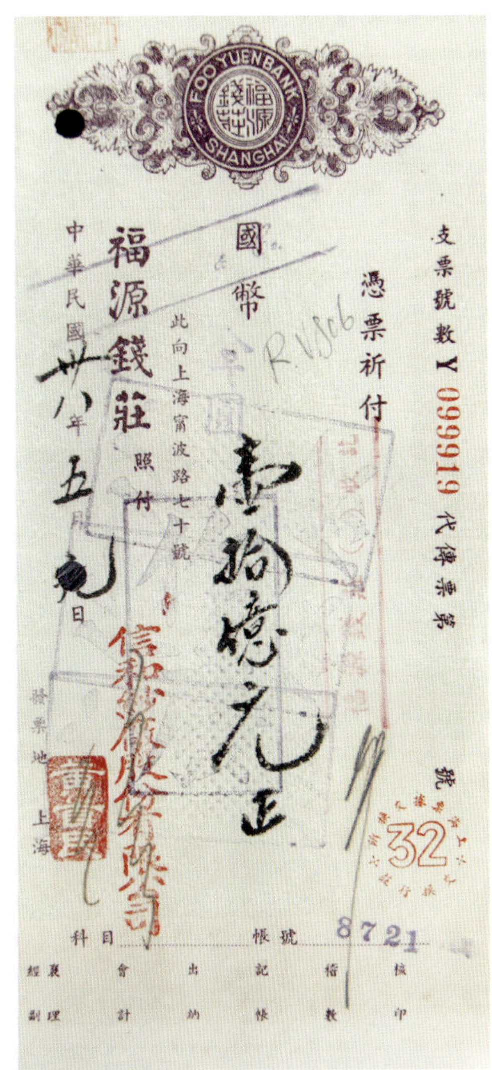

FOO YUEN BANK 福源錢莊 SHANGHAI

支票號數 Y 099919 代價票第 號

憑票祈付 國幣 壹拾億元正

此向上海甯波路七十號 福源錢莊 照付

中華民國 卅八 年 五 月 九 日

發票地 上海

信和紗廠股份有限公司

科目 帳號 8721

中国国货股份有限公司股票

China Merchandise Corp. Stock Certificate

1949 年

20.0 cm × 20.0 cm

社会征集 Acquired from local community member through donation

"九一八"以后，充斥上海市场的洋货给民族工业带来巨大压力，形势愈加严峻。宁波帮先行者高扬"倡导国货"的大旗，积极寻找商机，联手发展实业，抵制外货倾销，捍卫中国的经济权利，在 20 世纪 30 年代的上海上演了一场有声有色的商业反击战。1933 年，宁波帮人士方液仙、蒉延芳、任士刚等人投入资本 10 万元，在上海创办中国国货股份有限公司，商场设有绸缎、布匹等 40 个柜组。到 1937 年，又成立中国国货联营公司，并在重庆、福州等地增设分公司，对发展民族工业发挥了积极作用。

该股票为上海中国国货股份有限公司股东寅记的股票，共计股份一百万股，国币一千万元。上有公司宁波籍董事蒉延芳、叶友才、李康年签名。

In the wake of the September 18th Incident that led to Japan's occupation of Northeast China, the Shanghai market saw an influx of foreign goods, posing a significant challenge to domestic industries. The Ningbobang pioneers championed the cause of promoting Chinese-made products. In 1933, entrepreneurs from Ningbo, including Fang Yexian, Kui Yanfang, and Ren Shigang, invested 100,000 yuan to establish the China Merchandise Corp. in Shanghai. The company's department store had 40 counters selling silks, fabrics, and a wide array of goods.

This stock certificate belonged to Yin Ji, a shareholder in the corporation. It represents one million shares with a total value of ten million yuan of the national currency of the Republican era and carries the signatures of Kui Yanfang, Ye Youcai, and Li Kangnian, all of whom were from Ningbo.

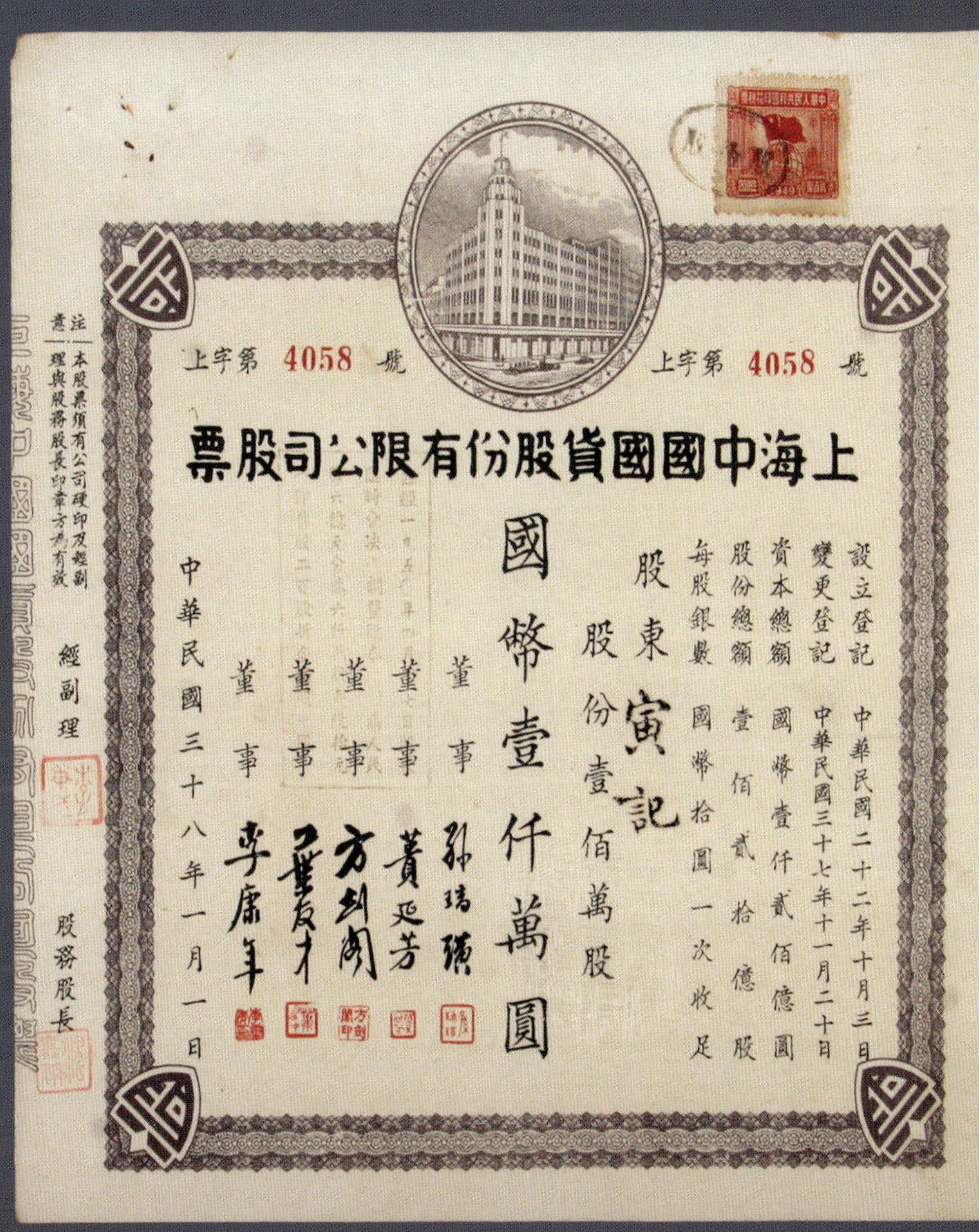

上字第 4058 號

上字第 4058 號

上海中國貨股份有限公司股票

設立登記　中華民國二十二年十月三日

變更登記　中華民國三十七年十一月二十日

資本總額　國幣壹仟貳佰億圓

股份總額　壹佰貳拾億股

每股銀數　國幣拾圓一次收足

股東　寅記

股份壹佰萬股

國幣壹仟萬圓

董事

董事

董事

董事

董事

中華民國三十八年一月一日

注意　一　本股票須有公司硬印及經副理與股務股長印章方為有效

經副理

股務股長

《银行周报》第 33 卷第 9 期

Volume 33, Issue 9 of the *Weekly Banking News*

1949 年
26.0 cm × 18.0 cm
储建国捐赠 Acquired from Chu Jianguo through donation

此刊物为 1949 年 2 月 28 日发行的《银行周报》第 33 卷第 9 期，为银行制度研究专号，对上海证券交易所的复业、禁止金银外运的意义、存款准备金代用品折价及存准金与交换户存息问题等内容进行了论述。

《银行周报》是我国创办最早的金融专业刊物，于 1917 年 5 月发行创刊号，至 1950 年 3 月停刊，以周刊的形式出版发行，共计 34 卷 1635 期，其发行时间之长、发行期数之多，亦是民国时期金融刊物之最，为推动近代华资银行乃至金融业的发展做出了重要贡献。《银行周报》以报告金融消息、研究经济事务、供银行业从业者参考为宗旨，兼顾实用性和学术性。刊物设有《每周金融》《每周汇兑》《每周证券》《每周商情》等栏目，及时报道和反馈每周银行业情况，同时收录有关宏观经济和金融的评论文章以及欧美先进金融制度和理念的介绍。

This publication is the 9th issue of the 33rd volume of the *Weekly Banking News*, dated February 28, 1949. It serves as a specialized edition focusing on the study of banking systems. Topics covered include the reopening of the Shanghai Stock Exchange, the significance of prohibiting the export of gold and silver, the discounting of reserve deposit substitutes, and matters related to reserve deposits and exchange account deposits.

Weekly Banking News holds the distinction of being one of China's earliest financial publications. It made its debut in May 1917 and continued publishing until March 1950. Presented as a weekly periodical, it boasted a total of 34 volumes and 1,635 issues. This enduring publishing had a significant impact during the Republican era, making substantial contributions to the development of Chinese-owned banks and the Chinese financial sector as a whole.

The primary objectives of *Weekly Banking News* were to report financial news, analyze economic events, and provide valuable insights for professionals in the banking industry. It struck a balance between practicality and academic rigor, featuring sections on weekly finance, exchange rates, securities, and business developments. Additionally, it included commentary on macroeconomic and financial matters, as well as introductions to advanced financial systems and concepts from Europe and the US.

銀行周報

第三十三卷　第九期

民國六年創刊　總第一五八三號

中華民國三十八年二月二十八日發行

銀行制度研究專號

銀行學會編印

三星牌搪瓷蚊香盘

Sanxing Enamel Mosquito Incense Holder

民国时期

直径 15.0 cm × 1.0 cm

沈天祥捐赠 Acquired from Shen Tianxiang through donation

蓝底蚊香盘，盘中印有“中国化学工业社　三星牌蚊烟香”商标，中心印有“三星”商标。“三星”取“福、禄、寿”三星吉祥之意。

1912 年，镇海人方液仙（1893—1940）在上海创办中国化学工业社，这是中国日用化工之滥觞。为提振销售，特别是强化与外商的竞争力量，方液仙打出“国人爱国，请用国货三星蚊香”的广告语，通过报纸、招贴画等形式广为宣传。在民众爱国热情的支持下，三星蚊香生意日渐兴隆，不仅畅销国内，而且远销南洋各埠，成功打破了日本野猪牌蚊香的市场垄断地位。在 1926 年美国费城世界博览会上，三星牌蚊香荣获香类丙等金奖。

This blue enamel mosquito incense holder is emblazoned with the words “China Chemical Works, Sanxing Mosquito Incense Coil”, accompanied by the Sanxing logo of three stars, representing prosperity, wealth, and longevity.

In 1912, Fang Yexian (1893-1940), a native of Zhenhai, Ningbo, founded China Chemical Works in Shanghai, a milestone in the formation of China’s modern consumer chemical products industry.

亚浦耳灯泡

Oppel Light Bulb

民国时期

直径 6.5 cm × 11.5 cm

沈天祥捐赠 Acquired from Shen Tianxiang through donation

亚浦耳灯泡厂成立于 1923 年，由宁波帮人士胡西园创办，是中国第一家生产灯泡的工厂。中华人民共和国成立后定名为亚明灯泡厂，产品商标名称从“亚浦耳”变更为“亚”。时至今日，亚明灯泡厂仍然是全国最大的光源生产基地之一，“亚”字品牌更是家喻户晓的著名民族品牌。

胡西园（1897—1981），镇海柴桥（今属北仑）人。少年就读于镇海中学时，便对工艺制造怀有浓厚兴趣，后考入浙江高等工业学校。毕业后，只身闯荡上海，1921 年研制出我国第一只白炽灯泡，一举打破外商垄断中国电灯泡市场的局面。胡西园也被誉为“中国灯泡之父”“中国电光源之父”和“中国照明电器工业的开拓者”。

The Oppel Light Bulb Factory was founded in 1923 by Hu Xiyuan, a member of the Ningbobang. It was the first factory in China to produce light bulbs. After the founding of the People’s Republic of China, it was renamed as the Yaming Light Bulb Factory. To this day, Yaming remains one of the largest lighting equipment producers in China.

中国统一呢绒纺织厂广告

Tung Yih Woollen Factory Advertisement

民国时期

26.0 cm × 18.0 cm

陈子元捐赠 Acquired from Chen Ziyuan through donation

1931年，陈贤本等人创办达隆呢绒厂，用进口毛纱织造精纺哔叽、华达呢、花呢等，该厂成为上海最早生产精纺呢绒的毛织厂。翌年“一·二八”事变爆发，该厂以“一·二八”为产品商标，顺应国人心理，因而产品虽初出茅庐，却很有销路。

In 1931, Chen Xianben and his associates established Tung Yih Woollen Factory, which specialized in the production of fine worsted and woolen fabrics using imported woolen yarn.

华生牌电风扇

Huasheng Electric Fan

民国时期

44.0 cm × 22.0 cm × 53.0 cm

社会征集 Acquired from local community members through donation

1914 年，杨济川、叶友才、袁宗耀三人筹集资金，以杨济川为主，仿照美国奇异电风扇制成中国第一台电风扇。1916 年，三人又集资在上海四川北路横滨桥创办了华生电器制造厂，由袁宗耀负责财务，杨济川主持生产，叶友才任经理。1924 年，在周家嘴路新建路口购地建造新厂房，正式生产华生牌电风扇，成为我国第一家自研自制的电扇厂。1926 年，华生牌电风扇参加美国费城世界博览会，荣获丁等银奖。其名“华生”，有中华民族自力更生之意。

In 1914, Yang Jichuan, Ye Youcai, and Yuan Zongyao raised funds to create China's first electric fan, inspired by America's GE electric fan. In 1916, they established the Huasheng Electrical Manufacturing Factory in Shanghai, with Yuan Zongyao handling the finances, Yang Jichuan overseeing production, and Ye Youcai as the manager. In 1924, a new factory was built by them, producing electric fans under the brand Huasheng, which became the first Chinese company to design and manufacture such an appliance.

童涵春堂药罐

Tong Han Chun Tang Medicine Jar

民国时期

直径 6.0 cm × 6.5 cm

社会征集 Acquired from local community member through donation

上海童涵春堂国药号始创于清乾隆四十八年（1783），是今日上海的一家百年老店、名店。创始人童善长（1745—1817）是宁波庄桥童朝阳家族的第 27 世孙。童氏家族财力雄厚。童善长从小聪明伶俐，成人后继承祖业，仍在庄桥一带经商。然而他并不满足于守成祖业，外出跑码头来到上海，接手竺涵春药店，将其改名为童涵春堂，亲自主持店务并出任经理。该店最初地址在上海县城小东门瓮城地段。

Shanghai's Tong Han Chun Tang Chinese Medicine Store, founded in 1783 during the Qing Dynasty, is a century-old prestigious establishment. Its founder, Tong Shanchang, was a descendant of the affluent Tong Chaoyang family in Zhuangqiao, Ningbo. Tong Shanchang, expanded the family business to Shanghai, where he took over the Zhu Han Chun Medicine Store, renamed it Tong Han Chun Tang, and handled the store's management.

“人造自来血” 药瓶

“Chilai” Blood Tonic Bottle

民国时期

6.5 cm × 4.0 cm × 16.0 cm

社会征集 Acquired from local community member through donation

“人造自来血” 是五洲药房的主要产品之一，在 1915 年美国巴拿马太平洋万国博览会中获得银奖。

五洲药房由黄楚九、夏瑞芳等人于 1907 年在上海创设。宁波人项松茂接任五洲药房经理后，不仅全力筹集资金，而且积极扩大经营，自制了一系列成药。其中包括治疗贫血症的 “人造自来血”、健胃补虚的 “补天汁”、清热解毒的 “海波药” 等。特别是 “人造自来血”，因质量优于其他药房的同类产品，且比进口的西药便宜很多，很受消费者欢迎，产量逐年上升，成为五洲药房的王牌产品。1913 年，“人造自来血” 在香港及东南亚各地注册，销往南洋各埠，继而进入欧美市场。1915 年，德国商人开设普恩药局，出售补血药片，使用 “人造自来血” 商标，企图鱼目混珠。项松茂有极强的产权意识，他发现后立即与德商严正交涉，并向工部局巡捕房提出诉讼，最后胜诉。五洲药房亦因此名声大振。

The International Dispensary Co., Ltd. was founded in Shanghai in 1907 by Huang Chujiu, Xia Ruifang, and their business associates. When Xiang Songmao, a native of Ningbo, became the manager, he not only raised more capital for the company but also expanded the range of proprietary medicines. Notably, the “Chilai” Blood Tonic gained popularity for its quality and affordability, leading to increased production and export to Southeast Asia, Hong Kong, and eventually Europe and the US by 1913.

老凤祥银项圈

Lao Feng Xiang Silver Neck Ring

民国时期

直径 16.0 cm

社会征集 Acquired from local community member through donation

上海老凤祥银楼始创于 1848 年，是中国珠宝首饰业传承至今历史最悠久的"中华老字号"，由镇海郑氏十七房郑熙创办。最初的"凤祥银楼"位于上海老城厢的南市大东门，取"凤祥"招牌，寓意女性的至善至美，以及对顾客的美好祝愿，也象征着首饰本身工艺的精美超群。

Shanghai's Lao Feng Xiang Jewelry, founded in 1848, is the oldest and most prestigious Chinese heritage brand in the jewelry industry. Established by Zheng Xi, a seventeenth-generation descendant of the Zheng family from Zhenhai, the original store was located in Shanghai's old town.

胡立范印章

Hu Lifan's Seal

民国时期

直径 1.4 cm × 3.0 cm

胡运焕捐赠 Acquired from Hu Yunhuan through donation

胡立范（？—1926），祖籍宁波，上海绮藻堂布业公所总董胡访鹤之子，学贯中西，早年便崭露头角，展现出了商业天赋，出任华记洋行总经理，深受商行业主信任。民国十五年（1926），积劳成疾，不幸早逝。这是他使用过的印章。

Hu Lifan, originally from Ningbo, was the son of Hu Fanghe, the Chairman of the Shanghai Qizaotang Textile Industry Association. He received a comprehensive education, which blended Chinese and Western learning, and showed remarkable business acumen from a young age. He held the position of General Manager at Hua Ji Trading Company and enjoyed the trust of the business owners. In 1926, he succumbed to illness after years of hard work, passing away at a young age. This was the seal he used.

张继光使用过的量尺、瓷碗

Ruler and Porcelain Bowl Used by Zhang Jiguang

民国时期

① 34.0 cm × 5.5 cm × 4.5 cm ② 31.2 cm × 3.3 cm ③直径 19.5 cm × 5.5 cm

张乾源捐赠 Acquired from Zhang Qianyuan through donation

张继光是宁波鄞县傅家漕人，近代上海建筑业的开拓者。在 20 世纪初的 30 余年间，张继光参与设计、建造的大楼大多集中在上海外滩和北京东路的金融区，如东方汇理银行大厦、中国实业银行、大清银行、日本领事馆、纱布交易所、盐业银行等，目前多为文保单位。他也是宁波灵桥发起筹建者之一，并在建造过程中积极奔走，出力甚巨。该量尺为建筑业专用，由英国知名量尺制造商史丹利公司制造，张继光一直贴身使用。该瓷碗为林忠震赠张继光，白釉寿桃纹。

张继光之子张乾源继承其父衣钵，投身于建筑业，著有《建筑综合论》。第三代中的张永勤也选择建筑业作为终身追求。张继光家族被业内誉为“建筑世家”。

Zhang Jiguang was a pioneering figure in the modern Shanghai construction industry. Hailing from the Fujiacao area of Yin County, Ningbo, he played a significant role in designing numerous buildings in Shanghai’s Bund area and the financial district on Beijing East Road in the early 20th century. Many of these buildings are now protected historical sites. Zhang Jiguang was also one of the advocators of the Ling Bridge construction project in Ningbo. This ruler, manufactured by the well-known British company Stanley, served as a professional architectural tool that Zhang Jiguang kept with him at all times. And this white glazed longevity peach pattern porcelain bowl was presented to Zhang Jiguang by Lin Zhongzhen.

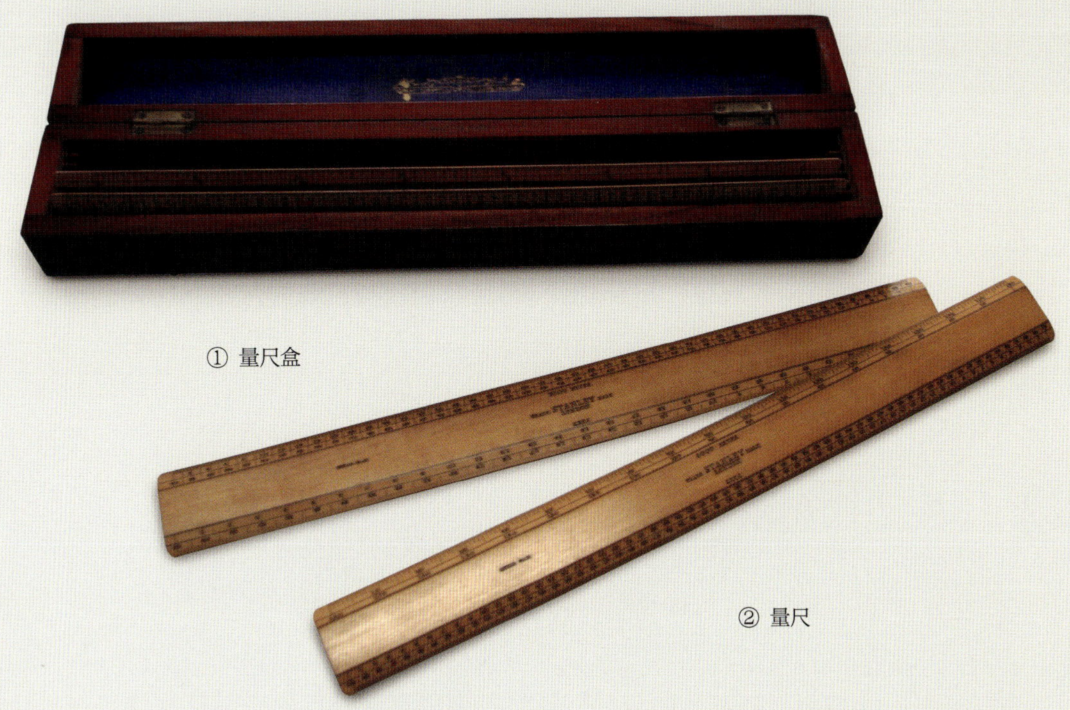

① 量尺盒

② 量尺

③ 瓷碗

亨达利怀表
L. Vrard & Co. Pocket Watch

民国时期

直径 4.0 cm

王辉捐赠 Acquired from Wang Hui through donation

1876 年，鄞县人孙廷源创设美华利钟表行，该店为我国创建最早的民族钟表店之一。1902 年，孙梅堂继承父业任总经理，后于 1905 年在宁波创设制钟工厂，首创国产时钟，并在 1915 年美国巴拿马太平洋万国博览会上荣获金质奖章及优等奖状，为我国在世界钟表领域争得一席之地。1917 年，孙梅堂兼并法商开设的亨达利钟表店，事业鼎盛期在上海、天津等地开设有 25 家分店。孙梅堂因此被誉为“钟表大王”。

In 1876, Sun Tingyuan, a native of Yin County, Ningbo, established the Mei Hua Li Clock Shop, one of the earliest clock shops in China. Sun Meitang took over his father's position as the general manager in 1902, and in 1905 founded a clock manufacturing factory in Ningbo, pioneering domestically produced clocks. In 1915, at the Panama-Pacific International Exposition, he was awarded a gold medal and a first-class certificate, securing a place for China in the world of horology. In 1917, Sun Meitang acquired the French-owned L. Vrard & Co. During the peak of his career, he operated 25 branches in Shanghai, Tianjin, and many other locations.

协大祥市尺
Ruler Used by Xie Da Xiang Textile Store

民国时期

33.3 cm × 1.7 cm

孙福龄捐赠 Acquired from Sun Fuling through donation

近现代，由宁波人唱主角的“三大祥”（协大祥绸布店、宝大祥绸布店、信大祥绸布店）闻名上海滩，尤以 1912 年成立的协大祥历史最悠久，实力最雄厚。“三大祥”的发展，见证了上海绸布行业发展的历史，都获得“中华老字号”的称号。

捐赠人孙福龄，1934 年生于宁波，未出满月即随家人前往上海生活。少年时代进入上海宝大祥绸布店，1980 年调上海协大祥商厦任办公室主管。退休后曾返聘黄浦协大祥公司任审计多年。

In the late 19th and early 20th centuries, the Bund had three highly popular textile stores, all owned by Ningbo merchants. The largest and oldest was the Xie Da Xiang Textile Store, which had been founded in 1912 and stood as testament to the growth of the textile industry in Shanghai.

Sun Fuling was born in Ningbo in 1934 and moved to Shanghai when he was less than a month old. As a young man, he worked at the Bao Da Xiang Silk and Fabric Store in Shanghai. In 1980, he assumed a managerial role at the Shanghai Xie Da Xiang Commercial Building. After retirement, he was rehired as an auditor at the Huangpu Xie Da Xiang Company, a position he held for several years.

老宁绍轮招贴画

Ningbo-Shaoxing Steamer Poster

民国时期

48.6 cm × 34.4 cm

乐兴华捐赠 Acquired from Le Xinghua through donation

1908 年虞洽卿等联络宁波、绍兴旅沪商人合资创办宁绍商轮公司，得到广大旅沪宁绍商人的广泛响应，几天之内就募得股金 28 万元，不足之数由虞氏向四明银行贷款。公司向福州马尾造船厂购得 2600 吨位轮船一艘，取名“宁绍”，并在上海、宁波设码头，建栈埠，经营沪甬线客货运输。该招贴画或用于招揽客户。

宁绍轮开航后，挂牌“立永洋五角”，以示永不涨价。太古公司和东方公司合谋降价为三角，并以另赠毛巾、肥皂来招揽乘客，想以此挤垮宁绍公司。在此情况下，宁波旅沪同乡会发动宁绍商人组织宁绍航业维持会，募集现洋 10 多万元，补贴宁绍公司。沪甬两地的商人还相约，凡需海运货物尽量交托宁绍公司承运。相持数月，终于战胜外资轮运企业的倾轧，之后又购进甬兴轮与宁绍轮“两船一来一往，逐日无间”。1914 年宁绍公司在汉口、九江等地建置码头、栈埠，开辟宁绍轮长江新航线。

In 1908, in an attempt to break up the monopoly that foreign-invested companies had over the Shanghai-Ningbo shipping route, Ningbo and Shaoxing merchants in Shanghai, led by Yu Qiaqing, jointly established the Ningbo-Shaoxing Steamship Company. This initiative received widespread support from the local merchants, and within a few days, they raised a capital of 280,000 silver yuan, with Yu Qiaqing obtaining the remaining amount through a loan from Siming Bank. The company purchased a 2,600-ton ship from the Fuzhou Mawei Shipyard, named it “Ningshao,” and built their own docks in Shanghai and Ningbo. This poster was an advertisement for the new shipping route.

老寧紹

“提倡国货　挽回利权”瓷盘

Porcelain Plate with *Ti Chang Guo Huo, Wan Hui Li Quan* (“Promote Domestic Products, Restore National Rights”) Inscription

民国时期

直径 19.0 cm × 3.2 cm

金国铭捐赠 Acquired from Jin Guoming through donation

中国国货运动始于 20 世纪初期，在其 30 多年的发展历程中，旨在发展生产、推销国货、抵制洋货倾销、推进民族工商业发展，不但是近代中国发展时间最长、影响最广的社会运动之一，而且是近代中国人民反帝爱国运动的重要组成部分。

在国货运动中，宁波帮凭借着在各行业中的领先地位，高举“提倡国货”的大旗，敢为人先，携手并进，积极发展实业，抵制洋货倾销，涌现出了三友实业社、中国化学工业社、大中华橡胶厂等一大批优秀民族企业，对国货运动的开展起到了巨大的推动作用。

这款瓷盘正是国货运动期间的产品，瓷盘上写有“提倡国货　挽回利权”，通过将口号、理念融入产品的形式激发民众重视国货、助力民族工商业发展的热情。

In the early 1900s, there was a thirty-year “national product movement” in China, during which the population demonstrated their support for domestic industries and domestic products as a form of resistance against the dumping of foreign products into the Chinese market. It was one of the longest-lasting and most impactful social movements in modern China and proved critical in the Chinese struggle against foreign imperialism.

This porcelain plate was a product of this social movement. Inscribed with the slogan “Promote Domestic Products, Restore National Rights”, this product called upon citizens to purchase domestic products and support domestic industries.

中国化学工业社雪花精瓶

China Chemical Works Skin Cream Bottle

民国时期

直径 3.5 cm × 5.7 cm

金国铭捐赠 Acquired from Jin Guoming through donation

此雪花精由方液仙创办的中国化学工业社生产，是民国时期的化妆用品。

方液仙，宁波镇海人，近代著名爱国实业家，被誉为“国货大王”。方液仙出身名门，父母分别来自宁波帮望族镇海柏墅方家和镇海小港李家。恰逢洋货倾销、民族工业积弱之时，方液仙毅然走上实业救国之路，于 1912 年在上海创办了中国化学工业社。创业早期，中国化学工业社主要生产牙粉、雪花精等，此后不断扩大研发和生产，成功试制出国内首支牙膏。20 世纪 30 年代，产品已扩至牙膏、肥皂、蚊香、化妆品、调味品、化工原料和玻璃器皿等七大类 200 多个规格品种，其中三星牌牙膏更是家喻户晓的明星产品。在方液仙的带领下，中国化学工业社逐渐发展成为当时中国日用化学工业规模最大的厂家之一，真正做到了与洋货轻工产品相抗衡，是民族工业发展中的一面旗帜。

This skin cream, a beauty product, was manufactured by China Chemical Works, a company founded by an industrialist from Ningbo named Fang Yexian.

大中华火柴公司火花

China Match Co., Ltd. Matchbox

民国时期

9.0 cm × 7.2 cm

收购 Acquired through purchase

刘鸿生（1888—1956），浙江定海人，中国近代著名爱国实业家。其经营领域遍布轻重工业、运输业、商业和金融业，创立了近代中国数一数二的民族企业集团。20 世纪初，在孙中山实业救国思想影响下，刘鸿生积极投身于民族工业。1930 年，为了与洋人洋火抗衡，刘鸿生将荧昌、鸿生、中华三家民族火柴厂合并，组建大中华火柴有限公司，使大中华火柴畅销大半个中国，打破了洋火垄断中国市场的局面，他也因此赢得了“火柴大王”的美誉。

Liu Hongsheng (1888-1956), from Dinghai, Zhejiang, was a prominent Chinese patriot and industrialist. In the early 1900s, inspired by Sun Yat-sen's ideas of industrialization for national restoration, Liu Hongsheng became actively involved in entrepreneurship. He founded one of the most influential Chinese business conglomerates of the time. His wide-ranging business interests spanned heavy and light industries, transportation, commerce, and finance.

In 1930, in response to foreign competition in the matchstick industry, Liu Hongsheng merged three Chinese-owned matchstick factories – Yingchang, Hongsheng, and Zhonghua – into the China Match Co., Ltd. This strategic move allowed China Match to gain a strong foothold in the Chinese market, breaking the foreign monopoly and earning Liu Hongsheng the nickname “Matchstick King”.

三友实业社门市部广告纸

Sanyou Industrial Company Advertisement

民国时期

61.0 cm × 45.0 cm

储建国捐赠 Acquired from Chu Jianguo through donation

三友实业社《三角志》广告册

Sanyou Industrial Company Brochure *San Jiao Zhi*

1936 年

18.0 cm × 13.0 cm

陈欢夸捐赠 Acquired from Chen Huankua through donation

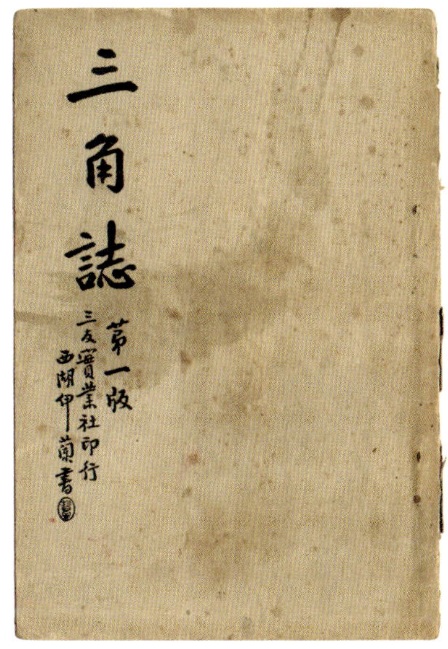

1912 年，宁波慈溪人陈万运等在上海创办三友实业社，生产“金星牌”洋烛芯。1917 年三友实业社开始生产“三角牌”毛巾，与日商的“铁锚”牌毛巾抗衡，成为上海织巾业的发轫产品。经过反复试验和技术改进，“三角牌”毛巾质量不断提升，深受顾客喜爱，畅销全国。1926 年三友实业社参加了费城世界博览会，“三角牌”毛巾以优异的品质荣获丙等金奖章（纺织品类）。除毛巾外，三友实业社还生产被单、被面、床毯、窗帘等产品，在供应国内市场的同时，还大量销往海外，成为当时民族工业品牌的旗帜。

三友实业社注重广告宣传，这两件藏品介绍了三友实业社出品的各类产品，收录了诸多颇具创意的广告，从侧面展现出三友实业的发展沿革和经营智慧。

In 1912, a group of businesspeople led by Chen Wanyun from Cixi, Ningbo, founded the Sanyou Industrial Company in Shanghai. They initially produced “Golden Star Brand” candle wicks. In 1917, the company expanded its production to include “Sanjiao Brand” towels, which became a cornerstone product in Shanghai’s textile industry. Through continuous testing and technological enhancements, the quality of “Sanjiao Brand” towels improved significantly, earning favor among customers and achieving nationwide popularity.

In addition to towels, Sanyou Industrial Company diversified its production to include items like sheets, quilt covers, blankets, and curtains. While catering to the domestic market, they also exported a substantial volume of their products overseas, establishing themselves as a prominent brand in China at the time. The Sanyou Industrial Company placed a strong emphasis on advertising and promotion.

遍布全国

Impact Across the Mainland

小港李家坤三房李祖龄夫人王颖资嫁衣

Wedding Robe of Wang Yingzi, wife of Lee Zuling from the Li family of Xiaogang

1927 年

120.0 cm × 70.0 cm

李宜华捐赠 Acquired from Li Yihua through donation

该物品为小港李家李祖龄夫人王颖资出嫁时的嫁衣，其长女李宜华捐赠给宁波帮博物馆。

清末至民国是小港李家发展的重要阶段，家族通过联姻的方式实现了强强联合，扩大了家族影响力和产业范围。这个时期的李家出现了首批去海外留学的子弟，李祖龄即为其中一员。

李祖龄（1904—1957），德国莱茵纺织专科学校毕业，回国后，在外交部、实业部、审计部、交通部等处任职。李祖龄长姐嫁与时任参议院议长王家襄（1872—1928）。1927年，经王家襄介绍，李祖龄与王颖资成婚。王颖资（1904—2011），原名王荫聪，王式通（1864—1931）幼女，幼承家学，知书达理，接受了高等教育，一生勤俭、博爱。

This wedding robe belonged to Wang Yingzi, wife of Lee Zuling of the Li family of Xiaogang. It was donated to Ningbobang Museum by their eldest daughter, Li Yihua.

During the late 19th and early 20th centuries, the Li family of Xiaogang experienced a pivotal period of growth. The family broadened its influence and industrial reach by strategically marrying into other influential families, thereby forging powerful alliances. Additionally, this time marked the beginning of the Li family's members pursuing education abroad, with Lee Zuling being one of the first to do so.

Lee Zuling (1904-1957) completed his studies at the Rhein Textile Engineering School in Germany. After returning to China, he assumed various significant roles within the Ministry of Foreign Affairs, the Ministry of Industry, the Audit Department, the Ministry of Transportation, and several other governmental departments. His elder sister was wed to Wang Jiaxiang (1872-1928), a prominent politician of the era. In 1927, Lee Zuling married Wang Yingzi through Wang Jiaxiang's introduction. Wang Yingzi (1904-2011), formerly known as Wang Yincong and the youngest daughter of Wang Shitong (1864-1931), was raised in an educated family. She received a higher education and devoted her life to philanthropy.

三北轮埠公司汉口分公司的水脚收条

Shipping Fee Receipt from the Hankou Branch of the San Peh Steam Navigation Co., Ltd.

1935 年

26.0 cm × 10.5 cm

收购 Acquired from purchase

三北轮船公司成立于 1913 年，由中国近代爱国民族资本家、航运业巨子、宁波人虞洽卿独资创立。次年更名为三北轮埠股份有限公司。1915 年，三北轮埠公司汉口分公司成立，并于 1922 年在汉口沿江大道洞庭小路口新建四层办公大楼与仓库堆栈等设施，该建筑由宁波帮人士沈祝三的汉协盛营造厂承建，1922 年建成。在列强林立的时代，这家民族航运公司的出现使长江航道上终于有了中国人自己的巨轮。1953 年，三北轮埠公司上海总部归入公私合营的上海轮船公司，包括武汉在内的其他城市的三北轮船分公司也退出历史舞台。

The San Peh Steamship Company was founded in 1913 as a sole proprietorship by Yu Qiaqing, a shipping magnate from Ningbo. The following year, it was renamed as the San Peh Steam Navigation Co., Ltd. A Hankou branch was established in 1915. In 1922, a new four-story office building and warehouse facilities were constructed at the intersection of Dongting Xiaolu and the Yangtze River Road in Hankou. This building was constructed by the Ningbo-based entrepreneur Shen Zhushan's Han Xie Sheng Construction Company.

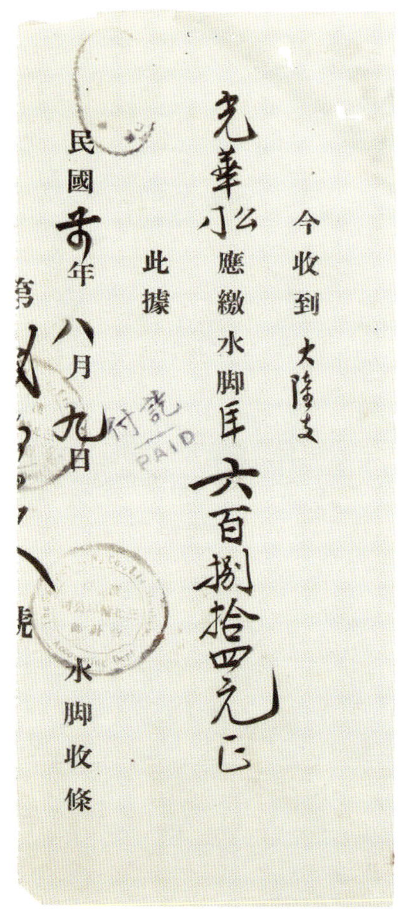
今收到 大陸支
光華公司 應繳水脚洋 六百捌拾四元正
此據
民國廿四年八月九日
付訖 PAID
水脚收條

康乐寒私立汉口宁波小学专任教员的聘书

Appointment Letter for Kang Lehan as a Teacher at the Hankou Ningbo Elementary School

1948 年

38. 0 cm × 26. 5 cm

陈勇捐赠 Acquired from Chen Yong through donation

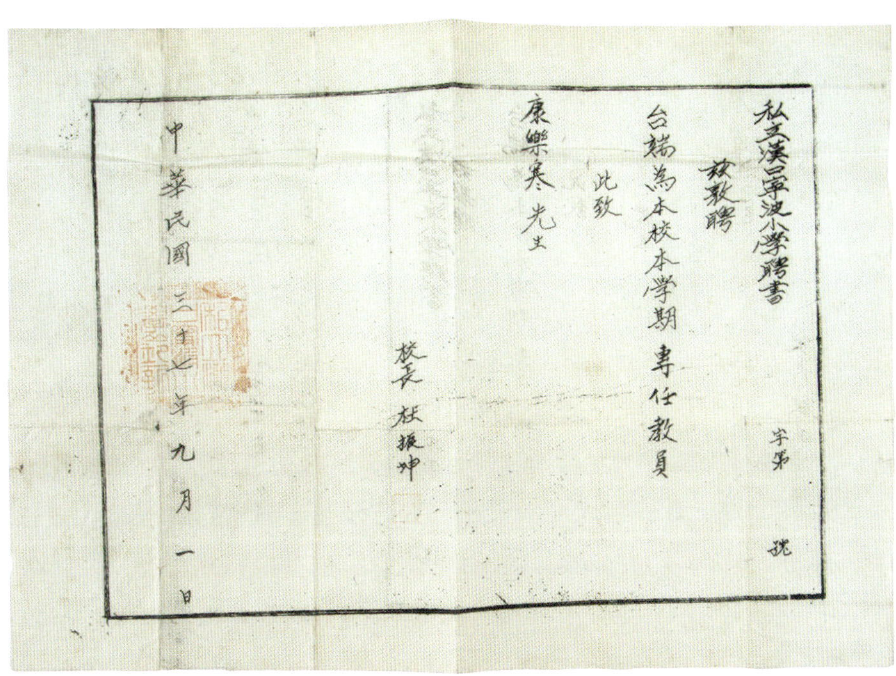

私立漢口寧波小學聘書 字第 號

茲敦聘

台端為本校本學期專任教員

此致

康樂寒先生

校長 杜振坤

中華民國三十七年九月一日

宁波旅汉小学最早于 1912 年由宁波会馆主事盛竹书和唐爱陆创办，据 1920 年《夏口县志》记载，当时该校位于汉口第四区德华里。后来该小学改名私立汉口宁波小学，随宁波会馆搬迁，就在隔壁与其紧密相连。大革命时期，宁波旅汉小学一度是汉口党团活动的中心，收容了大批宁波籍党团人士来汉避难，他们在此任教，编写刊物，传播进步思想。

The Hankou Ningbo Elementary School was founded in 1912 by Sheng Zhushu and Tang Ailu, leaders of the Ningbo business guild in Hankou. In the mid-1920s, the school briefly became a hub for CPC activity in Hankou, providing shelter for many CPC members of Ningbo origin. These party members also taught, disseminated their own publications, and spread progressive ideas at the school.

汉口包平和鞋帽庄制鞋工具

Shoemaking Tools of Bao Ping He Shoe and Hat Shop

民国时期

一套六件

包玉坤捐赠 Acquired from Bao Yukun through donation

清光绪年间，镇海横河堰包氏后人包振镳在汉口繁华地段的前花楼街开设包平和鞋帽庄，采用前店后厂形式，按照中国传统家族手工作坊的模式经营。1912 年，包振镳之子包兆龙进入汉口包平和鞋帽庄做学徒，学习下料、裁剪、贴膀、滚口到配底的全套制鞋工艺，后子承父业成为包平和鞋帽庄店主。包平和鞋帽庄生产布鞋、凉鞋、拖鞋、棉鞋等各式鞋靴以满足顾客在不同季节的穿着需求。同时，还兼营帽子、围巾、袜子、扇子、煤油灯等百货。

1931 年，包兆龙之子包玉刚从家乡宁波来到汉口，在父亲的包平和鞋帽庄学生意。包兆龙原本想让包玉刚继承父业，但年轻的包玉刚对金融业产生了强烈的兴趣，他利用空余时间进修英语、会计和经营知识。他向父亲提出要到英商安利洋行保险部工作，包兆龙见儿子志存高远，欣然同意。从在汉口包平和鞋帽庄协助父亲打理生意到成为汉口英商安利洋行保险部的一名实习生，包玉刚开启了在金融领域的奋斗历程，这段宝贵的经历为他今后走上船王之路、实现人生理想打下坚实的基础。

In the late 1800s, Bao Zhenbiao, a descendant of the Bao family from Hengheyan in Zhenhai, established the Bao Ping He Shoe and Hat Shop in a busy Hankou neighborhood. In 1912, Bao's son, Bao Zhaolong, joined the shop as an apprentice, eventually taking the reins and becoming the proprietor.

The Bao Ping He Shoe and Hat Shop crafted a wide array of footwear, including cloth shoes, sandals, slippers, and cotton shoes, catering to customers' seasonal needs. They also stocked items like hats, scarves, socks, fans, and kerosene lamps.

Bao Zhaolong's son, Sir Y.K. Pao, went on to become a shipping tycoon with his highly-successful Worldwide Shipping Group in Hong Kong.

汉阳阜成厂制造的宁波钱业会馆红砖瓦

Red Brick Tiles Manufactured by Hankow Han Yah Shing Agents for the Banking Guildhall of Ningbo (Qianye Huiguan)

民国时期

38.0 cm × 24.0 cm × 5.0 cm

宁波市钱币学会捐赠 Acquired from the Ningbo Numismatic Society through donation

位于宁波战船街10号的钱业会馆，是中国现存最为完好的金融业会馆建筑之一，也是全国唯一保存完整的钱庄业历史文化遗迹。

该砖瓦由宁波帮营造业翘楚沈祝三创办的汉阳阜成机器砖瓦厂制造。历史上，由汉阳裕记、阜成、华新等砖瓦厂生产的各类砖瓦，因为质地优良，声名远播，被时人称为“汉阳瓦”，主导长江流域市场。砖瓦上印有汉阳阜成厂的中英文商标，一方面彰显了厂家信誉，另一方面也体现了厂家对于产品质量的信心。1906年，德国商人在汉开办德源砖瓦厂，首次在武汉使用德式窑（后称轮窑）烧制红砖红瓦。后来沈祝三收购德源，创办阜成，在轮窑焙烧基础上，采用蒸汽机为动力制砖，是当时先进技术的代表，先后为武大珞珈山上的“老十八栋”别墅、汉口江滩的租界老房子等提供砖瓦，是近代武汉建筑变局的生动细节。

此外，沈祝三还在汉口创设汉协盛营造厂，逐渐发展成为武汉地区最有名的营造厂，在武汉等地留下了一大批包括武汉大学主体建筑、四明银行、璇宫饭店等武汉近代代表性建筑。

The building at 10 Zhanchuan Street in Ningbo, known as the Banking Guildhall of Ningbo, stands as one of the best-preserved architectural gems in China’s financial history. It is a true testament to the heritage of banking institutions in the country.

The bricks and tiles used in its construction were manufactured by the Hankow Han Yah Shing Agents, a prominent player in China’s construction industry. Historically, their bricks and tiles, known as “Hankow Tiles”, gained widespread recognition for their excellent quality and dominated the Yangtze River region markets.

These bricks and tiles proudly bear the bilingual trademark of Hankow Han Yah Shing Agents, symbolizing both the manufacturer’s reputation and their unwavering confidence in the quality of their products.

同仁堂乐氏家族合影

Tong Ren Tang Le Family Photo

69.0 cm × 18.0 cm

张健飞捐赠 Acquired from Zhang Jianfei through donation

在早期，宁波商人便开始尝试异地经营。慈城人乐显扬（号尊育）于清康熙八年（1669）在北京创办了同仁堂，以制售丸、散、膏、丹著称于世，曾供奉御药房和承办官药。清末民初，同仁堂铺东乐氏家族正处在兴旺时期，购买了包括清恭王府前院（现郭沫若故居所在地）在内的多处皇家的王府园林。该合影为乐氏家族后人乐季繁全家福，拍摄于清恭王府。

In 1669, Le Xianyang, a native of Cicheng, founded Tong Ren Tang in Beijing. The pharmacy became famous for its production and sale of pills, powders, ointments, and elixirs. At one point in time, Tong Ren Tang even supplied the imperial pharmacy. These early ventures paved the way for the later expansion of Ningbo merchants' businesses across China.

科学仪器馆股份有限公司汉口分馆发票

Invoice Issued by the Hankou Branch of the China Educational Supply Association, Ltd.

民国时期

22.0 cm × 15.0 cm

收购 Acquired from purchase

1925 年，美国芝加哥大学电气工程硕士、曾在美国西屋电气制造公司任职的镇海人丁佐成回国后到上海创业，在博物院路 20 号（今虎丘路 131 号）虎丘公寓二楼租了两间写字间，创办中华科学仪器馆，开始仪表制造。1927 年，该馆改为大华科学仪器股份有限公司，是中国第一家自主生产仪器仪表的企业。

丁佐成（1897—1966），宁波镇海人，仪表专家，中国现代仪器仪表业的先驱，组织生产了第一只国产电表，为中国仪表工业的发展做出了重要贡献。

In 1925, Ding Zuocheng (1897-1966), a native of Zhenhai, Ningbo, returned to China after completing his master's degree in electrical engineering at the University of Chicago and working for the Westinghouse Electric Manufacturing Company. He set up his business in Shanghai, leasing two office rooms on the second floor of the Huqiu Apartments at 20 Bowuyuan Road (now 131 Huqiu Road). There, he founded the Chinese Science Instrument Hall and began manufacturing scientific instruments and equipment. In 1927, the institution was transformed into the China Educational Supply Association, Ltd. making it the first Chinese company to independently produce scientific instruments. Ding Zuocheng is widely recognized as a pioneer in China's scientific instrument manufacturing industry, and his leadership resulted in the production of China's first domestically made electric meter, a significant milestone for the industry.

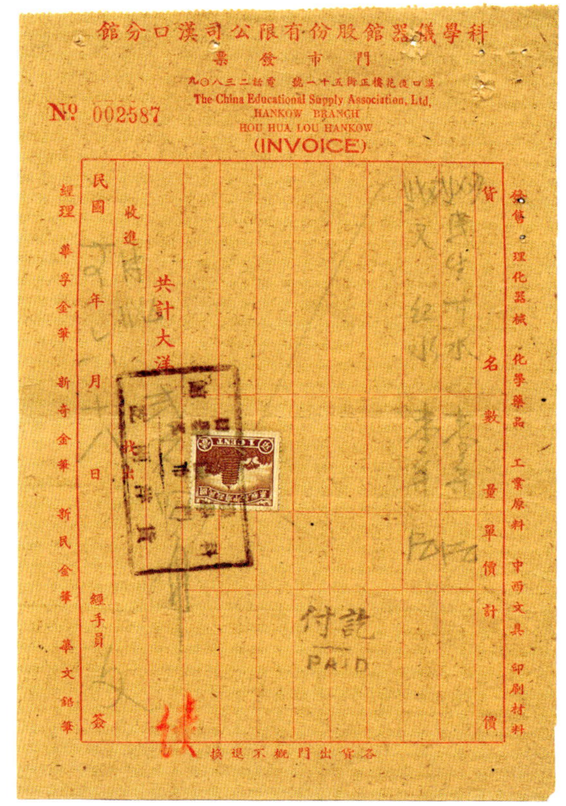

科學儀器館股份有限公司漢口分館
門市發票
漢口後花樓正街五十一號 電話二三八〇九
The China Educational Supply Association, Ltd,
HANKOW BRANCH
HOU HUA LOU HANKOW
(INVOICE)
№ 002587
發售 理化器械 化學藥品 工業原料 中西文具 印刷材料
貨名 數量 單價 計價
經理 華孚金筆 新奇金筆 新民金筆 華文鉛筆
民國 年 月 日
收進
共計大洋
經手員 簽
付訖 PAID
各貨出門概不退換

余名钰著《铸铁》

Iron Forging by Yu Mingyu

1953 年

21.5 cm × 14.8 cm × 1.0 cm

社会征集 Acquired from local community member through donation

余名钰（1896—1962）被誉为民国时期中国的“钢铁大王”。抗战爆发后，大鑫钢铁厂总经理余名钰将生产设备辗转武汉运至重庆，与民生公司、金城银行合资在重庆组建渝鑫钢铁厂股份有限公司，自任总经理兼总工程师，该厂是抗战时期大后方中的大型民营钢铁工业企业。1938 年至 1939 年，渝鑫厂基本以制造军火为主，生产炸弹、手榴弹和山炮。1939 年后，转以民用生产为主。从 1939 年到 1945 年，共生产钢 6057 吨、铁 5886 吨，生产的武器和弹药有力地支援了前线的抗日斗争。

Yu Mingyu (1896-1962) was widely recognized as the “Steel Tycoon” of the Republican era. At the start of the Anti-Japanese War, Yu Mingyu, the general manager of the Daxin Iron and Steel Factory, orchestrated the relocation of production equipment first to Wuhan and later Chongqing. There, he formed a joint venture with Minsheng Company and Jincheng Bank, giving birth to the Yuxin Iron and Steel Factory Co., Ltd. Yu Mingyu assumed the roles of general manager and chief engineer. This factory emerged as a significant privately-owned steel industry enterprise in the wartime rear areas.

Between 1938 and 1939, the Yuxin Factory primarily focused on manufacturing munitions, such as bombs, hand grenades, and mountain artillery. After 1939, the production shifted its primary focus to civilian goods. Over the period spanning 1939 to 1945, the factory collectively produced 6,057 tons of steel and 5,886 tons of iron, providing crucial support for the front lines of the war.

《武汉市志 · 城市建设　建筑业》稿本

Manuscript of *Wuhan City Chronicles: Urban Construction - Construction Industry*

1986 年

25.7 cm × 18.6 cm × 2.1 cm

康云龙捐赠 Acquired from Kang Yunlong through donation

宁波和武汉渊源深厚。历史上，宁波人怀着勇于拼搏、开拓创新的精神溯江至汉，在其中西交融的城市发展史中，谱写出至诚至真的篇章。

这两本史料集中体现了宁波帮和武汉建筑业同呼吸、共发展的历史，对当时武汉的营造厂、设计师进行了详细研究和记载，呈现了宁波帮承建大量武汉近代建筑的翔实信息，例如沈祝三的汉协盛营造厂、李祖贤的六合公司、魏清涛的魏清记营造厂、康炘生的康生记营造厂等。

《武汉著名的近代建筑概况表（1861—1949）》稿本

Manuscript of *Overview of Wuhan's Famous Modern Buildings (1861-1949)*

1986年

25.6 cm × 18.2 cm × 0.7 cm

康云龙捐赠 Acquired from Kang Yunlong through donation

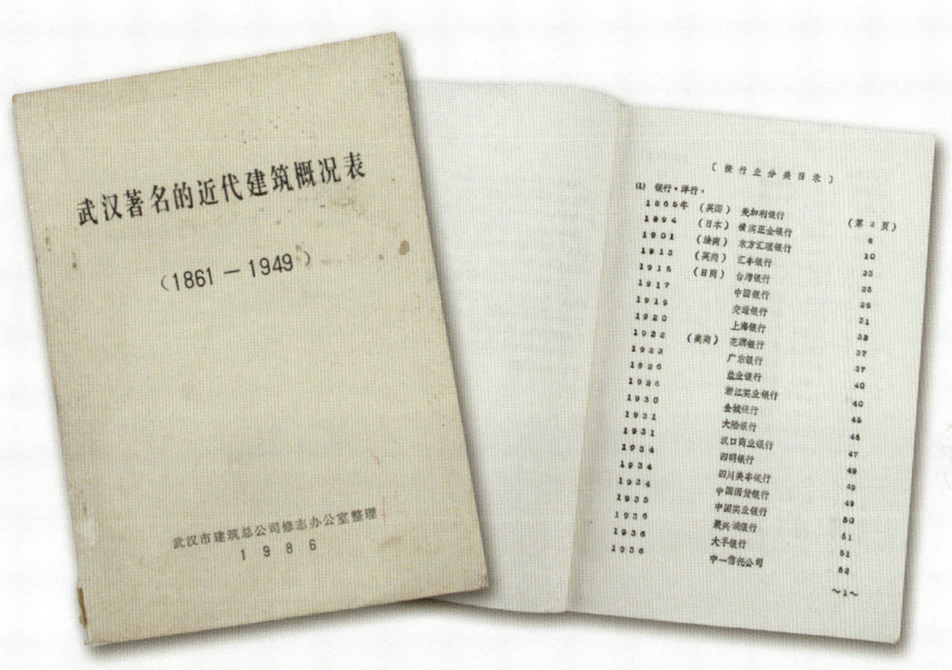

Ningbo has deep-rooted ties with Wuhan. In the realm of city construction, the life stories and resilient spirit of Ningbo's builders and designers have left an indelible mark on Wuhan's cityscape through various construction projects and architectural designs.

These two books are a testament to the shared history of Ningbo merchants and the development of Wuhan's construction industry. They meticulously document and explore the construction firms and architects in Wuhan during a particular period in history, providing insight into how Ningbo merchants contributed significantly to Wuhan's modern urban environment.

童萼塘使用过的眼底镜、医嘱手写卡片

Tong Etang's Ophthalmoscope and Handwritten Prescriptions

①直径 4.0 cm × 24.0 cm ②10.9 cm × 10.3 cm

童晓欣、童晓荣捐赠 Acquired from Tong Xiaoxin and Tong Xiaorong through donation

童萼塘（1933—2009），祖籍宁波慈溪，出身医学世家，著名神经病学专家，华中科技大学同济医学院附属协和医院神经科创始人。

20 世纪 70 年代，童萼塘深入中国农村调查研究，发现了由粗制棉油（含棉酚）引起的低钾软病，阐明了发病机理，提出了防治措施，改变了广大中国农村人口食用粗制棉油的生活方式，根除了由粗制棉油引起的低钾软病的发病和死亡。他主持的低血钾软病研究曾获国家科技进步二等奖。

童萼塘在极其艰苦的条件下，从无到有地创建了武汉协和医院神经内科，并将其培育成为湖北省重点学科。他在疑难疾病诊治方面具有独到的见解，在运动障碍性疾病领域和神经康复学领域的研究造诣博大精深。

2003 年 3 月退休后，童萼塘仍坚持工作在临床第一线。为了方便病患，童萼塘手写了几百张医嘱说明卡，制作了专门的印章，将疾病的名称、症状、服药方法等一一列出，这些卡片和印章被誉为“连心卡”“便民章”。在 76 岁高龄之际，他仍旧坚持每天坐诊，名医门诊结束后，就到普通门诊义务诊病。2009 年 7 月 4 日，童萼塘意外离世。他的学生、患者，乃至医院物业员工、保洁阿姨上千人自发吊唁悼念。

Tong Etang (1933-2009), originally from Cixi, Ningbo, came from a family of doctors and was a renowned expert in neurology. He was the founder of the Department of Neurology, Union Hospital, Tongji Medical College, Huazhong University of Science and Technology. In the 1970s, Tong conducted in-depth research in rural China and discovered cases of hypokalemic myopathy caused by the consumption of crudely processed cottonseed oil which contains gossypol. Tong elucidated the disease's pathogenesis and proposed prevention and treatment measures. This changed the dietary habits of the vast rural population in China, eradicating the incidence and mortality of hypokalemic myopathy. The research Tong led on hypokalemic myopathy won the Second Prize of National Science and Technology Progress Award.

Amidst formidable challenges, Tong established the Department of Neurology at Wuhan Union Hospital and transformed it into a pivotal discipline within Hubei Province. He possessed distinctive insights into the diagnosis and treatment of complex diseases, making significant contributions to the study of movement disorders and the advancement of neurological rehabilitation.

Following his retirement in March 2003, Tong persisted in his clinical work, manually writing hundreds of prescriptions to aid his patients. Even at the age of 76, he steadfastly continued to see patients every day. After concluding his sessions in the specialist outpatient department, he voluntarily served in the general outpatient clinic. Tong unexpectedly passed away on July 4, 2009, leaving a legacy that prompted spontaneous mourning and tributes from thousands of people, including his students, patients, and even the hospital's maintenance and cleaning staff.

① 眼底镜

有忧郁症状的病员的家属请注意：

1. 现在治疗"忧郁症状"的药物很多，效果也比较好，副作用较少而且即使有也较轻，容易解决。但要想用得好，一般至少要半个月以后才显效；一个月以后才有明显疗效。药物一定要吃足量，不能少吃，而且要坚持用较长时间，否则容易又再加重。

2. 有忧郁的病员，相当一部分会有"自杀"的念头，因为他(她)们的精神症状不像其他精神病那样重（如精神错乱），所以要想自杀也容易成功。所以这种病员最好住院治疗（得护理好，不会发生自杀）；如果不住院在家里一定要有人日夜陪伴不能离人，吃药要看着病人吞下去，所有药物

② 医嘱手写卡片

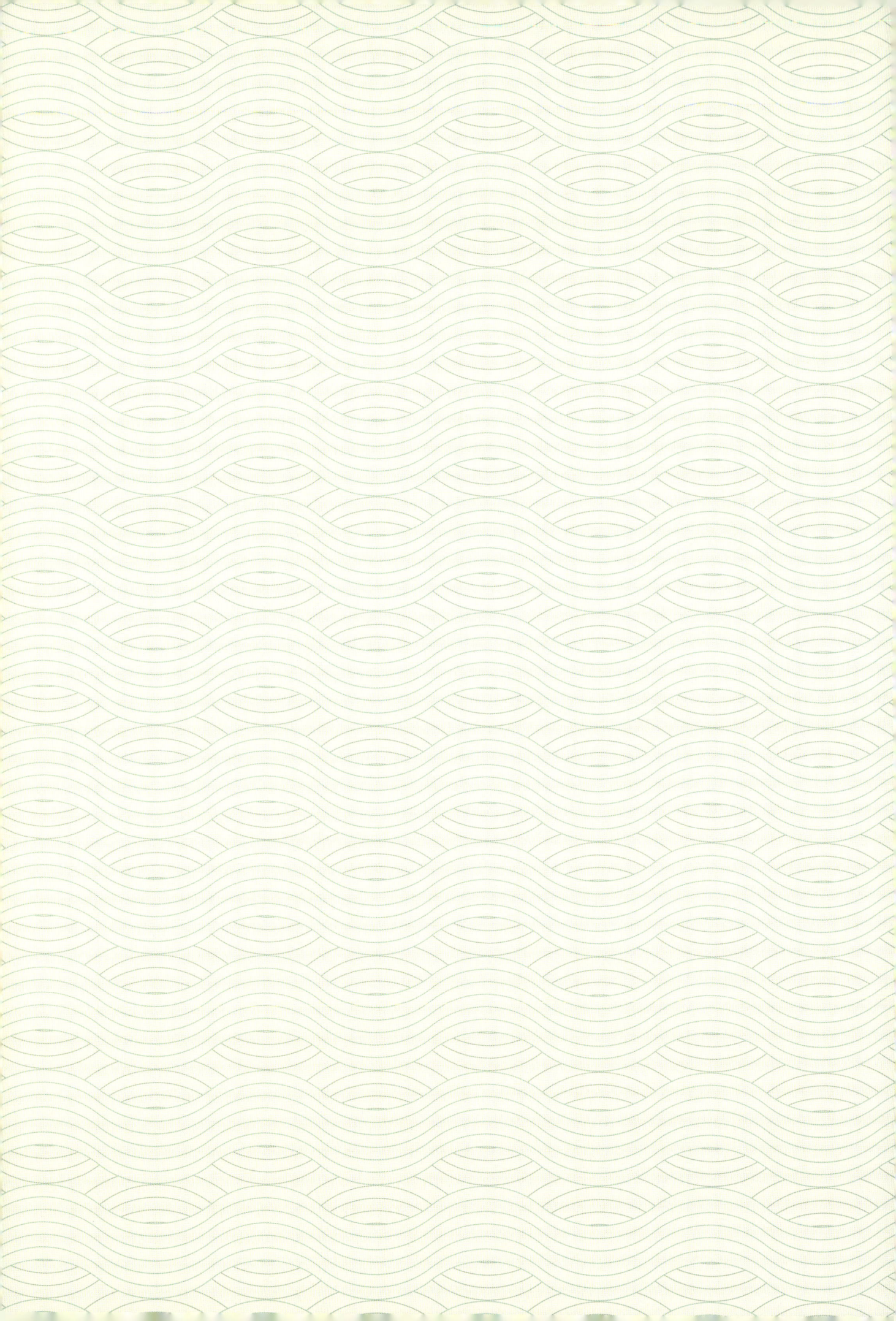

驰骋港台

Prominence in Hong Kong and Taiwan

姚胥锑私立沪江大学商学院毕业证书

Graduation Certificate of Yao Xuti from the Business School of Shanghai College

1947 年

48.0 cm × 32.0 cm

姚锦华捐赠 Acquired from Yao Jinhua through donation

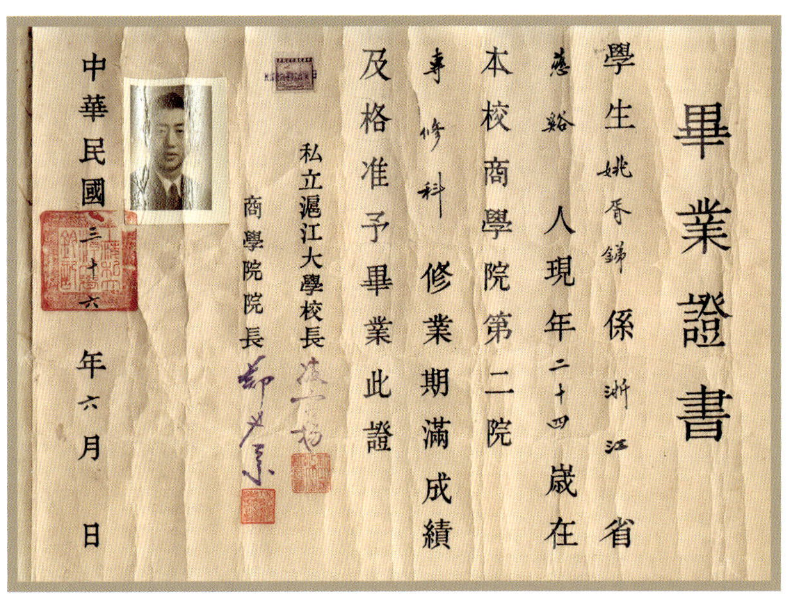

畢業證書

學生姚胥銻係浙江省慈谿人現年二十四歲在本校商學院第二院專修科修業期滿成績及格准予畢業此證

私立滬江大學校長

商學院院長

中華民國三十六年六月日

姚祥兴（1924—2011），原名姚胥锑，祖籍宁波庄桥。曾任香港祥丰企业有限公司董事长，香港甬港联谊会永远名誉会长，宁波市政协第十届、十一届港澳委员。

姚祥兴于 20 世纪 50 年代赴香港经商，事业有成后，多次为祖国和家乡的教育卫生等社会公益事业慷慨解囊。自 1984 年以来，姚祥兴多次回宁波考察，先后捐资助建宁波祥星幼儿园、宁波祥星医院、奉化西坞中学祥星教学楼等 10 余个公益福利项目。2005 年，姚祥兴夫妇在宁波大学捐资设立“姚祥兴、邹星缘助学基金”。

该证书为 1947 年 6 月姚祥兴（姚胥锑）从私立沪江大学商学院毕业的证书。沪江大学创办于 1906 年，是 20 世纪上半叶上海著名的综合性大学，学校以文理商科著称。

Yao Xiangxing (1924-2011), originally named Yao Xuti and hailing from Zhuangqiao, Ningbo, was the Chairman of Hong Kong's J. S. Yao Co., Ltd. In the 1950s, he embarked on a successful business journey in Hong Kong. He also got into philanthropy, making multiple donations to support social welfare projects in Ningbo, particularly in education and healthcare.

This is Yao's graduation certificate from the Business School of Shanghai College, dated June 1947. Founded in 1906, Shanghai College was a prominent comprehensive institution in Shanghai during the first half of the 20th century, with a strong reputation in fields such as liberal arts, science, and commerce.

张渭熊使用过的旅行箱

Travel Case Used by Zhang Weixiong

1948 年

74.0 cm × 45.0 cm × 20.0 cm

张蓓、张范捐赠 Acquired from Zhang Bei and Zhang Fan through donation

张渭熊，宁波人，曾在董浩云的“天龙”轮上担任报务助理，后升任三副。

1946 年，董浩云在上海成立中国航运信托公司，为践行“象征国力、交流文化、活动经济”的愿望，从 1947 年到 1948 年，“天龙”轮穿越大西洋、“通平”轮穿越太平洋，开创了中国远洋航业的壮举。此后，中国船的踪迹遂遍及世界各大洋。

作为“天龙”轮的三副，张渭熊以严谨认真、一丝不苟的工作态度为“天龙”轮保驾护航，实现了中国远洋航运环球航行的壮举。张渭熊在“天龙”轮航行途中所使用的这只旅行箱是中国远洋航业壮举的见证。

Zhang Weixiong, Ningbo native, served as an assistant on C.Y. Tung's vessel *Heavenly Dragon* and was later promoted to Third Officer. In 1946, C.Y. Tung established the Orient Overseas Container Line in Shanghai with the goal of revitalizing national strength, promoting cultural exchange, and facilitating trade. From 1947 to 1948, the *Heavenly Dragon* successfully crossed the Atlantic and C.Y. Tung's another vessel *Tongping* crossed the Pacific, marking a significant milestone in China's long-distance shipping industry.

This travel case would have accompanied Zhang on his many journeys as third officer of the *Heavenly Dragon*, be they as far away as the Atlantic or to locations closer to home.

王宽诚的香港中华总商会永远名誉会董证书

Honorary Director Certificate Issued to Kwan-cheng Wong by the Chinese General Chamber of Commerce, Hong Kong

1953 年

30.5 cm × 26.5 cm

王宽诚家族捐赠 Acquired from Kwan-cheng Wong's family through donation

香港中華總商會
THE CHINESE GENERAL CHAMBER OF COMMERCE
HONG KONG

永遠名譽會董證書 籌字第58號

王寬誠先生經遵照會章加入為本會永遠名譽會董相應發給本證書以資證明此證

右給王寬誠先生存執

會長 高卓雄

副會長 黃炳英 許庇穀

公曆壹九五三年七月一日

王宽诚（1907—1986），香港中华总商会原会长。毕生爱国爱乡，积极投身祖国建设，创办了"王宽诚教育基金会"，支持国家选派留学生，培养高科技人才。2018 年 12 月 18 日，党中央、国务院授予王宽诚"改革先锋"称号。

中华人民共和国成立初期，由于受到西方势力的封锁，外部可利用资源有限。王宽诚听闻国家需要进口棉花等物资，便在广东投资华侨投资公司，开展进出口贸易业务，产生的盈利全部用于支援国内建设。他甚至出售了自己在香港的房地产，购买国内急需物资，辗转运入中国内地。这一时期，王宽诚经常往返于香港、广州两地，为祖国的进出口贸易事业不遗余力、积极奔走，这张 1954 年的往返内地通行证便是珍贵见证。

香港中华总商会成立于 1900 年，是香港历史最长以及最具规模的商会之一。王宽诚自 1958 年担任该会副会长以来，共领导该会 13 届，成为该会百年史上担任副会长、会长时间最长的人之一。他在任职期间，为港胞民生福祉、香港

王宽诚往返内地通行证

Kwan-cheng Wong's Travel Pass to the Chinese Mainland

1954 年

19.5 cm × 13.0 cm

王宽诚家族捐赠 Acquired from Kwan-cheng Wong's family through donation

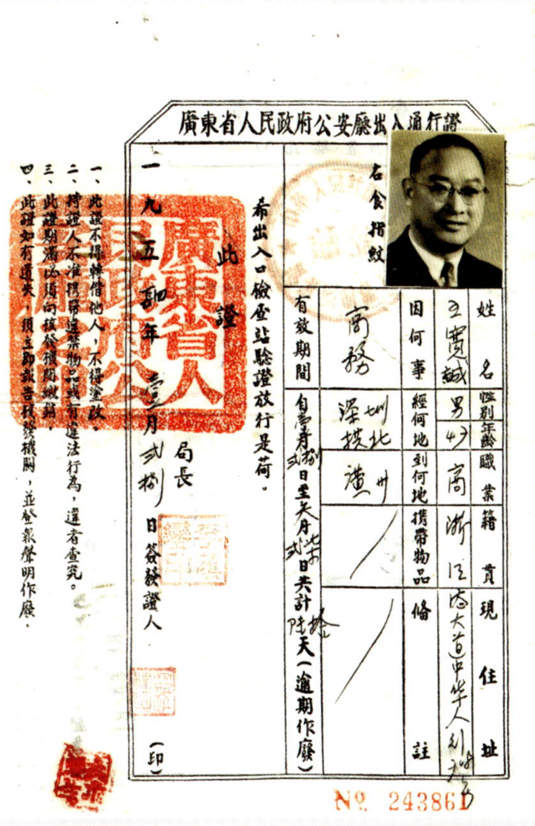

廣東省人民政府公安廳出入通行證

右食指紋

姓名	性別	年齡	職業	籍貫	現住址
王寬誠	男	47	商	浙江	

因何事	商務
經何地	深圳
到何地	廣州
攜帶物品	/
備註	/

有效期間 自壹月式拾日至叁月式拾日共計陸拾天（逾期作廢）

希出入口檢查站驗證放行是荷。

此證

局長

一九五四年壹月式拾日簽發

發證人

（印）

一、此證不得轉借他人，不得塗改。

二、持證人不准攜帶違禁物品或有違法行為，違者查究。

三、此證期滿必須向核發機關繳銷。

四、此證如有遺失，須立即報告核發機關，並登報聲明作廢。

No. 243861

与内地的交流做出了特殊贡献。

香港历来缺水，1963 年又出现大旱，港胞饱受缺水之苦。由王宽诚领导的香港中华总商会联合港九工会联合会向内地请求救援，中央拨出专款高速建成东深供水工程，从此结束了香港长期缺水的历史。在香港回归进程中，王宽诚出任基本法咨委会副主任，对香港的稳定发挥了积极作用。

Kwan-cheng Wong (1907-1986), was the former President of the Chinese General Chamber of Commerce in Hong Kong. Throughout his life, he had a deep sense of patriotism and dedicated his time to charity projects in Ningbo, his family's city of origin. He established the "Kwan-cheng Wong Education Foundation", which funded Chinese students studies abroad, nurturing high-tech talents for the country.

“东菊”号下水典礼银斧

Ceremonial Silver Axe from the Launching of the *Eastern Kiku*

1965年

39.0 cm × 19.0 cm × 7.0 cm

包陪庆捐赠 Acquired from Anna Pui-Hing Pao Sohmen through donation

20世纪60年代初，“东菊”号在日本下水，包玉刚夫人黄秀英主持典礼，并用此银斧砍断船绳。银斧置于一木盒中，盒盖的内面写有“M/V EASTERNKIKU”“BUILT BY：THE HAKODATE DOCK CO., LTD., HAKODATE, JAPAN.”的英文字样。银斧的手柄上除“东菊”号的英文名称外，还刻有“LAUNCHED ON 10TH FEBRUARY, 1965”。

包玉刚交往广泛，与各国政要保持良好关系，常邀请一些国家的元首夫人或皇室成员参加船舶下水典礼。当时的英国西敏斯特公爵夫人、新加坡总理李光耀夫人、美国国务卿基辛格夫人、英国玛格丽特公主、英国首相撒切尔夫人等都曾参加过包玉刚船舶下水典礼。

In the early 1960s, the ship *Eastern Kiku* was launched in Japan. Huang Sue-Ing, wife of Sir Y.K. Pao, presided over the ceremony, using this silver axe to cut the rope tethering the ship to the dock. The axe was later stored in a wooden box, which had the English text “M/V EASTERN-KIKU” and “BUILT BY: THE HAKODATE DOCK CO., LTD., HAKODATE, JAPAN.” inscribed on the inside of the lid. The axe handle featured the name of the ship, “EASTERN KIKU”, and the inscription “LAUNCHED ON 10TH FEBRUARY, 1965.”

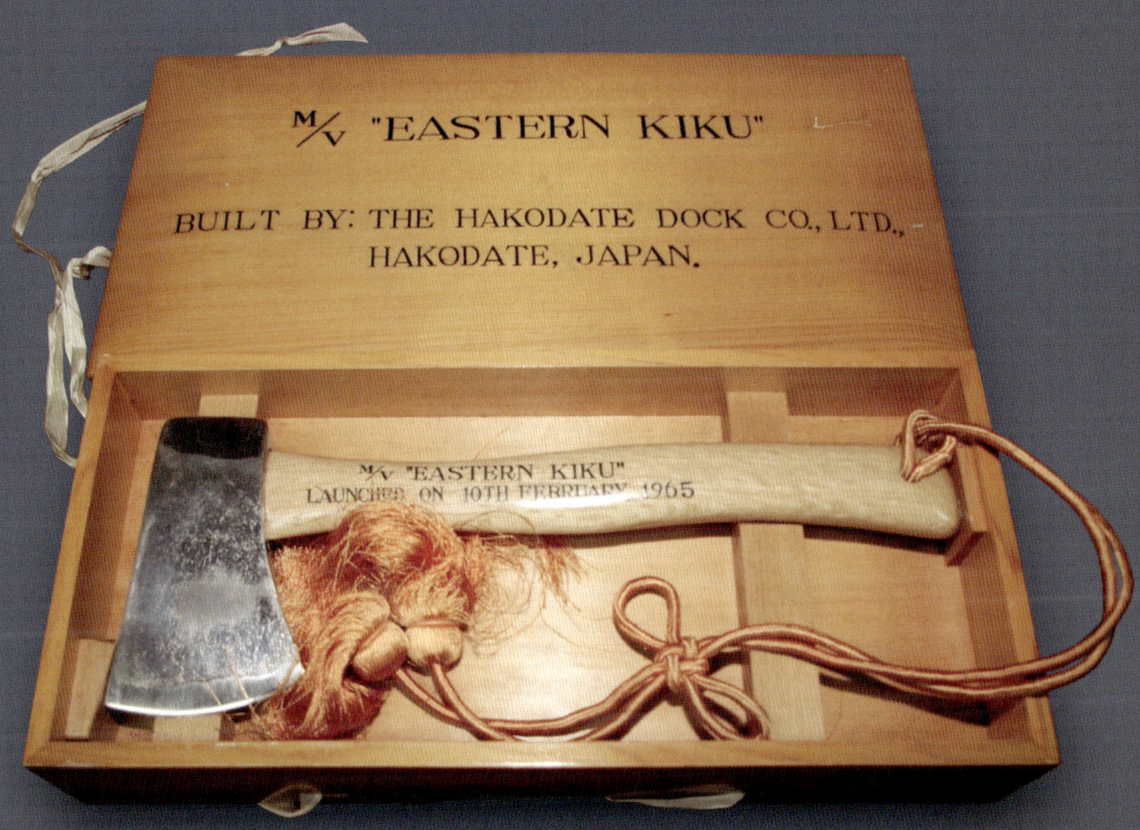
M/V "EASTERN KIKU"
BUILT BY: THE HAKODATE DOCK CO., LTD.,
HAKODATE, JAPAN.
M/V "EASTERN KIKU"
LAUNCHED ON 10TH FEBRUARY 1965

李达三当选为港九无线电联会会长的任命书

Appointment Letter of Li Dak Sum as President of the Radio Association of Hong Kong

1971 年

35.0 cm × 24.0 cm

李达三捐赠 Acquired from Li Dak Sum through donation

港九無線電聯會
RADIO ASSOCIATION OF HONG KONG

選任書 （選字第一九一號）

本會第十九屆會董業經照章選出
全體公推
李達三 先生為本屆會長
任期 由一九七一年七月一日起
至一九七三年六月底止
謹致選任書藉資存照

第十九屆選舉委員會主席

一九七一年七月一日

李达三，1921 年出生于宁波鄞县，毕业于复旦大学会计系。1949 年，李达三南下香港创立乐声公司，涉足电器业，取得日本声宝电器在中国香港、新加坡和马来西亚的总代理权，之后又与声宝合资在马来西亚建立生产基地，出口彩电等电器。20 世纪 80 年代后期在海外开拓卡尔登酒店集团，成为酒店业巨子。

李达三热心社会事务，担任港九无线电联会会长期间，以深远的目光和宽厚的胸怀，敦睦乡谊、守望相助、风雨携手、情系故里，为香港电子器材业及视听器材业的推动和发展贡献良多。

Li Dak Sum, born in 1921 in Yin County, Ningbo. In 1949, he relocated to Hong Kong and founded Roxy Radio and Electric company entering the electronics retail industry.In the late 1980s, he expanded overseas and became a magnate in the hotel industry by becoming the Chairman of the Carlton Group of Hotels.

Li was actively involved in philanthropy. During his tenure as the President of the Radio Association of Hong Kong, he contributed significantly to the growth of the electronics and audio-visual equipment industries in Hong Kong.

《诺丁汉大学与李达三博士及叶耀珍女士的友谊与互相支持协议》

Agreement of Friendship and Support between Dr. Li Dak Sum and Mrs. Li Yip Yio Chin and the University of Nottingham

30.0 cm × 21.0 cm

李达三捐赠 Acquired from Li Dak Sum through donation

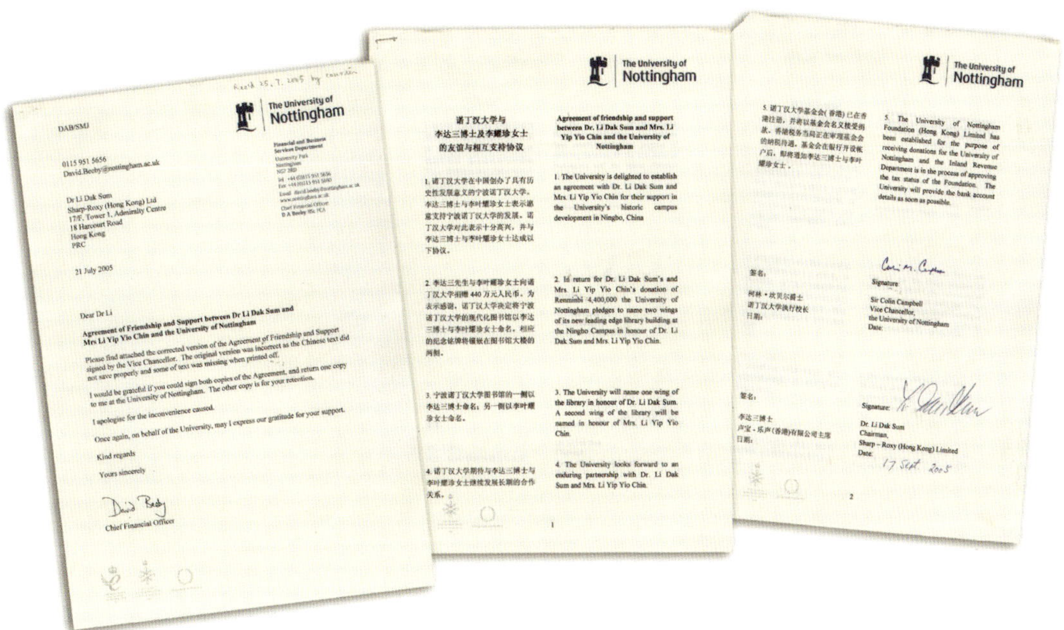

Rec'd 25.7.2005 by courier

The University of Nottingham

DAB/SMJ

0115 951 5656
David.Beeby@nottingham.ac.uk

Financial and Business Services Department
University Park
Nottingham
NG7 2RD

Dr Li Dak Sum
Sharp-Roxy (Hong Kong) Ltd
17/F, Tower 1, Admiralty Centre
18 Harcourt Road
Hong Kong
PRC

21 July 2005

Dear Dr Li

Agreement of Friendship and Support between Dr Li Dak Sum and Mrs Li Yip Yio Chin and the University of Nottingham

Please find attached the corrected version of the Agreement of Friendship and Support signed by the Vice Chancellor. The original version was incorrect as the Chinese text did not save properly and some of text was missing when printed off.

I would be grateful if you could sign both copies of the Agreement, and return one copy to me at the University of Nottingham. The other copy is for your retention.

I apologise for the inconvenience caused.

Once again, on behalf of the University, may I express our gratitude for your support.

Kind regards

Yours sincerely

David Beeby

Chief Financial Officer

The University of Nottingham

诺丁汉大学与李达三博士及李耀珍女士的友谊与相互支持协议

1. 诺丁汉大学在中国创办了具有历史性发展意义的宁波诺丁汉大学。李达三博士与李叶耀珍女士表示愿意支持宁波诺丁汉大学的发展。诺丁汉大学对此表示十分高兴，并与李达三博士与李叶耀珍女士达成以下协议。

2. 李达三先生与李叶耀珍女士向诺丁汉大学捐赠440万元人民币。为表示感谢，诺丁汉大学决定将宁波诺丁汉大学的现代化图书馆以李达三博士与李叶耀珍女士命名。相应的纪念铭牌将镶嵌在图书馆大楼的两侧。

3. 宁波诺丁汉大学图书馆的一侧以李达三博士命名；另一侧以李叶耀珍女士命名。

4. 诺丁汉大学期待与李达三博士与李叶耀珍女士继续发展长期的合作关系。

Agreement of friendship and support between Dr. Li Dak Sum and Mrs. Li Yip Yio Chin and the University of Nottingham

1. The University is delighted to establish an agreement with Dr. Li Dak Sum and Mrs. Li Yip Yio Chin for their support in the University's historic campus development in Ningbo, China

2. In return for Dr. Li Dak Sum's and Mrs. Li Yip Yio Chin's donation of Renminbi 4,400,000 the University of Nottingham pledges to name two wings of its new leading edge library building at the Ningbo Campus in honour of Dr. Li Dak Sum and Mrs. Li Yip Yio Chin.

3. The University will name one wing of the library in honour of Dr. Li Dak Sum. A second wing of the library will be named in honour of Mrs. Li Yip Yio Chin.

4. The University looks forward to an enduring partnership with Dr. Li Dak Sum and Mrs. Li Yip Yio Chin.

1

The University of Nottingham

5. 诺丁汉大学基金会(香港)已在香港注册，并将以基金会名义接受捐款。香港税务当局正在审理基金会的纳税待遇。基金会在银行开设帐户后，即将通知李达三博士与李叶耀珍女士。

5. The University of Nottingham Foundation (Hong Kong) Limited has been established for the purpose of receiving donations for the University of Nottingham and the Inland Revenue Department is in the process of approving the tax status of the Foundation. The University will provide the bank account details as soon as possible.

签名：

柯林·坎贝尔爵士
诺丁汉大学执行校长
日期：

Signature: Colin M. Campbell

Sir Colin Campbell
Vice Chancellor,
the University of Nottingham
Date:

签名：

李达三博士
声宝-乐声(香港)有限公司主席
日期：

Signature:

Dr. Li Dak Sum
Chairman,
Sharp – Roxy (Hong Kong) Limited
Date: 17 Sept. 2005

2

事业有成之后，李达三不忘回馈社会、回报祖国。他与夫人叶耀珍、长孙李本俊在浙江、香港等地捐款捐物、造福桑梓，支持祖国教育、福利等事业。在宁波，他们先后捐建宁波大学、宁波诺丁汉大学教学楼，设立各类奖学金以及李达三叶耀珍伉俪李本俊体育发展基金。

Li was both a highly accomplished businessperson and a generous philanthropist. Along with his wife Yip Yio Chin and eldest grandson Kenneth Li, he invested in numerous goodwill projects across China. In Ningbo, their contributions have played a crucial role in supporting the construction of new buildings at Ningbo University and the University of Nottingham Ningbo China, and setting up scholarships. The Li Dak Sum Yip Yio Chin Kenneth Li Sports Development Fund was set up to support Ningbo's athletic endeavors.

《海上巨人号下水礼》电影胶片

Film Reel of the *Launch Ceremony of the Ship Seawise Giant*

1981 年

直径 35.0 cm × 2.5 cm

董浩云资料室捐赠 Acquired from the C. Y. Tung Archives through donation

电影胶片记录了“海上巨人”号下水典礼的盛况，宁波帮航运巨子董浩云为制片人。

董浩云祖籍浙江舟山，由其创办的中国东方海外货柜航运公司拥有 150 多艘船舶，总吨位超过 1100 万吨，他个人也成为世界最大独立船东。1981 年，公司旗下的“海上巨人”号正式下水。该船长 458 米，以其重达 56 万吨的总承载量成为当时世界上最大的船只。经商之余，董浩云对音乐、文学、戏剧、摄影都有浓厚的兴趣。特别是电影，由他编导的《超级邮轮史诗》曾两次荣获国际奖项。

董浩云使用过的打字机

C. Y. Tung's Typewriter

20 世纪

50.0 cm × 35.0 cm × 30.0 cm

董浩云资料室捐赠 Acquired from the C. Y. Tung Archives through donation

The film footage captured the grand ceremony of the launch of the Ship *Seawise Giant*, with shipping magnate C.Y. Tung as the producer. C.Y. Tung, originally from Zhoushan, Zhejiang, founded the Orient Overseas Container Line. At the peak of his career, he owned a shipping fleet with over 150 freight ships, and his fleet's cargo capacity exceeded 11 million tons. In 1981, the company's *Seawise Giant* was officially launched. This ship was 458 meters long, and with its impressive tonnage of 560,000 DWT, it was the world's largest vessel of its time.

“世谊”号航海天文钟

Marine Chronometer on the *Shiyi*

1982 年

木盒 19.0 cm × 18.3 cm × 17.0 cm；钟直径 14.0 cm × 7.0 cm

包陪庆捐赠 Acquired from Anna Pui-Hing Pao Sohmen through donation

“世谊”号是世界船王包玉刚创办的香港环球航运集团向上海江南造船厂订造的一艘 2.7 万吨散装船。在 20 世纪 80 年代的中英谈判中，“世谊”号发挥了特殊作用。

1982 年，中英谈判陷入僵局。包玉刚与时任英国首相撒切尔夫人会面时，向英方开出造价不菲的船舶订单，并邀请撒切尔夫人来中国参加船舶下水命名典礼。1983 年，撒切尔夫人应约以非官方身份到上海参加江南造船厂“世谊”号下水剪彩。这作为契机，进一步促进了中英双方的沟通。

The *Shiyi* was a 27,000-ton bulk carrier commissioned by Hong Kong’s Worldwide Shipping Group (founded by shipping magnate Sir Y.K. Pao) from the Shanghai Jiangnan Shipyard. During negotiations in the 1980s between China and Britain regarding the sovereignty of Hong Kong, the *Shiyi* played an unexpectedly crucial role.

In 1982, as Sino-British negotiations reached an impasse, Sir Y. K. Pao met with then-Prime Minister of the United Kingdom Margaret Thatcher. He offered a substantial shipbuilding order to the British side and extended an invitation for Mrs. Thatcher to participate in the ship’s naming and launch ceremony in China. In 1983, Thatcher accepted the invitation in a non-official capacity and joined the launch event for the *Shiyi* at the Jiangnan Shipyard. This occasion facilitated further communication between China and the UK.

上海江南造船厂制造的“世沪”号模型

Model of the *Shihu* Built by Shanghai Jiangnan Shipyard

1982 年

75.0 cm × 18.0 cm × 23.0 cm

包陪庆捐赠 Acquired from Anna Pui-Hing Pao Sohmen through donation

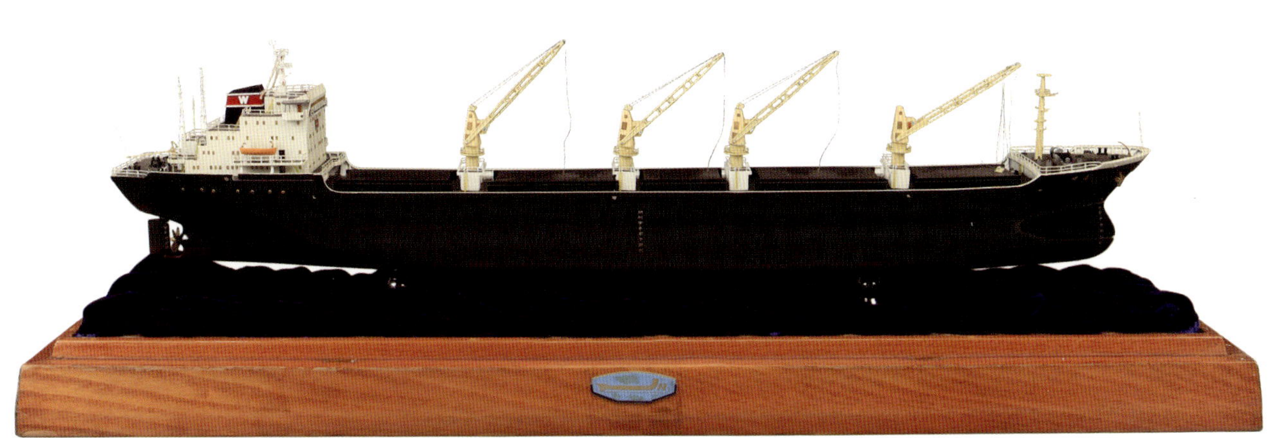

1980 年，包玉刚创办的香港环球航运集团向上海江南造船厂订造了两条 2.7 万吨散装船——“世沪”号和“世谊”号。包玉刚希望以此为契机，推动中国造船业迈向国际。

1982 年 6 月 10 日，“世沪”号举行下水典礼。菲律宾总统夫人伊梅尔达 · 马科斯应邀主持仪式并亲自为这艘货轮命名。香港环球航运集团主席包玉刚和上海市市长汪道涵、外交部顾问韩念龙、中国船舶工业总公司董事长柴树藩等出席了典礼。“世沪”号成为 1982 年 5 月成立的中国船舶工业总公司的首条出口船舶。

“世沪”号在随后的远航生涯中经受了多次大风大浪的考验，引领中国造船业打开了国际市场的大门，从此国外航运界订单接踵而来。“世沪”号于 1982 年 9 月获得国家质量金质奖，被美国、日本和中国香港的造船界、航运界人士誉为“可与世界上任何一条船的质量媲美”。

In 1980, Hong Kong's Worldwide Shipping Group, founded by Sir Y.K. Pao, commissioned two 27,000-ton bulk carriers from the Shanghai Jiangnan Shipyard, the *Shihu* and the *Shiyi*. Sir Y.K. Pao intended to leverage this opportunity to propel China's shipbuilding industry onto the global stage.

安子介发明的写字机

Typewriter Invented by An Zijie

1988 年

35.5 cm × 31.5 cm × 13.0 cm

安宇昭捐赠 Acquired from An Yuzhao through donation

安子介（1912—2000），祖籍宁波定海，1912 年 6 月出生于上海，是杰出的社会活动家、著名爱国人士、香港知名实业家、中国人民政治协商会议第九届全国委员会副主席。

安子介在大力兴办实业的同时，继承中国童蒙识字教育传统，并努力推动其现代化进程。1979 年起，他孜孜不倦地向世界推广汉字，编撰的《解开汉字之谜》等 21 本汉字学专著成为外国人学习汉字的热门书。1988 年发明“安子介写字机”和安氏数字编码汉字输入法，让中文输入更为便利。安子介以其对社会的卓越贡献成为爱国爱港人士的一面旗帜。

An Zijie (1912-2000) was born in June 1912 in Shanghai to a family that hailed from Dinghai, Ningbo. He was a prominent social activist, a well-known patriot, and a successful Hong Kong industrialist.

From 1979 onwards, An Zijie dedicated himself to promoting Chinese language worldwide. In 1988, he introduced the “An Zijie Typewriter” and pioneered the An Zijie Digital Code Chinese Character Input Method, which greatly enhanced the efficiency of Chinese character input for users.

邱进益在“汪辜会谈”中使用过的钢笔

Pen Used by Qiu Jinyi During the Wang–Koo Summit

1993 年

直径 1.6 cm × 13.6 cm

邱进益捐赠 Acquired from Qiu Jinyi through donation

邱进益，生于 1936 年，祖籍慈溪。1993 年 3 月出任海峡交流基金会副董事长兼秘书长。同年应海峡两岸关系协会邀请，邱进益一行与海协会常务副会长唐树备进行“汪辜会谈”预备性磋商，草签了《两岸公证书使用查证协议》《两岸挂号函件查询、补偿事宜协议》，后又抵达新加坡，为“汪辜会谈”做最后的准备。

2013 年，邱进益向宁波帮博物馆捐赠了他参加“汪辜会谈”时所使用过的物品。这支在会谈中使用的钢笔尤为珍贵，是这一历史事件的实物见证。

Qiu Jinyi was born in 1936 to a family from Cixi, Ningbo. In March 1993, he assumed the position of Vice Chairman and Secretary-General of the Straits Exchange Foundation. In the same year, he was invited by the Association for Relations Across the Taiwan Straits to engage in preparatory discussions for the Wang-Koo Summit with Tang Shubei, the Association's Executive Deputy Chairman. Following this, he traveled to Singapore for the Summit's final preparations.

In 2013, Qiu made a significant donation to Ningbobang Museum, including items he had used during the Summit. Among these, a pen used during the negotiations holds particular value as a tangible witness to this historic event.

“瑞仑”轮纪念银牌

Commemorative Silver Medal of the *Lowlands Beilun*

1999 年

直径 12.0 cm

顾建纲捐赠 Acquired from Gu Jiangang through donation

1926 年，顾宗瑞（1886—1972）投身航运业，成立泰昌祥轮船行，以独立船东的身份经营航运业，泰昌祥成为中国最早的轮船公司之一。1949 年，顾宗瑞迁居香港，拓展航路，带领顾氏集团迎来了快速发展期。为顺应行业发展之势，1983 年顾氏集团重组为万利和泰昌祥（香港）两个独立的公司。

该银牌为“瑞仑”轮命名典礼的纪念品。“瑞仑”轮是 1999 年下水的好望角型散货轮，该船名取自顾氏家乡北仑港，其首航目的地即为北仑港。在外发展，顾宗瑞始终惦记着生养自己的故土，他再三嘱咐子嗣要爱国爱乡、造福桑梓。顾氏家族第二代、第三代在家乡捐建医院、学校，助力家乡港口建设，推动甬港交流合作，为宁波的发展做出了杰出贡献。

In 1926, C.S. Koo (1886-1972), as an independent ship owner, founded the Tai Chong Hsiang Steamship Company, one of China's earliest shipping firms. This commemorative silver medal was from the naming ceremony of the *Lowlands Beilun*, a Capesize bulk carrier launched in 1999. Its name was inspired by Gu's hometown, Beilun Port. Its inaugural voyage destination was also Beilun Port.

NAMING CEREMONY

曹光彪获得的沃顿商学院院长奖章及证书

The Warton School Dean's Medal and Certificate Awarded to K.P. Chao

2004 年

53.0 cm × 33.0 cm

曹其东捐赠 Acquired from Cao Qidong through donation

曹光彪(1921—2021),鄞县下应镇曹隘人,香港永新集团创始人,港龙航空发起者和创办人。曹光彪爱国爱港,将个人发展与国家繁荣紧密相连,热忱公益,重视科教,捐资设立多项高科技基金。国际永久编号 4566 号的小行星被命名为“曹光彪星”。

1978 年,曹光彪率先在珠海创办香洲毛纺厂。他开创的“三来一补”(来料加工、来样加工、来件装配和补偿贸易)亦领中国补偿贸易之先。2004 年,美国宾夕法尼亚大学沃顿商学院向他颁授“沃顿院长勋章”,以表彰他在中国改革开放中的重要推动作用。作为全球最负盛名的商学院,沃顿从 1983 年起设立院长奖章,旨在表彰在企业、公共服务以及学术领域做出突出成就的领袖人物。

Chao Kuang Piu (1921-2021), originally from Caoga in Xiaying Town, Yin County, Ningbo, was the founder of Novel Enterprises in Hong Kong and the visionary behind the establishment of Dragonair. In 1978, Chao founded the Xiangzhou Wollen Spinning Factory in Zhuhai. He pioneered an innovative business model that includes processing materials provided by foreign clients, processing goods based on samples provided by foreign clients, and assembling components provided by foreign clients, along with compensation trade. In 2004, the Wharton School of the University of Pennsylvania awarded him the prestigious Wharton Dean's Medal in recognition of his vital role in driving China's reform and opening-up.

永新光学生产的嫦娥探测器光学镜头

Optical Lens for Chang'e Probe Manufactured by Yongxin Optics

①直径 4.0 cm × 2.5 cm ②直径 4.0 cm × 3.2 cm

永新光学捐赠 Acquired from Yongxin Optical through donation

①

②

1997 年，曹光彪在宁波创立永新光学股份有限公司，从生产教育显微镜起步，扎根光学精密制造领域，专注于光学显微镜、光学元件组件的研发、生产和销售，产品主要出口到欧美、日本、新加坡等地，拥有多个自主品牌。

2019 年 1 月 3 日 10 时 26 分，嫦娥四号探测器成功在月球背面的南极－艾特肯盆地着陆，实现人类探测器首次在月球背面的软着陆，并通过“鹊桥号”中继卫星传回了世界第一张近距离拍摄的月背影像图。“嫦娥四号”降落月球第一眼近距离看清月球背面神秘世界的“眼睛”——光学镜头即由永新光学制造，记录下了中国航天事业发展的历史性时刻。

In 1997, Chao Kuang Piu founded Yongxin Optics Co., Ltd. in Ningbo. Originally producing educational microscopes, the company has since established itself in the field of precision optical manufacturing. They specialize in the research, production, and sales of optical microscopes and optical component assemblies, with their products primarily exported to Europe, the United States, Japan, Singapore, and other regions. They also have multiple proprietary brands.

On January 3, 2019, at 10:26 a.m., the Chang'e-4 lunar probe successfully landed in the South Pole-Aitken Basin on the far side of the moon. This marked the first time a human-made lunar probe had achieved a soft landing on the moon's far side. Through the relay satellite "Queqiao", it transmitted the world's first close-up image of the lunar far side. The "eye" that provided this close-up view of the mysterious world on the moon's far side was an optical lens manufactured by none other than Yongxin Optics.

赵安中穿过的毛衣

Sweater Worn by Chao An Chung

60.0 cm × 135.0 cm

赵安中家族捐赠 Acquired from the Chao An Chung family through donation

赵安中（1918—2007），出生于镇海骆驼，从学徒起家，辗转各地拼搏创业，终于在“知天命之年”获得事业的成功。其生前担任香港荣华纺织有限公司董事长，香港浙江省同乡会联合会、香港甬港联谊会、宁波旅港同乡会名誉会长等职。

赵安中在事业成功之后，热心社会公益，倾其所有投身“希望工程”，以母亲林杏琴命名的捐资助学项目几乎遍及浙江省所有的贫困乡镇。在助学上，赵安中慷慨解囊，而他对自己的生活几乎到了苛刻的地步。他穿过的毛衣上打满了补丁却不舍得扔掉，把节俭体现到了极致。

Chao An Chung (1918-2007), from Luotuo, Zhenhai, began his career as an apprentice and worked his way up through entrepreneurial ventures across China and other regions. Notably, he served as the Chairman of Wing Wah Textile Co., Ltd. in Hong Kong and held honorary positions in various associations, including the Ningbo Residents Association Hong Kong.

Even after achieving great success in his career, Chao An Chung remained deeply committed to philanthropy. He was especially passionate about supporting education, and his dedication extended to his personal life. His well-worn sweaters, adorned with patches, were a testament to his frugality and reluctance to waste.

应昌期发明并使用过的围棋桌

Go Table Invented and Used by Ing Chang-Ki

67.0 cm × 60.0 cm × 70.0 cm

应明皓捐赠 Acquired from Ying Minghao through donation

应昌期(1917—1997),生于宁波慈城,台湾金融界、实业界著名人士,应氏围棋计点制创造人,被誉为"黑白世界的诺贝尔""20世纪中国围棋之父"。

围棋是应昌期生活中不可或缺的一部分。在台北市重庆南路的家中,除客厅外,应昌期还布置了一间颇具规模的弈棋室——五窗填满斋,可同时容纳五六对人下棋。棋室中布置了六张棋桌,均由精致美观的镶贝壳柚木制作而成。棋桌设计构思精妙,平时俨如茶几,要对弈时,只需将桌面一翻便成棋桌,两侧又安置了两个旋转抽屉,可放棋子、茶杯、烟灰缸等,美观便捷。

2008年,应昌期之子应明皓先生将五窗填满斋中的一张围棋桌捐赠予筹建中的宁波帮博物馆。

Ing Chang-Ki (1917-1997), from Cicheng, Ningbo, was a prominent figure in Taiwan's financial and industrial circles. He was the ingenious mind behind the Ing rules of Go.

His design for this Go table is nothing short of remarkable. During everyday use, it serves as an elegant tea table. When the time comes for a game, one simply flips the tabletop to reveal the Go board. Two rotating drawers on each side provide convenient storage for game pieces, teacups, ashtrays, and other small items, seamlessly blending practicality with aesthetic appeal.

通利琴行早期打制的 CONCONE 钢琴

CONCONE Piano Produced by Tom Lee Music During its Early Years

150.0 cm × 60.0 cm × 130.0 cm

李孙文英捐赠 Acquired from Li-Sun Wenying through donation

通利琴行于 1953 年在香港成立，由李孙文英与其夫李子文共同创办。李孙文英，宁波鄞州区人，1952 年移居香港。琴行初创时，主要业务为制造及装配钢琴，20 世纪 60 年代成为香港最大的钢琴制造商。1962 年，通利琴行开始生产自家品牌 CONCONE 直身钢琴，外形精巧，采用柚木制造，桃木色，高 108 厘米，每月约生产 10 多部，主要在香港销售，推出后广受欢迎，直至 70 年代逐渐减少生产。如今，通利琴行业务范围日益扩大，服务网络遍及中国及加拿大的各大城市，也是全东南亚规模庞大的乐器经销商之一。

2006 年 9 月，一位顾客经通利服务部维修 CONCONE 钢琴。由于这部钢琴的结构、音色各方面依然良好，并对通利琴行有莫大意义，因此，通利琴行回收这部钢琴，并于 2009 年捐赠给宁波帮博物馆。

Tom Lee Music was established in Hong Kong in 1953 by the efforts of Li-Sun Wenying and her husband Li Ziwen. Li-Sun Wenying, originally from Yinzhou District, Ningbo, relocated to Hong Kong in 1952. In its early years, Tom Lee Music primarily engaged in the manufacturing and assembly of pianos, eventually becoming the largest piano manufacturer in Hong Kong during the 1960s. By 1962, Tom Lee Music had ventured into producing its own brand of upright pianos named CONCONE. Presently, Tom Lee Music has expanded its business scope, with a service network covering major cities in China and Canada, while also solidifying its position as one of the largest musical instrument distributors in Southeast Asia.

In September 2006, a customer had a CONCONE piano repaired by Tom Lee's service department. Impressed by the piano's enduring structure and tone, and recognizing the significance of Tom Lee Music, the customer decided to return the piano to Tom Lee Music. In 2009, Tom Lee Music donated this piano to Ningbobang Museum.

闻儒根使用过的 ROLLEICORD 相机
ROLLEICORD Camera Used by Wen Rugen

11.0 cm × 10.0 cm × 15.0 cm

闻儒根家人捐赠 Acquired from the Wen Rugen Family through donation

闻儒根（1920—2002），宁波樟村人，著名香港实业家。1950 年，闻儒根到香港创业，起初经营小规模的五金业务，后改行经营钟表。1969 年，他成立永联行贸易有限公司，生意日渐兴隆，所经营的 AROMA（奥威马）和 CLOWAT（确利华）钟表畅销世界。自 20 世纪 80 年代起，闻儒根多次回乡，在苏浙沪一带捐建了教育、卫生类的公益项目 60 多个。

闻儒根年轻时酷爱摄影，到香港创业后不久就买下了这台 ROLLEICORD 相机，用以记录与家人的温馨时光。这台相机伴随了闻家子女们的成长，也见证了先生不遗余力捐资家乡公益事业的桑梓情怀。

Wen Rugen (1920-2002), originally from Zhangcun, Ningbo, was a well-known Hong Kong industrialist. He began his entrepreneurial journey in Hong Kong in 1950, starting with a small hardware business, later transitioning to the watchmaking industry. In 1969, he founded Wing Luen Hong Trading Co., Ltd., whose AROMA and CLOWAT timepieces saw success worldwide. Since the 1980s, Wen Rugen made several return visits to his hometown, generously contributing to over 60 philanthropic projects in education and healthcare across the Yangtze River Delta.

In his youth, Wen Rugen was passionate about photography. Shortly after establishing himself in Hong Kong, he purchased a ROLLEICORD camera, using it to capture cherished moments with his family. This camera remained a constant companion as it witnessed his children's growth and other milestones throughout Wen's life.

“嘉新奖学金”奖杯

“Jiaxin Scholarship” Trophy

10.0 cm × 6.5 cm × 36.0 cm

张敏钰家族捐赠 Acquired from the Zhang Minyu Family through donation

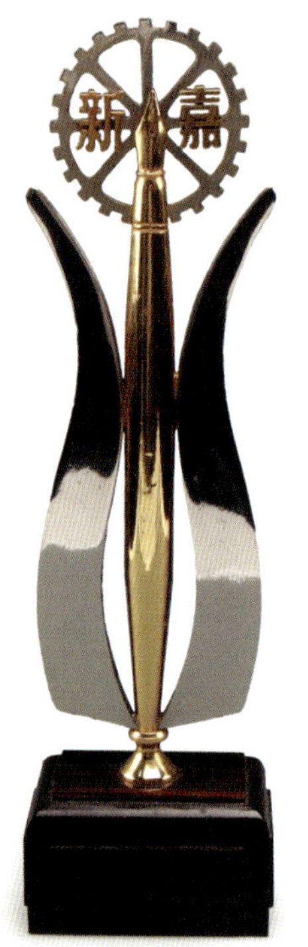

张敏钰使用过的樟木箱

Camphor Wood Chest Used by Zhang Minyu

90.0 cm × 48.0 cm × 42.0 cm

张敏钰家族捐赠 Acquired from the Zhang Minyu Family through donation

张敏钰（1913—2008），出生于宁波霞浦，台湾著名宁波帮实业家。张敏钰早年在上海经营纺织业，后赴台发展。1954 年在台创设嘉新水泥股份公司，逐渐发展成为台湾水泥业翘楚，被誉为“水泥大王”。

1960 年，张敏钰以公司盈余设置了“嘉新奖学金”，后发展为嘉新文化基金会，成为台湾第一个私人创办的基金会，致力于推动文教事业，泽被万千学子。

张敏钰一生情系家乡，多次回乡助建学校、医院、敬老院等，为宁波的发展做出了重要贡献。

Zhang Minyu (1913-2008), born in Xiapu, Ningbo, was a prominent business figure in Taiwan. In his early years, Zhang was involved in the textile industry in Shanghai before venturing south. He established the Jiaxin Cement Company in 1954, gradually transforming it into a leading player in the local cement industry, earning him the title of “Cement King”.

In 1960, Zhang allocated company profits to establish the Jiaxin Scholarship, which later evolved into the Jiaxin Cultural Foundation. It became the first privately initiated foundation in Taiwan, dedicated to advancing cultural and educational causes and benefiting countless students.

Throughout his life, Zhang Minyu maintained strong ties to his hometown, contributing significantly to Ningbo’s development by supporting the construction of schools, hospitals, nursing homes, and other charitable projects during multiple visits.

王统元香港纱厂玫瑰纪念品

Souvenir Rose of Wong Toong Yuen's Hong Kong Cotton Mills

17.0 cm × 10.5 cm × 5.0 cm

梁王培芳、王培丽捐赠 Acquired from Liangwang Peifang and Wang Peili through donation

王统元，香港纱厂创办人，“上海纺织大王”之一。在上海，以王统元为代表的王氏家族与以荣毅仁为代表的荣氏家族同属中国民营纺织业的巨头。王统元的父亲王启宇在上海创办的达丰染织厂曾是中国最早的染织企业。

1949 年，王统元在香港创办了香港纱厂，该厂是当时香港规模最大的现代化纺织企业之一，他本人成为香港纺织业的大亨，多次担任香港棉纺业同业公会主席，他艰苦创业的历程也被载入香港大型历史文献——《香江历程》。1971 年至 1975 年，王统元担任香港宁波同乡会第三、第四任会长，同时他积极从事香港的公益事业，捐资兴建宁波公学、香港中文大学何善衡工程大楼王统元堂等，获委任为香港非官守太平绅士。

Wong Toong Yuen was a textile magnate in Shanghai in the 1940s, who founded the Hong Kong Cotton Mills in Hong Kong in 1949. Hong Kong Cotton Mills was the largest textile factory of its time, utilizing the latest technology.

南丰纱厂棉纱拉力测试仪

Cotton Yarn Tension Testing Equipment from Nan Fung Cotton Mills

46.0 cm × 26.0 cm × 44.0 cm

陈廷骅捐赠 Acquired from Chen Din Hwa through donation

陈廷骅（1923—2012），出生于宁波，香港著名实业家，享有“香港棉纱大王”的美誉。1954 年，陈廷骅在香港创办南丰纱厂有限公司。1969 年，陈廷骅将南丰纱厂改组成为南丰纺织联合公司，1970 年上市。

陈廷骅热心教育事业，鼎力支持“希望工程”项目。自 1993 年起，他通过陈廷骅基金会向中国青少年发展基金会捐助、捐建希望小学 600 所，累计捐款达 1.2 亿元。这是“希望工程”在香港获得的最大一笔捐款。

南丰纺织有限公司相关资料

Newspaper Article Featuring Nan Fung Textile Co., Ltd.

56.0 cm × 39.0 cm

陈廷骅捐赠 Acquired from Chen Din Hwa through donation

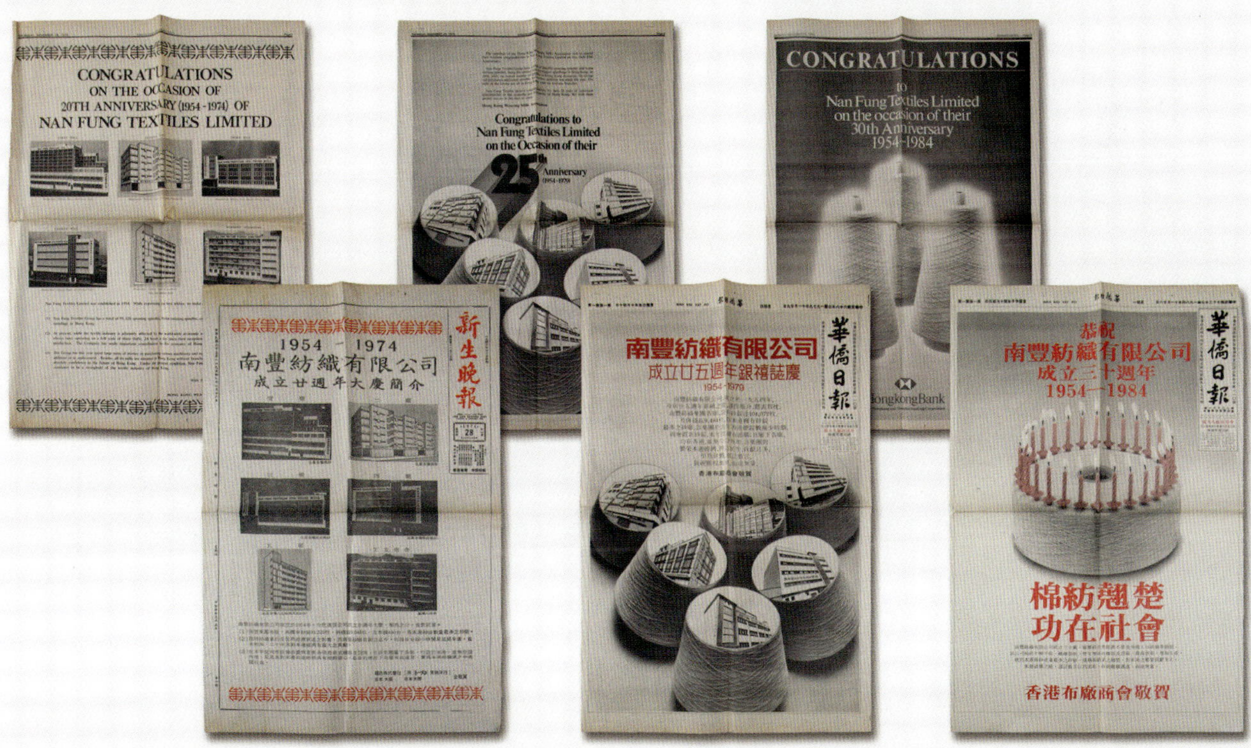

CONGRATULATIONS
ON THE OCCASION OF
20TH ANNIVERSARY (1954-1974) OF
NAN FUNG TEXTILES LIMITED

Congratulations to
Nan Fung Textiles Limited
on the Occasion of their
25th Anniversary
1954-1979

CONGRATULATIONS
to
Nan Fung Textiles Limited
on the occasion of their
30th Anniversary
1954-1984
HongkongBank

新生晚報
1954 - 1974
南豐紡織有限公司
成立廿週年大慶簡介

華僑日報
南豐紡織有限公司
成立廿五週年銀禧誌慶
1954-1979

華僑日報
恭祝
南豐紡織有限公司
成立三十週年
1954—1984
棉紡翹楚
功在社會
香港布廠商會敬賀

Chen Din Hwa (1923-2012), born in Ningbo, was a renowned Hong Kong industrialist, widely recognized as the "King of Cotton Yarn". In 1954, Chen established Nan Fung Textiles, which went public in 1970.

Chen was a strong advocate for education access and provided substantial support to "the Hope Project" on the Chinese mainland. Starting in 1993, he made generous donations through the Chen Din Hwa Foundation to the China Youth Development Foundation, contributing to the establishment and development of 600 Hope Primary Schools. His cumulative donations amounted to 120 million yuan, making him the largest donor to "the Hope Project" in Hong Kong.

朱绣山使用过的放大镜、皮公文包

Magnifying Glass and Leather Briefcase Used by Chu Shou Shan

20 世纪

① 6.3 cm × 5.3 cm × 1.0 cm ② 7.4 cm × 5.7 cm × 0.8 cm ③ 43.5 cm × 38.0 cm × 6.0 cm

朱黄龙捐赠 Acquired from Zhu Huanglong through donation

① 放大镜（方形）

② 放大镜（圆形）

③ 皮公文包

朱绣山（1919—2005），宁波市鄞州区高桥镇藕缆桥人。台湾著名实业家，曾任台北市宁波同乡会顾问。

朱绣山 1947 年迁居台湾，同年创办台湾台新染织公司，并由纺织拓展到制衣、化工、航运及国际贸易等领域。他一生乐善好施，热忱社会公益。1993 年起，在宁波助建多所医院、学校、安老院，设立医疗救助金、学生奖助学金等。朱绣山重视贫困山区孩童教育及西部地区生态建设，于 2000 年起在贵州、陕西、甘肃的偏远山区助建学校，在陕北黄土高原筑建水坝植树造林，在延安南泥湾兴建水库灌溉农田。

Chu Shou Shan (1919-2005), originally from Oulanqiao in Gaoqiao Town, Yinzhou district, was a prominent industrialist with roots in Ningbo who later settled in Taiwan.

Chu Shou Shan moved to Taiwan in 1947, founded Taiwan Taixin Dyeing & Weaving Company at the same year. Chu Shou Shan had been very generous all his life and was a man of public spirit. He had offered aids to build many hospitals, schools, nursing homes at Ningbo from 1993, and established medical aid fund, student awards and grants, etc. Chu Shou Shan attached great importance to children's education in poor mountainous areas and ecological construction in western regions. He had been to the poverty mountain areas in Guizhou, Shaanxi and Gansu, offering aids to build schools since 2000. He also carried out the water and soil conservation projects in west part of China.

俞翊焘使用过的公文包、老式机械案秤

Briefcase and Vintage Mechanical Scale Used by Yu Yitao

①45.0 cm × 19.0 cm × 30.0 cm ②39.0 cm × 17.5 cm

俞家琛捐赠 Acquired from Yu Jiachen through donation

① 公文包

② 老式机械案秤

1989 年，镇海籍台胞俞立梓在老家蛟川街道捐资兴建乔梓小学以解决当地学生就学问题。“乔”，“南有乔木，不可休思”；“梓”，“梓里也”。“乔梓”两字，饱含着俞立梓浓浓的爱乡之情。

俞立梓的长子俞翊焘，在台湾从事帽子加工外销行业，曾任台湾地区帽子输出同业公会总会理事达 16 年。从 20 世纪 90 年代起，俞翊焘先后捐资助建乔梓小学、招宝山鳌柱塔、渡假桥村路等项目。2018 年俞翊焘去世后，其子俞家琛接过祖辈反哺家乡的接力棒，持续为乔梓小学“梓芽 · 鼎育”奖学金提供资金支持。近 30 年来，俞氏家族三代人传承接力，在家乡累积捐资助建 10 余个项目，拳拳赤子之心可见一斑。

该公文包为俞翊焘日常办公差旅使用，陪伴他往返于甬台两地，见证了俞翊焘捐资兴教的桑梓情怀。

Yu Yitao, originally from Zhenhai, Ningbo, was involved in the hat processing and export industry in Taiwan. Since the 1990s, Yu has generously funded various infrastructure projects in Ningbo, including the founding of Qiaozi Primary School, the restoration of Aozhu Tower at Zhaobaoshan, and the construction of village roads at Dujiaqiao. Over the past three decades, three generations of the Yu family have upheld this noble philanthropic tradition.

This briefcase served as Yu Yitao's companion for his daily office work and travel, accompanying him between Ningbo and Taiwan.

胡嘉烈赠沈友梅储物盒

Storage Case Gifted by Woo Kai Lea to Sun Yew-May

26.5 cm × 18.0 cm × 8.0 cm

沈曼霖捐赠 Acquired from Shen Manlin through donation

沈友梅（1904—1994），出生于鄞县茅山乡后沈家村，曾任台北市宁波同乡会会长。沈友梅一生投身教育、办学、抗日救亡宣传、办报写作，唤醒民众。民国时期，曾任宁波日报社社长，先后创办花园小学、鄞县乡村师范学校（茅山中学前身）、定象两县联立战时初中学生补习学校等。辗转到台湾后，连续 9 年担任台北市宁波同乡会理事长（第五届至第八届）。1990 年后，他回到家乡宁波定居，在宁波大学、茅山中学设立“沈氏奖学金”，积极推动甬台两地交往。

胡嘉烈（1911—1977），鄞县茅山乡胡家坟人，著名新加坡侨商。他热心公益事业，关心桑梓，捐助三江小学、三江公墓，发起成立新加坡宁波同乡会，在家乡设慈善机构片云堂，实行粮食平粜，资助胡家坟小学，捐资修建花园村豫章桥和太平桥等。

该储物盒盖外刻“SUN YEW-MAY”，盖内贴有金属铭牌，上刻“Compliments from Woo Kai Lea”，为胡嘉烈赠沈友梅的定制款。

Sun Yew-May (1904-1994), from Houshenjia Village in Maoshan Town, Yin county, notably held the position of president of the Taipei Ningbo Association. Throughout his lifetime, Sun Yew-May dedicated himself to supporting education and journalism. In the Republican era, he was the president of *Ningbo Daily* and was instrumental in establishing various educational institutions, such as Huayuan Elementary School, Yin County Rural Normal School (which later became Maoshan Middle School), and a wartime supplementary school for junior high students from Dinghai and Xiangshan counties. After relocating to Taiwan, he was elected chairman of the Taipei Ningbo Association from its fifth through eighth terms, serving for nine years in a row. In the 1990s, he returned to Ningbo, his birthplace, where he founded scholarships at Ningbo University and Maoshan Middle School, vigorously fostering ties between Ningbo and Taiwan.

Woo Kai Lea (1911-1977), of Hujiafen in Maoshan Town, Yin county, was a distinguished Singaporean-Chinese entrepreneur, known for his philanthropic endeavors and deep connection to his homeland. His contributions included support for Sanjiang Elementary School and the Sanjiang Public Cemetery, the establishment of the Singapore Ningbo Guild, and the creation of the charitable organization Pianyuntang. Through Pianyuntang, he provided grain subsidies, aided the Hujiafen Elementary School, and financed the construction of Yuzhang Bridge and Taiping Bridge in Huayuan Village, demonstrating his commitment to the well-being and development of his home community.

The exterior of this storage case's lid is engraved with "SUN YEW-MAY". The case features an interior metal nameplate inscribed with "Compliments from Woo Kai Lea". This custom-made piece was a personal gift from Woo to Sun.

宁波大学海运学院赠魏绍相的船模

Ship Model Gifted by the Faculty of Maritime Transportation of Ningbo University to Wei Shaoxiang

2003 年

37.0 cm × 8.5 cm × 13.5 cm

魏绍相捐赠 Acquired from Wei Shaoxiang through donation

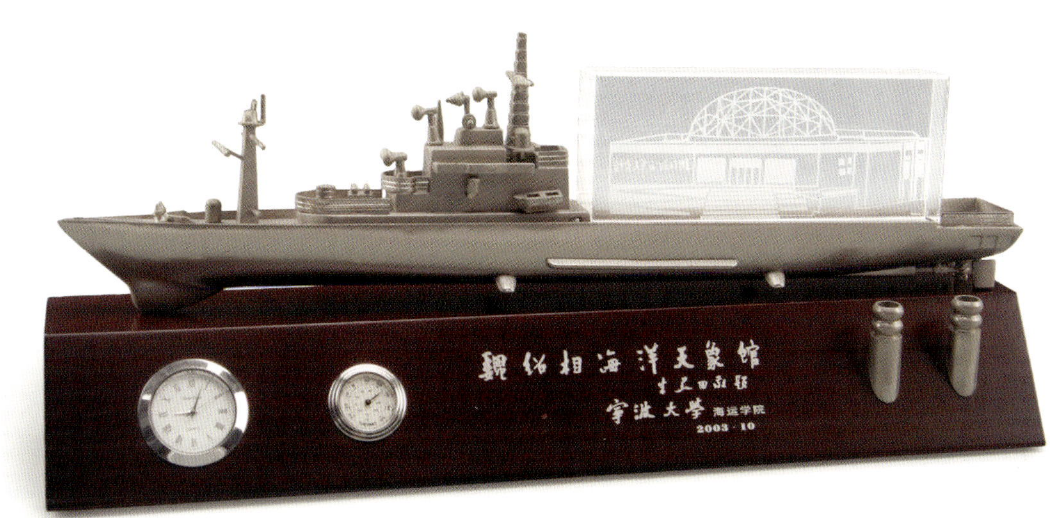

魏绍相（1925—2023），宁波余姚牟山镇魏家村人，香港甬港联谊会永远名誉会长、香港恒丰喉业有限公司董事长。1940 年辍学赴上海经商。1948 年赴港。1976 年创办恒丰公司，经营五金、水管等建筑材料的贸易业务。

魏绍相情系家乡、捐资助学。自 1996 年首次到访宁波大学之后，魏绍相先后捐资魏绍相馆、魏绍相计算机信息中心、魏绍相临床技能中心等项目，为宁波大学的建设和发展倾注了大量心血。此外，他还向家乡余姚以及浙江大学等捐助了多个项目。宁波大学魏绍相海洋天象馆建成于 2003 年。

Wei Shaoxiang (1925-2023), originally from Weijia Village in Moushan Town, Yuyao, Ningbo, held the positions of Permanent Honorary Chairman of the Ningbo Hong Kong Fellowship Association (Hong Kong) and Chairman of Hang Fung Pipes Company Ltd.. His business career began in 1940 when he left school to pursue commercial endeavors in Shanghai. By 1948, Wei had relocated to Hong Kong, where he founded Hang Fung Pipes in 1976. His enterprise specialized in the trading of hardware, water pipes, and various building materials.

Wei Shaoxiang maintained a profound bond with his hometown and was notably philanthropic in supporting education. From his initial visit to Ningbo University in 1996, he contributed to numerous initiatives, including the establishment of Wei Shaoxiang Hall, Wei Shaoxiang IT Center, and Wei Shaoxiang Clinical Skills Center. These contributions played a pivotal role in the expansion and enhancement of Ningbo University. Beyond the university, he also supported various projects in Yuyao and at Zhejiang University, among other places. one of his notable contributions, the Wei Shaoxiang Marine Celestial Observatory at Ningbo University, was completed in 2003.

走向世界

Global Renown

陈纪林和陈顺庆的护照

Passports of Chen Jilin and Chen Chun Ching

① 1924 年 ② 1932 年

① 21.0 cm × 16.0 cm ② 22.0 cm × 16.0 cm

陈名豪捐赠 Acquired from Chen Minghao through donation

1915 年，陈纪林作为海员随北德公司轮船前往德国汉堡，后创办德国第一家华人侨团汉堡中华会馆并担任会长。其子陈顺庆后受公推继任，继续热心会务。1958 年，其孙陈名豪赴汉堡继承家业，逐渐成为汉堡市享有威望的侨领。陈氏家族三代均致力于联络、服务侨胞，他们心系故土，回馈家乡，多次为家乡捐助基础设施并支持扶贫助困活动。

这几本护照饱含陈家三代人在异国他乡艰苦创业以及维护华侨权益、热心为侨胞服务的心路历程，是旅德宁波帮人士扎根异乡、艰苦奋斗的历史见证。

In 1915, Chen Jilin traveled to Hamburg, Germany as a humble seaman. He later became the founding president of the Hamburg Chinese Association, the first Chinese expatriate organization in Germany. His son, Chen Chun Ching, was elected as his successor and continued to be active in the association's affairs. In 1958, Chen's grandson, Chen Minghao, took over the family legacy and gradually became a respected figure among the Chinese community in Hamburg.

Across three generations, the Chen family has been dedicated to connecting and serving their fellow expatriates. They maintained strong ties to Ningbo, contributing to the development of local infrastructure and participating in poverty alleviation efforts. These passports were used by the Chen family on their travels between China and Germany.

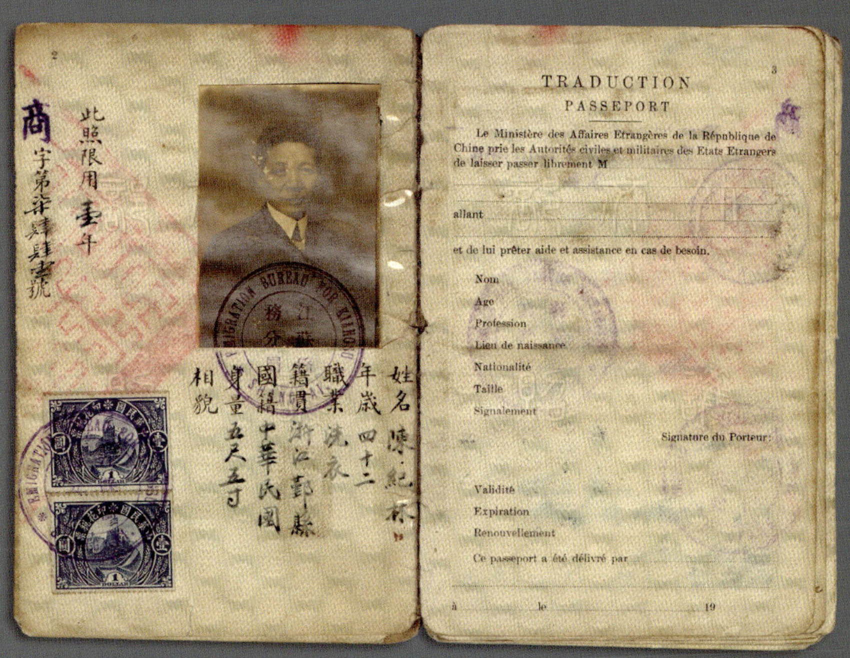

① 陈纪林护照

② 陈顺庆护照

范岁久的丹麦王国护照和私人账本

Danish Kingdom Passport and Private Ledger of Fan Suijiu

1935 年

① 14.0 cm × 10.2 cm × 0.3 cm ② 18.0 cm × 11.8 cm × 1.5 cm

范汉民捐赠 Acquired from Fan Hanmin through donation

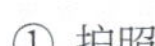

① 护照

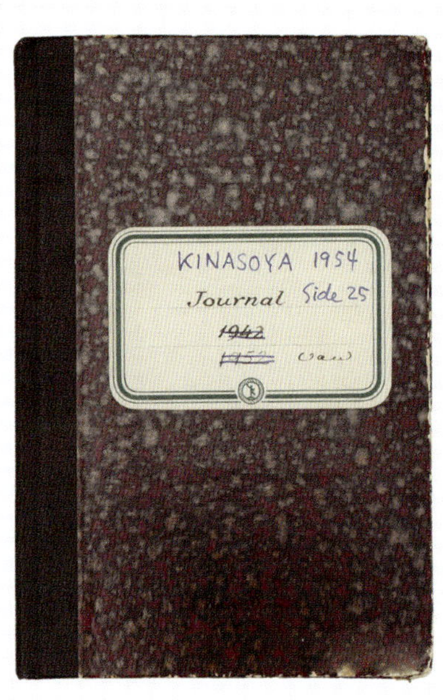

② 账本

范岁久（1912—2003），祖籍宁波慈溪，1935 年只身远赴北欧留学，先后获得硕士和博士学位。他是最早留学丹麦的中国人之一，是丹麦大龙食品公司（Daloon）的创始人，将中国传统饮食文化传播至世界。他将自己的企业命名为"大龙"，饱含着对祖国的无限眷恋；将两个儿子取名为"本德""汉明"，以示永不忘本；在事业有成后毅然创立大龙基金，为祖国和家乡的公益事业慷慨解囊；他还为中丹两国的友好往来奉献力量，被推选为丹麦华人协会终身名誉会长。

范岁久使用过的博朗牌收音机

Braun Radio Used by Fan Suijiu

36.1 cm × 13.5 cm × 25.0 cm

范汉民捐赠 Acquired from Fan Hanmin through donation

在异国创业的范岁久情系祖国，思乡甚笃，于 1960 年购买当时价格昂贵的博朗牌收音机，专门用来收听中国短波新闻。2016 年 8 月，这台收音机由范岁久之子范汉民先生捐赠给宁波帮博物馆。

Fan Suijiu (1912-2003), originally from Cixi, Ningbo, was one of the first Chinese international students to study in Denmark. He began his studies in 1935, earning a master's degree and a PhD. Fan later went on to establish his own food company, Daloon, becoming known as the "Spring Roll King of Denmark" during his lifetime.

In 1960, Fan purchased this Braun radio to tune in to shortwave Chinese news broadcasts. In August 2016, this radio was generously donated to Ningbobang Museum by Fan Suijiu's son, Fan Hanmin.

包从兴在非洲创业的相关物品

T.H. Pao's Personal Items from His Time in Africa

一套多件

包惠明捐赠 Acquired from Bao Huiming through donation

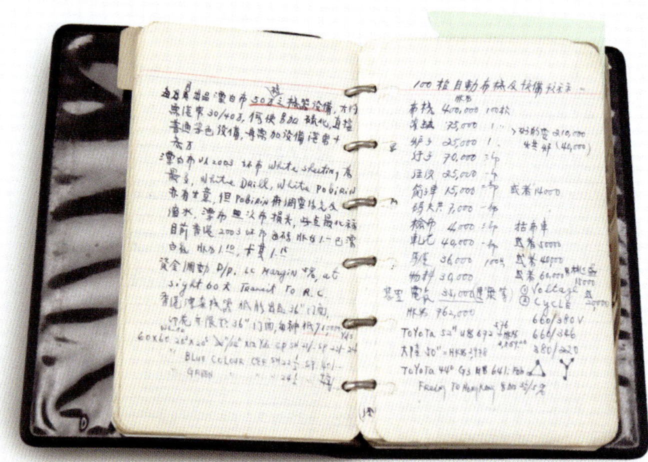

包从兴(1922—2013)，香港著名实业家、慈善家及社会活动家，宁波旅港同乡会永远名誉会长、香港苏浙同乡会永远名誉会长、香港甬港联谊会名誉会长。少时就读于叶氏中兴小学。1948 年，赴香港创办友宁纺织投资有限公司。1960 年，他在加纳创办非洲第一家新式纺织厂——加纳纺织厂，短短几年内便形成了集种植、纺纱、织布、印染、制衣于一体的纺织企业集团，成为当时西非纺织业之冠。周恩来总理访问非洲时在加纳接见了包从兴，称赞他在第三世界开拓创业的精神。

该组藏品为包从兴在非洲创业时的相关物品。印花布为包从兴创办的加纳纺织厂所生产的产品。

T.H. Pao (1922-2013) was a renowned entrepreneur and philanthropist. In 1960, he established the Ghana Textile Manufacturing Co., Ltd., the first modern textile factory in Africa. Within a short span of time, this venture evolved into a comprehensive textile conglomerate active in cotton planting, spinning, weaving, printing, dyeing, and garment manufacturing. During his visit to Africa, Premier Zhou Enlai met with Pao in Ghana and commended his business success. The materials in this collection are personal items used by Pao during his time on the continent. The fabrics are products of Ghana Textile Manufacturing Co., Ltd.

戴祖贻使用过的西装包和裁剪工具

Suit Bag and Tailoring Tools Used by Dai Zuyi

①60.0 cm × 44.0 cm × 20.0 cm　②一套多件

戴祖贻捐赠 Acquired from Dai Zuyi through donation

① 西装包

作为上海著名西服店培罗蒙创办者许达昌的第一嫡传弟子，戴祖贻在日本承袭经营培罗蒙半个多世纪，在日本服装界享有很高的地位和声誉，以至于客户们称他为“培罗蒙”先生（Mr. Baromon）。戴祖贻在传承红帮技艺的基础上不懈创新，先后考察英、美、法、意等多国服装市场，学习先进工艺，在技术、版型、风格、材料上精益求精，以中华民族精雕细琢、注重细节的“工匠精神”在异国他乡铸造了“培罗蒙”的辉煌，赢得了广泛赞誉。

该西装包为戴祖贻工作时专用。包内通过独特的设计方便西装的摆放和固定，减少了因旅途颠簸对西服造成伤害，同时包内设有多个夹层和口袋，用于放置领带、口袋巾等配饰以及其他差旅物品。该西装包陪伴戴祖贻行走于世界各国，见证了红帮名家开拓进取、名扬四海的辉煌。

② 裁剪工具

Dai Zuyi, a protege of Xu Dachang, the founder of the renowned Shanghai bespoke tailor Baromon, continued the Baromon legacy in Japan for over half a century. He held a prestigious and reputable position in the Japanese fashion industry, to the extent that his clients respectfully addressed him as "Mr. Baromon".

This suit bag was exclusively designed for holding a single suit. The interior features a system for securely storing and protecting the suit, minimizing damage from travel. Additionally, the bag includes multiple compartments and pockets for accessories like ties, pocket squares, as well as Dai's tailoring tools.

应行久使用过的劳斯莱斯银刺轿车

Rolls-Royce Silver Spur Used by Ying Xingjiu

1982 年

540.0 cm × 190.0 cm × 184.0 cm

应立人捐赠 Acquired from Ying Liren through donation

应行久（1914—2001），祖籍宁波镇海，1935 年考入上海沪江大学，于商学院攻读商科。1947 年赴美创业，开始时在纽约开了家小礼品店，由于经营有方，仅一年就发展到 3 家店。1973 年，他购下当时号称“世界最高的摩天大楼”——纽约世界贸易中心的顶层，成立幸运礼品公司。随着公司经营规模日益扩大，他又在纽约购下丰泽楼，经营中国菜肴，将公司的经营领域由小礼品延伸到餐饮业。他创办的大中集团也因此跻身美国华人十大财团之一。1979 年 6 月，应行久被推举为全美华侨总商会董事长，成为纽约华人社会中声誉卓著的代表人物。

20 世纪 70 年代，邓小平同志前往美国参加联合国大会和访问期间，应行久曾用自己的专车接待过邓小平。这辆车牌为“YING 888”的黑色劳斯莱斯轿车出厂于 1982 年，为应行久私人定制版。这辆车还曾接送过多位党和国家领导人，见证过许多重大历史时刻。2007 年 11 月，应行久之子应立人将此车捐赠给宁波帮博物馆。

Ying Xingjiu (1914-2001), originally from Zhenhai, Ningbo, entered the Business School of Shanghai College in 1935. In 1947, he opened a small gift shop in New York. Thanks to his keen business acumen, Ying expanded to three stores within just a year. In 1973, he purchased the top floor of the New York World Trade Center, which is the world's tallest skyscraper at that time, to establish his own company.

During the 1970s, when Deng Xiaoping visited the United States to attend the United Nations General Assembly and engage in diplomatic visits, Ying used his personal car to receive Deng. This black Rolls-Royce, bearing the license plate “YING888”, was custom-made for Ying in 1982 and had the honor of transporting several high-ranking Chinese leaders. In November 2007, his son, Ying Liren, graciously donated the vehicle to Ningbobang Museum.

MYFLORIDA.COM
YING 888
SUNSHINE STATE

张济民使用过的《英汉四用辞典》

A Daily Use English-Chinese Dictionary Used by Zhang Jimin

17.0 cm × 11.0 cm × 6.0 cm

张惠中捐赠 Acquired from Zhang Huizhong through donation

张济民（1920—2017），宁波镇海人，美籍华人实业家。1936 年，年仅 15 岁的张济民带着 20 瓮榨菜远涉南洋，后辗转日本闯入商海，创办日独药品株式会社，成为当时日本最大的华人企业。在日本，他用日文撰写的《我的经营观》成为当时经营管理的教科书。"知天命"之年，张济民又辗转美国开始新的创业。他手抄《美国税法大全》闯过了语言关，创办"西湖投资管理公司"，成为旧金山"湾区首富"。

张济民关心支持祖国发展，曾任美国华商总会第一任会长和中华人民共和国教育基金会第一任会长，创办美国"华声电视"，宣传报道中国改革开放情况，为促成上海与旧金山结为友好城市发挥了很大作用。

华声电视台监视器、编辑机

Monitor and Editing Machine of Hua Sheng Television Station

20 世纪

① 36.0 cm × 42.0 cm × 36.0 cm　② 42.5 cm × 49.0 cm × 19.0 cm

张惠中捐赠 Acquired from Zhang Huizhong through donation

① 监视器(上)　② 编辑机(下)

Zhang Jimin (1920-2017), originally from Zhenhai, Ningbo, was a Chinese-American entrepreneur. He set out on his entrepreneurial journey at the age of 15 when he left China in search of opportunities in Southeast Asia. His endeavors led him to establish a pharmaceutical company in Japan, which became the largest Chinese-owned enterprise in Japan at the time. In his fifties, he ventured to the United States, where he overcame language barriers and founded a successful investment company in San Francisco.

吴仙标美国特拉华州副州长专用 2 号车牌
“2 Lt. Governor Delaware” License Plate Owned by Shien Biau Woo

30.4 cm × 15.2 cm

吴仙标捐赠 Acquired from Shien Biau Woo through donation

吴仙标，祖籍宁波，是美国第一位留学生华人副州长。他是 1972 年中美建交后，周恩来总理首批邀请的华人华侨访华团成员之一。吴仙标长期致力于推动中美持久和互利的贸易合作关系，在他的支持与促成下，美国特拉华州最大的城市威尔明顿市与中国上海、宁波缔结为姐妹城市。宁波市还与特拉华州合作，建立船运业合作系统。

作为海外宁波帮的杰出代表，吴仙标于 2011 年回乡时将他在美国期间的相关物品捐赠给宁波帮博物馆，包括他担任美国特拉华州副州长时专用的这块 2 号车牌。

Shien Biau Woo (born August 13, 1937) is a Chinese-American professor and politician from Newark, Delaware. He served as the 21st lieutenant governor of Delaware. With Woo’s facilitation, Wilmington, the largest city in Delaware, became sister city of Shanghai and Ningbo.

In 2011, Woo donated a collection of personal items to Ningbobang Museum. These included the “2 Lt. Governor Delaware” license plate that he used during his time in office.

THE FIRST STATE
2
LT. GOVERNOR
DELAWARE
NOV
88

人文传承

LEGACY

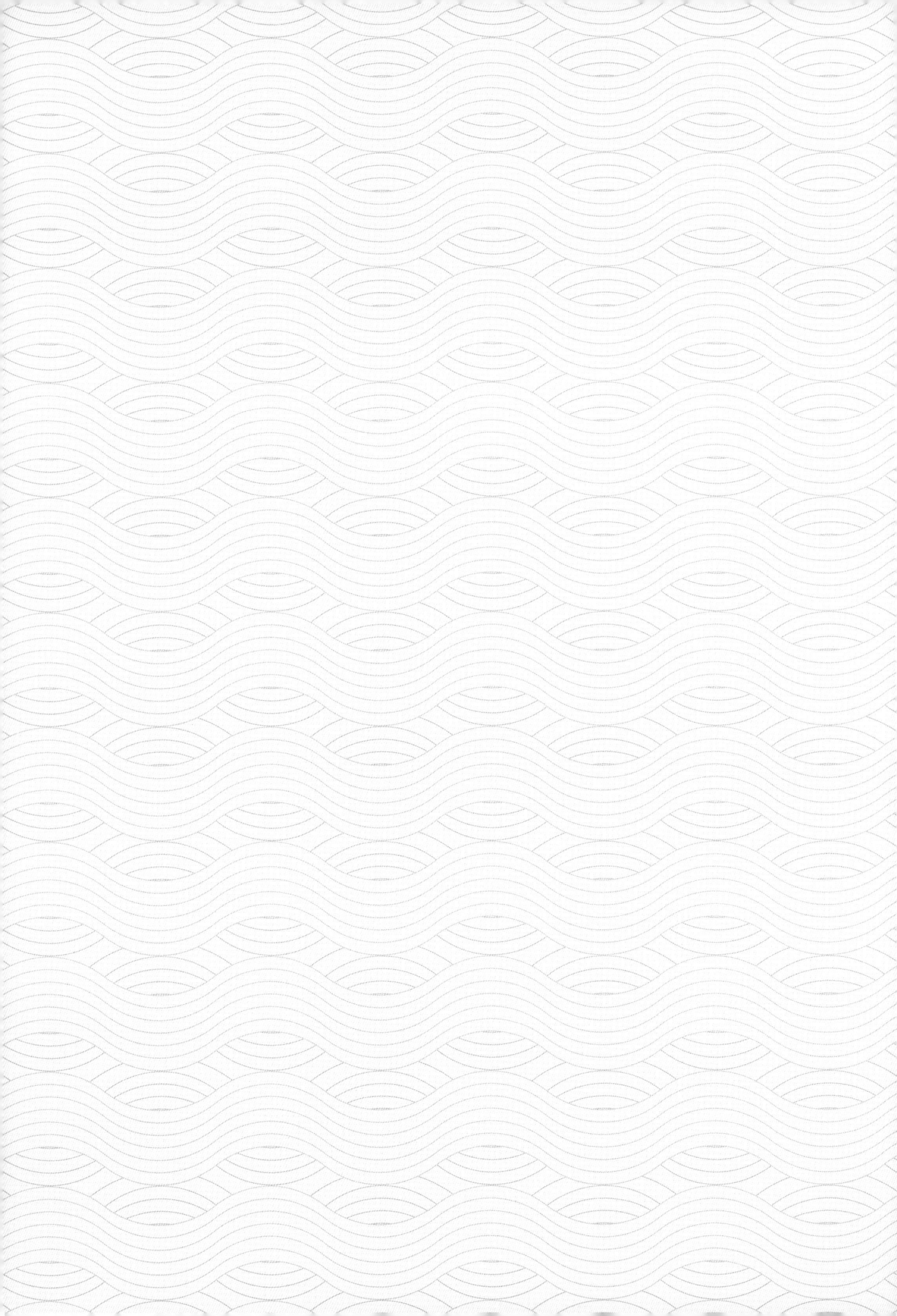

敦睦乡谊

Hometown Pride

四明公所董事会合影照片

Siming Association Board of Directors Group Photo

1934 年
47.5 cm × 35.5 cm
张乾源捐赠 Acquired from Zhang Qianyuan through donation

四明公所是旅沪宁波商人和手工业者的同乡组织。清嘉庆二年（1797），旅沪宁波绅商钱随、费元圭、潘凤占、王忠烈等以“联乡公谊而安旅榇”为名发起“一文愿捐”，于上海县城北郊购地 30 亩，嘉庆三年（1798）建成殡舍。嘉庆八年（1803），建成关帝殿，正门题额“四明公所”。后公所不断购地扩建，规模恢宏，“凡甬人旅沪各业各帮大率有会，而皆总汇于公所”。1874 年和 1898 年发生的两次“四明公所事件”中，甬人团结一心，成功抵制了法国人的无理要求，名震沪上。四明公所作为宁波人在上海成立的第一个同乡组织，标志着宁波人在上海站稳了脚跟。

这张合影记载了董事莅临四明公所董事会情况，合影前排坐者为九老：李詠裳、方式如、乐俊宝、陈良玉、虞洽卿、洪贤舫、方樵苓、葛虞臣、孙衡甫；后列立者为各董：方椒伯、孙梅堂、张继光、秦润卿、宋子奎、袁履登。

The Siming Association was founded in Shanghai by Ningbo merchants and tradespeople in the 18th century. As the first organization for the Ningbo business community in Shanghai, the Siming Association's founding signified the community's growing strength.

繼光先生惠存
余稱九老
遂邀集本公
董事會稱
各位董事合
一影以紀
而董事會同
湘雲及聯合
鄔君志豪
廷蓀周事未
蕊將莅攝合
台銜列左
前列坐者
為九老
李君詠裳
方君式如
樂君俊寶
陳君良玉
虞君洽卿
洪君賢舫
方君樵苓
葛弟虞臣
孫君衡甫
後列立者
為各董
方君椒伯
孫君梅堂
張君繼光
秦君潤卿
宋君子奎
袁君履登
甲戌孟春誌

唐熊楷书为胡访鹤七秩寿八条屏

Eight-Panel Calligraphy Work for the 70th Birthday of Hu Fanghe by Tang Xiong

1936 年

木盒 55.5 cm × 26.5 cm × 17.0 cm；寿屏 230.0 cm × 46.8 cm

胡运熹捐赠 Acquired from Hu Yunxi through donation

该物品为 1936 年上海市土布业同业公会为庆贺胡访鹤（时为上海绮藻堂布业公所总董）七十寿辰的贺礼，木盒刻有“上海朵云轩监制”“松柏同春”，盒内寿屏 8 卷。寿屏由杨家悌撰文，唐熊书，计 932 字，概述胡访鹤生平。

胡访鹤，祖籍宁波慈溪，15 岁时到上海，后从事土布经营，认为“土布为我国固有之工业，小则可以补救民主，广之可以启人爱国”，致力土布发展。有子立范，孙士栋。该物品为其后人胡运熹（时任美东三江公所主席）捐赠。

These eight scrolls are a gift presented in 1936 by the Shanghai Cotton Industry Guild to celebrate the 70th birthday of Hu Fanghe (b. 1866), a native of Cixi, Ningbo, who arrived in Shanghai at the age of 15 and was then the Chairman of the Shanghai Qizaotang Textile Industry Association. The scrolls contain a total of 932 characters. It provides a brief overview of Hu Fanghe's life.

慈谿胡訪鶴先生　七秩壽序

蓋聞有大德者必有大壽有大願者必有大成原以心性相因福由自造自造之端維何曰勤曰儉曰誠曰慎勤與儉致福之源誠與慎造福之基我

訪鶴胡先生敦本睦族克儉成家有大德而兼有大願焉歲丙子秋

（局部）

宁波旅沪同乡会第五届同乡集团结婚证书

Marriage Certificate from the 5th Group Wedding of the Ningbo Residents' Association in Shanghai

1939 年

56.0 cm × 37.8 cm

郑元龙捐赠 Acquired from Zheng Yuanlong through donation

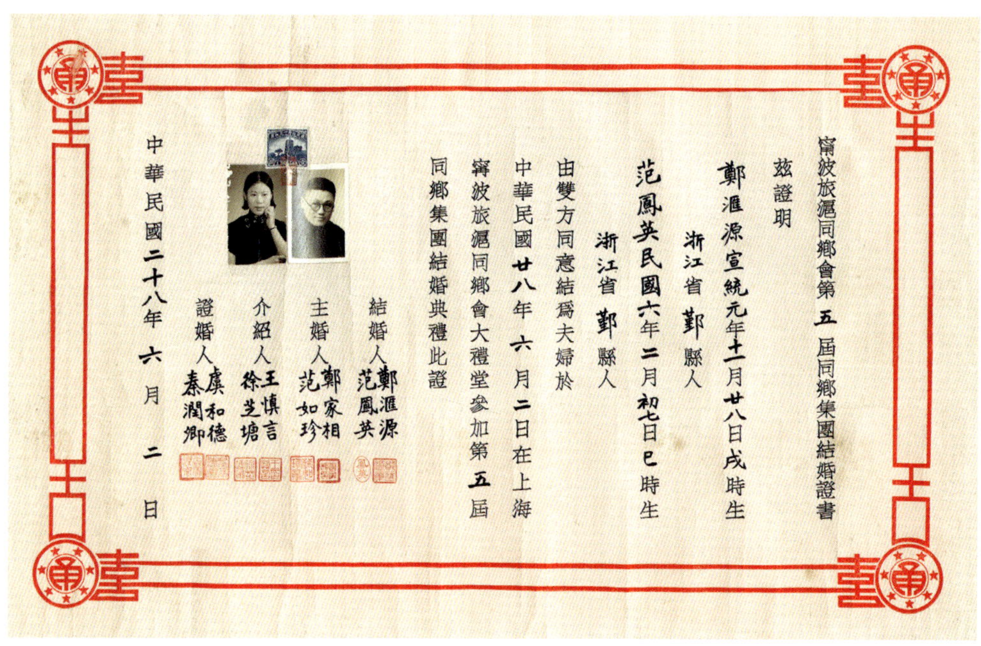

寧波旅滬同鄉會第五屆同鄉集團結婚證書

茲證明

鄭滙源宣統元年十一月廿八日戌時生

浙江省鄞縣人

范鳳英民國六年二月初七日巳時生

浙江省鄞縣人

由雙方同意結爲夫婦於

中華民國廿八年六月二日在上海

寧波旅滬同鄉會大禮堂參加第五屆

同鄉集團結婚典禮此證

結婚人 鄭滙源 范鳳英

主婚人 鄭家相 范如珍

介紹人 王慎言 徐芝塘

證婚人 虞和德 秦潤卿

中華民國二十八年六月二日

20 世纪 30 年代，上海兴起了以简单、经济、庄严为特点的集团婚礼。宁波旅沪同乡会专门成立了专务委员会筹备集团婚礼事项，并且制定了参加同乡集团婚礼的相关办法。从 1935 年开始，宁波旅沪同乡会每年举办一次同乡集团婚礼。按规定，凡年满 18 岁的宁波籍男子和年满 16 岁的宁波籍女子均可申请参加，举行婚礼前要向社会公布结婚登记人姓名，并由当时在同乡会中很有威望的人作为主婚人和证婚人。该集团结婚证书的结婚人为郑汇源、范凤英，证婚人为当时在上海滩颇有名望的宁波帮人士秦润卿、虞和德（虞洽卿）。

集团婚礼的举办，不仅体现了旅沪宁波人团结、节俭的精神，还进一步推动了婚礼仪式的改革，取得了良好的社会反响，成为一时风尚。

Starting from 1935, the Ningbo Residents' Association in Shanghai began organizing annual group weddings for its members. As per regulations, individuals who were Ningbo natives residing in Shanghai and met the age criteria of over 18 for men and over 16 for women were eligible to apply. The names of those registering for marriage were publicly announced before the wedding, and respected members within the association, who held significant prestige, acted as the officiants and witnesses. The couple listed on this group wedding certificate are Zheng Huiyuan and Fan Fengying, with Qin Runqing and Yu Hede (Yu Qiaqing), prominent figures in the Shanghai Ningbo community at the time, serving as the officiant and witness.

宁波旅沪同乡会永远名誉会董证书

Permanent Honorary Director Certificate of the Ningbo Residents' Association in Shanghai

1942 年

47.0 cm × 36.0 cm

储建国捐赠 Acquired from Chu Jianguo through donation

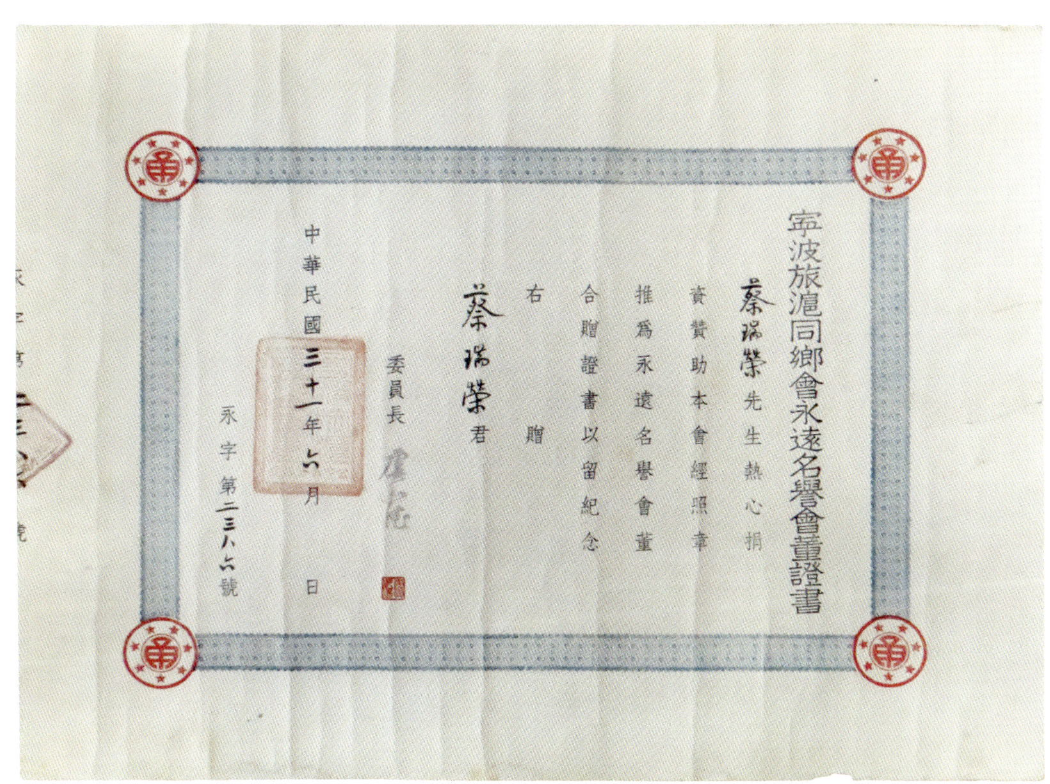

寗波旅滬同鄉會永遠名譽會董證書

蔡瑞榮先生熱心捐資贊助本會經照章推爲永遠名譽會董合贈證書以留紀念

右贈

蔡瑞榮君

委員長

中華民國三十一年六月 日

永字第二三八六號

清宣统元年(1909),慈溪人洪宝斋集宁波同乡数十人,在汉口路创建四明旅沪同乡会,后洪宝斋离沪,同乡会一度停辍。次年,施嵋青捐全部私产,与钱达三、谢蘅牕、陈韵泉、陈蓉馆、朱葆三、孙梅堂等捐资复兴,改名为“宁波旅沪同乡会”,设事务所于福州路 22 号。宣统三年(1911)同乡会成立,大会公推李徵五为会长,虞洽卿、朱葆三为副会长。该会以“团结同乡,发挥自治精神”为宗旨,积极致力于团结同乡、服务同乡、促进家乡建设等事业。

The Ningbo Residents' Association in Shanghai was founded in 1911 at 22 Fuzhou Road. Its mission was providing support and facilitate cohesion for Ningbo residents living in Shanghai.

美东纽约三江慈善公所同人庆祝一周年纪念摄影

Commemorative Photograph of the US East Coast New York San Kiang Charitable Association Celebrating its First Anniversary

1943 年

50.0 cm × 30.5 cm

美东纽约三江慈善公所捐赠 Acquired from the US East Coast New York San Kiang Charitable Association through donation

美东三江公所全称为美东纽约三江慈善公所，原为1929 年 6 月由旅美的浙江、江苏、江西籍人士发起成立的三江公所，创立时有会员七八十人，目前会员已发展到 1000 余人。公所有常设机构致力于慈善事业，对各慈善机构、社会教育和文化艺术团体均予捐助或做实质性协助，并设有“三江文教奖学基金”，从 1966 年起每年一次颁发给学业优异的三江子弟。公所对会员参与美国政治活动和竞选公职均予以积极鼓励和支持，如为美国首位华人副州长吴仙标的参选成功做出了贡献。公所积极推进与中国的联系，在 1997 年宁波遭受特大台风灾害时，曾组织会员捐款赈灾。

《美东纽约三江慈善公所成立七十周年纪念特刊》

Special Issue Commemorating the 70th Anniversary of the US East Coast New York San Kiang Charitable Association

28.0 cm × 21.5 cm

美东纽约三江慈善公所捐赠 Acquired from the US East Coast New York San Kiang Charitable Association through donation

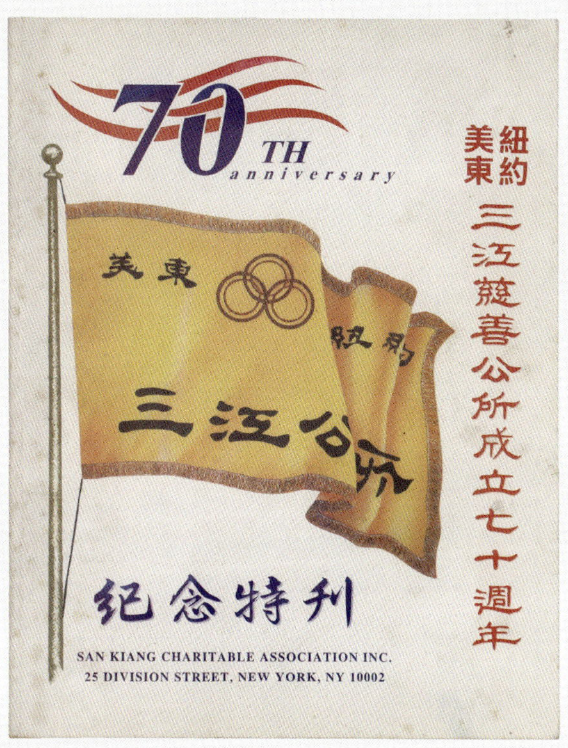

The US East Coast New York San Kiang Charitable Association was founded in June 1929 with an initial membership of around 70 to 80 people. Presently, membership has grown to over 1,000 individuals. The association maintains permanent institutions committed to charitable endeavors. They extend assistance and financial support to various charitable organizations, community education programs, and cultural and artistic groups. The association has also established a scholarship fund, awarding annual scholarships since 1966 to outstanding students from the Chinese-American community.

旅沪宁波人订婚证书

Engagement Certificate of a Ningbo Couple in Shanghai

1948 年

52.0 cm × 38.0 cm

储建国捐赠 Acquired from Chu Jianguo through donation

訂婚證書
李光耀係浙江省鎮海縣人
念叁歲丙寅年三月十八日辰時生
李蟾蘋係浙江省鄞縣人
念弍歲丁卯年十二月初三日巳時生
今由
王光前 朱福林 先生介紹謹詹於
中華民國叁拾柒年捌月拾日午
時在上海南市紫華路平安里
舉行訂婚儀式恭請
桂偉民 先生蒞場證明從茲締結良緣
訂成佳偶志同道合早經牢繫
赤繩意洽情投行看永偕白首
花好月圓欣燕爾之將詠海枯
石爛指鴛侶而先盟此約
訂婚人 李光耀 李蟾蘋
證明人 桂偉民
介紹人 王光前 朱福林
主婚人 李厚祖 李新章
中華民國叁拾柒年捌月拾日謹訂

该订婚证书的订婚人分别是镇海人李光耀和鄞县人李蟾蘋，时间为 1948 年 8 月。宁波、上海一苇可航，鸦片战争以后，上海快速发展成为全国乃至远东最大的工商城市与经济中心，是宁波人创业的首选之地。到清末，在上海的宁波人已达 40 万，约占当时上海居民总数的三分之一。到 20 世纪二三十年代，旅沪宁波人达百万之众。旅沪宁波人落地生根，融入上海社会之中，对上海城市性格的形成和塑造产生了深远影响，也使得沪甬两地社会生活具有较强的联系。至今许多上海家庭都有祖籍宁波的亲戚，两地在语言、饮食习惯等方面也具有相似性。

This is the engagement certificate of Li Guangyao, a native of Zhenhai, and Li Chanping, a native of Yin County, dated August 1948. In the early 1900s, Shanghai was already home to 400,000 Ningbo natives, constituting roughly a third of the city's total population at that time. In the 1920s and 1930s, the number of Ningbo locals in Shanghai swelled to a million. Even today, many Shanghai households maintain ties to Ningbo, sharing commonalities in language and culinary preferences, among other things.

王禹襄书冯幵撰宁波旅沪同乡会为乌母七十寿屏

Scrolls Written by Wang Yuxiang, With Text Composed by Feng Jian, for the 70th Birthday of Wu Yaqin' mother, Signed by 230 Members of the Ningbo Residents' Association in Shanghai

民国时期

木盒 55.0 cm × 23.0 cm × 29.0 cm；寿屏 202.0 cm × 43.5 cm

收购 Acquired through purchase

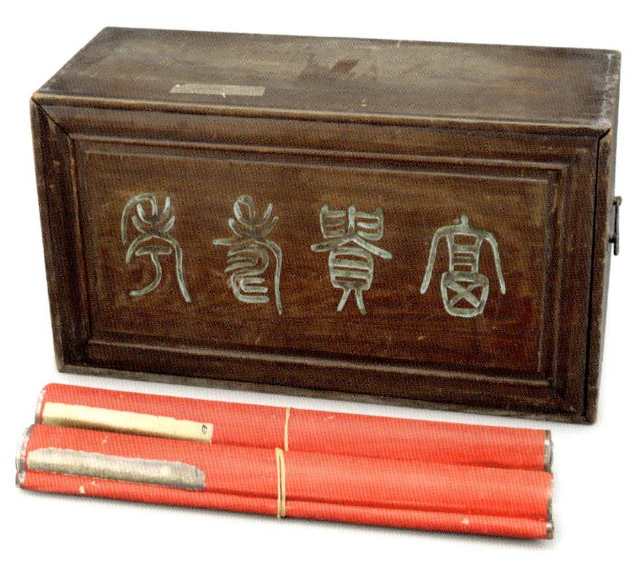

（局部）

寿屏共16幅长屏，讲述了乌母张孺人倾力将乌崖琴培养成才以及乌崖琴孝敬母亲的事迹，是宁波旅沪同乡会理事乌崖琴为庆祝母亲张孺人七十大寿的贺联，内容由冯幵撰、王禹襄书，共有同乡会同仁落款230人，对于研究民国时期宁波旅沪同乡会的人员构成、会务活动等具有重要历史价值。

乌崖琴（1889—1981），名人垚，宁波人。早期从事教育，曾任镇海县立高小校长、教育会会长。1921年任宁波旅沪同乡会理事，长期参与同乡会会务活动，负责管理学务20余年，其间同乡会小学从3所发展至10所。1922年以同乡会名义补助留法勤工俭学同乡学生，开同乡会设立助学金先河。抗战胜利后任上海储能中学校长，1949年后任上海市静安区政协委员。

These 16 long scrolls bear a congratulatory message from Wu Yaqin, a board member of the Ningbo Residents' Association in Shanghai, celebrating his mother's 70th birthday. It extolls her dedication to her son's development and describes acts of filial piety Wu has shown towards his mother. The text was composed by Feng Jian and inscribed by Wang Yuxiang. 230 members of the Association attached their signatures to the scrolls.

Wu Yaqin (1889-1981), a Ningbo native, initially worked in education and served as the principal of the Zhenhai County Elementary School. In 1921, he became a board member of the Ningbo Residents' Association in Shanghai.

宁波旅日同乡会铜牌

Bronze Plaque of the Japan Ningbo Association

1952 年

200.0 cm × 80.0 cm × 5.0 cm

宁波旅日同乡会捐赠 Acquired from the Japan Ningbo Association through donation

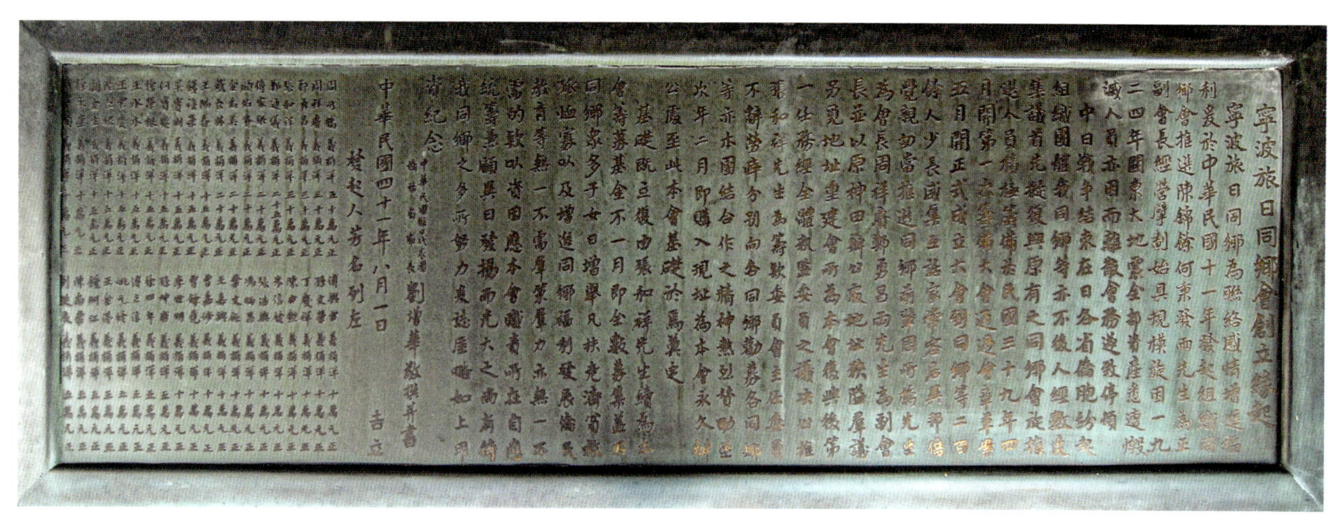

1922 年，陈锦徐、何秉发等人在日本东京发起创办宁波旅日同乡会，后因 1923 年关东大地震，会务中断。1950 年 5 月重建，1957 年 4 月取得财团法人资格，将会长制改为理事长制。张和祥、丁志明、长江启泰先后担任会长。宁波旅日同乡会以“敦睦乡谊、团结同乡、发展福利、为会员排忧解难”为宗旨，是日本具有较大影响的华侨华人社团，为发展日本与宁波的经济文化交流做了许多工作。

该铜牌记录了宁波旅日同乡会创立的缘起，及创会发起人名单与捐款数。

The Japan Ningbo Association was founded in Tokyo, Japan in 1922. This bronze plaque details the history of the Association's founding, listing the names of the founding members and the amount of donations they made.

《香港苏浙同乡会五十周年金禧纪念 1946—1996》

50th Anniversary Commemorative Booklet of the Kiangsu and Chekiang Residents (H.K.) Association

30.0 cm × 21.5 cm × 1.8 cm

香港苏浙沪同乡会捐赠 Acquired from the Kiangsu, Chekiang and Shanghai Residents (H.K.) Association through donation

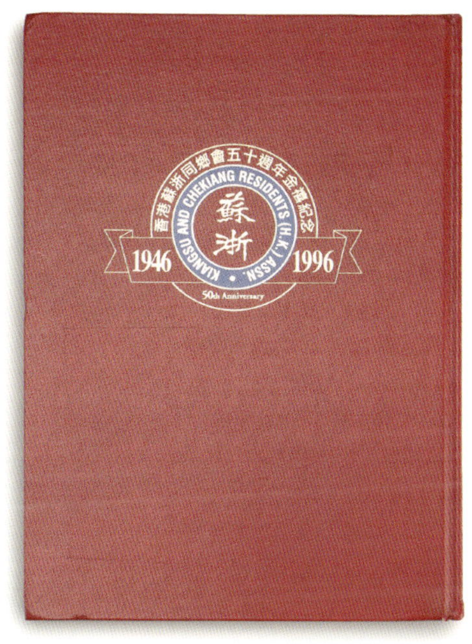

《香港苏浙沪同乡会六十周年钻禧纪念 1946—2006》

60th Anniversary Commemorative Booklet of the Kiangsu, Chekiang and Shanghai Residents (H.K.) Association

30.0 cm × 21.5 cm × 2.5 cm

香港苏浙沪同乡会捐赠 Acquired from the Kiangsu, Chekiang and Shanghai Residents (H.K.) Association through donation

香港苏浙沪同乡会(香港苏浙同乡会)于 1946 年 1 月 5 日成立，前身为 1939 年成立的旅港苏浙沪商人协会。首任会长为宁波籍人士阮维扬，宁波籍人士叶庚年、曹光彪也曾担任会长。会员主要是来自江苏、浙江、上海的旅港同胞。该会以团结乡侨、服务社会为宗旨，成立以来多次组团赴内地考察和交流，并积极捐助内地的公益事业，为祖国经济建设和各项事业的发展做出了积极的贡献。

The Kiangsu, Chekiang and Shanghai Residents (H.K.) Association, once called The Kiangsu and Chekiang Residents (H.K.) Association, was founded on January 5, 1946, with its members consisting primarily of individuals who had migrated to Hong Kong from Jiangsu, Zhejiang and Shanghai.

宁波旅港同乡会会钟

Ceremonial Bell of the Ning Po Residents Association Hong Kong

钟直径 11.0 cm × 18.0 cm；槌 26.0 cm × 9.0 cm

宁波旅港同乡会捐赠 Acquired from the Ning Po Residents Association Hong Kong through donation

香港宁波同乡会（原名宁波旅港同乡会）创办于 1967 年 4 月 9 日。20 世纪 50 年代初，大批宁波籍人士赴港谋生创业。为了互助合作，经多位乡贤的倡议及努力，于首次会员大会后成立同乡会，并由李达三博士担任创会会长。成员由在香港的宁波籍人士组成，王统元、曹伯中、包从兴、王惟翰、金如新、周亦卿、顾国华、李宗德、赵亨文、李本俊、范久祥等先后当选会长。

自创会以来，同乡会始终秉承“情系乡梓、守望互助，兴师办学、造福社会，立足香港、胸怀祖国”的创会宗旨，会务蒸蒸日上，成为香港社会较有影响的社团组织，为香港的繁荣、祖国的富强和家乡宁波的发展贡献良多。2009 年，宁波旅港同乡会改名为香港宁波同乡会。

The Ning Po Residents Association Hong Kong was established on April 9, 1967. In the early 1950s, numerous individuals originally from Ningbo relocated to Hong Kong in search of economic opportunities. In order to foster mutual support and collaboration, the association was founded following its inaugural members' assembly, with Dr. Li Dak-sum assuming the role of founding president.

寧波旅港同鄉會

宁波旅港同乡会历届会长名录石碑

Engraved Stone Tablet Inscribed with the Names of Past Presidents of the Ning Po Residents Association Hong Kong

49.0 cm × 2.0 cm × 85.0 cm

香港宁波同乡会捐赠 Acquired from the Ning Po Residents Association Hong Kong through donation

该石碑详细记录了截至 2015 年的香港宁波同乡会历任会长的名字和任期，包括李达三、王统元、曹伯中、包从兴、王惟翰等。在历任会长的带领下，同乡会蓬勃发展，凝聚力、吸引力和社会影响力日益提高，从一个几十人的团体发展成为一个有着数千会员并具有一定社会地位和声誉的社团。

This stone tablet provides a comprehensive record of the names and terms of office of past presidents of the Ning Po Residents Association Hong Kong up to the year 2015. The association flourished under the guidance of these former presidents, witnessing a growth in unity and social influence. It has evolved from a small group of a few dozen members into a well-respected organization with thousands of members, holding a prominent place in Hong Kong society.

香港甬港联谊会赠予宁波甬港联谊会的“造福桑梓”锦旗

Banner Presented by the Ningbo Hong Kong Fellowship Association (Hong Kong) to its Ningbo Counterpart

1980 年

120.0 cm × 77.0 cm

宁波甬港联谊会捐赠 Acquired from the Ningbo Hong Kong Fellowship Association (Ningbo) through donation

在改革开放初期，香港宁波帮人士王宽诚和宁波工商界人士俞佐宸共同倡议，以在甬港两地分别成立联谊会的方式，促进两地合作交流，推动宁波发展。

1980 年，宁波甬港联谊会成立大会在华侨饭店举行，香港甬港联谊会首任会长王宽诚率代表团前来祝贺，后向宁波甬港联谊会首任会长俞佐宸赠送“造福桑梓”锦旗，体现了两会的创会宗旨和共同目标。两会成立以来，不断加强交流合作，积极推动、促成港澳台及海外“宁波帮”和“帮宁波”人士在祖国和家乡开展经贸投资、科技合作、文化交流和慈善公益等事业，被誉为沟通宁波与香港之间的一座金桥，为宁波经济和社会发展、香港的繁荣稳定做出了重要贡献。

This banner, which bears the words “For the Benefit of Our Hometown”, was presented by the first president of the Ningbo Hong Kong Fellowship Association (Hong Kong), Kwan-cheng Wong, to his Ningbo counterpart Yu Zuochen during the organization’s inaugural ceremony in 1980.

香港宁波第二中学落成纪念册

Original of the Inaugural Records of the Ning Po No. 2 College in Hong Kong

1988 年

256.0 cm × 27.8 cm

梁王培芳、王培丽捐赠 Acquired from Liangwang Peifang and Wang Peili through donation

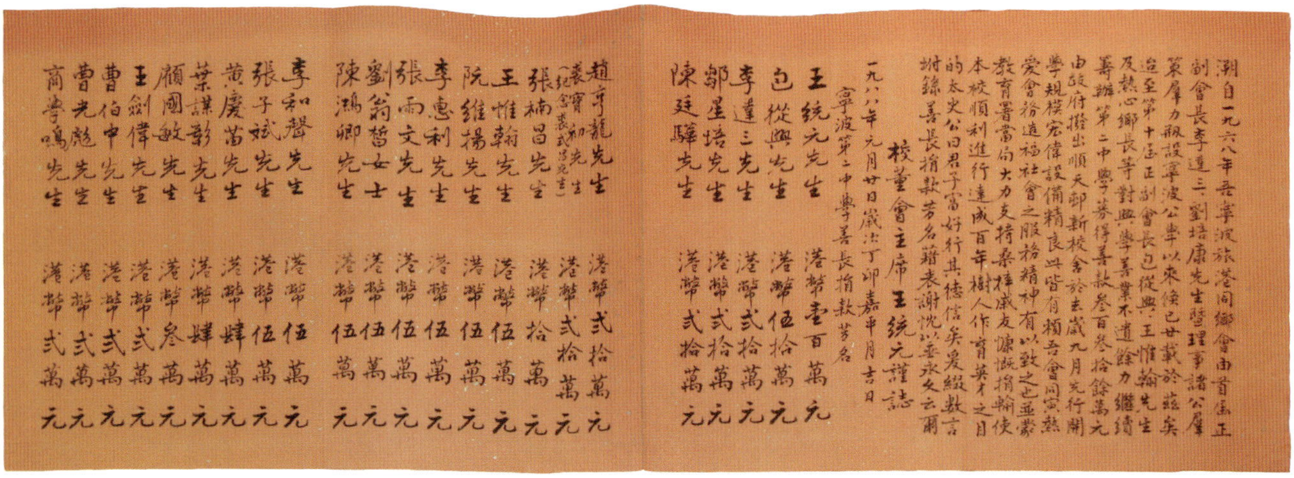

香港宁波第二中学地处香港观塘顺天村，是香港宁波同乡会继宁波公学之后创办的第二所政府津贴英文文法中学。1983 年，经会长包从兴、校董会主席王统元、校监李达三建议，香港宁波同乡会理监事会决定筹建宁波第二中学。同年，获香港政府拨款 200 万元作建校设备费用，同乡会与热心乡长捐款 330 多万元作学校补充设施与办学基金之用。1987 年 9 月，校舍启用并正式开课。该校办学重视培养学生的品德及自学能力，秉承“学生为本”的精神，在积极、愉快、融洽有序的学习环境下，发挥学生潜能，提升学生的素质和能力，使其成为正直、守法的公民。

该纪念册载有香港宁波第二中学校董会主席王统元先生的致辞及捐款乡长姓名，彰显了香港宁波同乡会乡长们热忱教育的殷切之情。

The Ning Po No. 2 College in Hong Kong is the second government-subsidized school founded by the Ning Po Residents Association Hong Kong.

The school was proposed in 1983 by Association President T. H. Pao and Association members Wong Toong Yuen, and Dr. Li Dak-sum, after which it was established by the Association's Board of Directors.

These records contain a message from Wong Toong Yuen, chairman of the school's council, and a list of generous donors.

世界中华宁波总商会纪念会徽

Lapel Pin of the International Ningbo Merchants Association

2009年

直径2.0 cm

世界中华宁波总商会捐赠 Acquired from the International Ningbo Merchants Association through donation

世界中华宁波总商会由香港宁波帮人士牵头，于2008年初在香港注册成立，并于2009年4月17日举行成立大会。商会以香港为总部，宁波为基地，建立环球联络平台，与世界各地宁波商会和侨胞保持密切联系、互通信息，参与社会公益服务，同时为会员提供各种商业咨询服务，为“宁波帮”和“帮宁波”人士发挥良好的桥梁和纽带作用。总商会会员遍布世界各地不同国家、不同城市、不同行业（如航运、制造、贸易、信息科技、房地产、金融、投资、旅游等）。

The International Ningbo Merchants Association was initiated by individuals of the Ningbobang in Hong Kong. It was officially registered in the SAR at the beginning of 2008 and held its inaugural meeting on April 17, 2009. The organization maintains close connections and information exchange with Ningbo chambers of commerce and overseas Ningbo compatriots around the world. The organization is involved in various philanthropic projects and provides a range of business consulting services to its members.

台北市宁波同乡会会旗、会刊

The Flag and Journal of Taipei Ningbo Association

① 143.0 cm × 97.0 cm ② 25.7 cm × 19.0 cm

台北市宁波同乡会捐赠 Acquired from the Taipei Ningbo Association through donation

① 会旗

②《宁波同乡》会刊

1947 年 8 月 28 日，台湾宁波籍人士叶启发、应昌期等 20 余人发起成立宁波旅台同乡会，后改称台北市宁波同乡会。水祥云、沈友梅等担任理事长。同乡会成立以来，本着"联络乡情乡谊，发扬自助精神，推进社会建设，协谋同乡福利"之宗旨，举办各项会务和社会公益活动，成为台湾地区颇有影响的社会组织。台北市宁波同乡会会旗由会名与会徽构成，会徽采用圆形设计，中间为"甬"字的变形，四周围绕六颗星，代表旧宁波府属六县。同乡会会刊《宁波同乡》于 1963 年 8 月 1 日创刊，发行人为理事长水祥云，主编人陈如一。

On August 28, 1947, more than 20 individuals of Ningbo origin in Taiwan initiated the establishment of the Taipei Ningbo Association. They organized various activities and philanthropic initiatives, making it a significant and influential social organization in Taiwan.

The Association flag consists of the its name and emblem. The emblem is designed in a circular shape with a modified " 甬 " (Yong) character in the center, surrounded by six stars, representing the six counties of the former Ningbo Prefecture. The association's journal, *Ningbo Compatriots*, was first published on August 1, 1963.

日本神户市财团法人三江会馆锦旗

Banner of San Kiang Association in Kobe, Japan

20 世纪

90.0 cm × 61.0 cm

姜成生捐赠 Acquired from Jiang Chengsheng through donation

日本神户三江会馆是最早的旅日华侨社团之一，其前身是三江公所。1912 年，在神户从事商业活动的江苏、江西、浙江籍侨胞动议成立了社团法人三江商业会（现称三江会馆），首任理事长为宁波籍旅日爱国侨领吴锦堂。

三江会馆的主要工作目标：一是资助三江子弟上学，照顾华侨中的老人、残疾人，并在三江华侨中开展继承民族文化的活动；二是经常组织与中国的交流活动，开展双向文化交流，推动中日友好往来。

In 1912, overseas Chinese from Jiangsu, Jiangxi, and Zhejiang engaged in business activities in Kobe, Japan came together to establish the San Kiang Association. The primary goals of the association were twofold: first, to support the education of Chinese descendants, provide care for elderly and disabled members of the overseas Chinese community, and promote the preservation of ethnic cultural traditions; second, to regularly organize exchange activities with China, fostering two-way cultural exchange and enhancing friendly relations between China and Japan.

留日华侨浙江同乡会会旗

Flag of Zhejiang Japan Association

20 世纪

63.0 cm × 49.0 cm

留日华侨浙江同乡会捐赠 Acquired from the Zhejiang Japan Association through donation

留日华侨浙江同乡会在中日邦交正常化之前的困难时期，历经数年的准备工作，于 1968 年 7 月正式成立，旨在通过同乡会的活动，加强爱国爱乡意识，加深同乡之间的亲睦和团结；维护同乡之间的共同利益和正当权利，接受华侨总会的领导和支持来共同解决同乡的事业和教育以及与侨居有关的法律问题；通过日常生活中必要的信息交换和日复一日的累积来促进中日友好；根据各自的能力为故乡浙江省的发展建设做出贡献。

The Zhejiang Japan Association was officially founded in July 1968. Its mission was to foster patriotism and hometown pride, promote closer bonds and unity among its members, and safeguard the shared interests and legitimate rights of its members.

纽约宁波同乡会会旗、胸章

Banner and Lapel Pins of New York Ningbo Association Inc.

20 世纪

① 50.0 cm × 50.0 cm ② 直径 3.0 cm ③ 直径 2.0 cm

纽约宁波同乡会捐赠 Acquired from the New York Ningbo Association Inc. through donation

① 会旗

② 大胸章

③ 小胸章

1999 年 11 月，旅居美国的宁波籍人士创办纽约宁波同乡会。该会成立以来，在聚集宁波侨胞、联络乡亲感情、团结兄弟侨团、促进中美友谊方面发挥了重要作用。

In November 1999, Ningbo natives residing in the United States established the New York Ningbo Association. Since its inception, the association has played a significant role in bringing together Ningbo compatriots, fostering unity, partnering with other overseas Chinese associations, and promoting Sino-American friendship.

加拿大宁波总商会会旗

Flag of the Ningbo Chamber of Commerce of Canada Society

152.0 cm × 90.0 cm

郑国英捐赠 Acquired from Zheng Guoying through donation

加拿大宁波总商会成立于 2018 年 5 月，是由在加拿大与宁波相关的企业家和企业、在宁波与加拿大相关的企业家和企业组成的加拿大全国性的专业商会和互助团体。在多伦多、蒙特利尔、上海、南京、宁波等地设有分会。同时在慈溪、余姚、镇海、北仑、奉化、象山、宁海设有商会联络处。

商会宗旨为充分发挥商会作为宁波与加拿大的经济纽带及桥梁的作用；代表并维护会员的合法权益，促进资源共享与经验交流，增进会员之间的互助及沟通；加强与政府、商务团体、企业等各界的交流合作，引导并帮助会员深度了解中国与加拿大的商业环境及背景，促进企业更快更强地发展，帮助会员创业、回馈社会；发挥商会的仲裁作用。

The Ningbo Chamber of Commerce of Canada Society, established in May 2018, is a nationwide professional organization and mutual assistance group comprising entrepreneurs and businesses in both Canada and Ningbo. The chamber has branches in cities like Toronto, Montreal, Shanghai, Nanjing and Ningbo, as well as liaison offices in Cixi, Yuyao, Zhenhai, Beilun, Fenghua, Xiangshan, and Ninghai.

《泰国江浙会馆成立 67 周年纪念特刊》

Special Issue Commemorating the 67th Anniversary of the Kung Jek Association of Thailand

27.0 cm × 19.3 cm × 1.5 cm

收购 Acquired through purchase

1923 年，张宝元、张兴宝两兄弟发起，沈章行、沈纪荣、张福堂、赵士林、苏庆和等几经磋商筹备，于 7 月 29 日正式成立泰国江浙会馆，并向政府申请注册后获批准。江浙会馆的成立，极大地提升了侨居泰国乡亲的凝聚力。江浙会馆广泛参与社会公共福利和慈善事业，团结广大侨胞，致力于华侨华人的福利事业。自中泰建交以来，会馆在中泰友好往来方面做了许多工作。

On July 29, 1923, the Kung Jek Association of Thailand was founded. It was spearheaded by brothers Zhang Baoyuan and Zhang Xingbao, along with collaborative efforts from Shen Zhangxing, Shen Jirong, Zhang Futang, Zhao Tulin, Su Qinghe, among others. Following a successful registration application with government approval, the association became a vital force in enhancing the unity of the Ningbo community in Thailand. Actively involved in a range of charitable activities, the association unites the broader overseas Chinese community and is dedicated to advancing the welfare of Chinese expatriates. Since the establishment of diplomatic relations between China and Thailand, the association has played a dynamic role in fostering enduring Sino-Thai friendships.

家国情怀

Patriotic Spirit

李锦关于上饶集中营回忆相关手稿

Manuscripts on Li Jin's Concentration Camp Experience in Shangrao

36.0 cm × 26.0 cm

李小威、徐佳欣捐赠 Acquired from Li Xiaowei and Xu Jiaxin through donation

上饶集中营女生队的斗争纪实
——忆女生队部分同志
自从1937年日本帝国主义发动"七七"
芦沟桥事变，对我国开始了大规模的侵略战争，
在这中华民族生死存亡的危难时刻，中国共产
党和国民党第二次合作，停止了内战，结束了

李锦（1923—2020），原名李采芝，出生于宁波小港，为宁波帮望族小港李家后人，父亲李善祥是著名宁波帮人士。

李锦年少时就读于素有矗立蛟门的"红色堡垒"之誉的蔚斗小学，接受了爱国主义思想的启蒙教育。1937 年七七事变后，14 岁的李锦跟随大哥李祖平（李光言）、二姐李幼兰（李又兰）等，参加了镇海县小港镇抗日救亡宣传队和救护队。1938 年 3 月，她在江西南昌参加了新四军战地服务团，曾在皖南前线做过民运工作，在战地服务团第三队随叶挺军长夜渡长江到皖北新四军第四、第五支队慰问演出和做群众工作，不久加入中国共产党。1941 年 1 月皖南事变，她被捕关入上饶集中营，后经其父李善祥活动，由地下党通过关系保释。1944 年底，回浙东四明山新四军三五支队。先后在

中华全国妇女联合会纪念章

Commemorative Medal of the All-China Women's Federation

(由上至下)直径 2.2 cm; 1.6 cm × 1.6 cm; 直径 2.4 cm; 2.5 cm × 2.2 cm; 2.3 cm × 2.3 cm

李小威、徐佳欣捐赠 Acquired from Li Xiaowei and Xu Jiaxin through donation

鲁迅学院、浙东日报社学习和工作。1945 年北撤时奉命隐蔽到辽宁锦州其父亲处，与地下党保持联系。中华人民共和国成立后，在锦州市妇联工作。1953 年调至北京全国妇联工作。1982 年离休。

Li Jin (1923-2020), originally named Li Caizhi, was born in Xiaogang, Ningbo. In March 1938, she joined the New Fourth Army Field Service Corps in Nanchang, Jiangxi, and shortly thereafter, she became a member of the CPC. In January 1941, during the Southern Anhui Incident, she was arrested and placed in a concentration camp in Shangrao, Jiangxi. Thanks to the efforts of her father, Li Shanxiang, and connections within the underground Party, she was released. After the founding of the People's Republic of China, she worked for the Women's Federation in Jinzhou. In 1953, she was transferred to work for the All-China Women's Federation in Beijing.

冯玉祥赠卢绪章对联

Couplet Gifted by Feng Yuxiang to Lu Xuzhang

1946 年

175.5 cm × 44.7 cm

卢绪章家族捐赠 Acquired from the Lu Xuzhang Family through donation

该对联是冯玉祥为祝贺卢绪章荣任民安保险公司总经理所写，上联“人民为主宰”，下联“科学是救星”。

1933 年，宁波人卢绪章与田鸣皋、杨延修、张平、郑栋林在上海发起成立广大华行，开展药品、医疗器械的零售批发业务，旨在为抗日救亡活动提供经济保障。1943 年，卢绪章在重庆参与创办了民安保险公司，并以广大华行和民安保险公司为掩护，建立了党的秘密工作机构，受中共中央南方局和周恩来同志的直接领导。

在战争年代，广大华行和民安保险卓有成效地开展了党的统战工作和经济工作，不但为党提供了大量经费和紧缺物资，还培养了一批富有经验的金融保险骨干，胜利完成了上级党组织交给的各项任务，为争取抗战胜利、加速全国解放提供了有力支持。

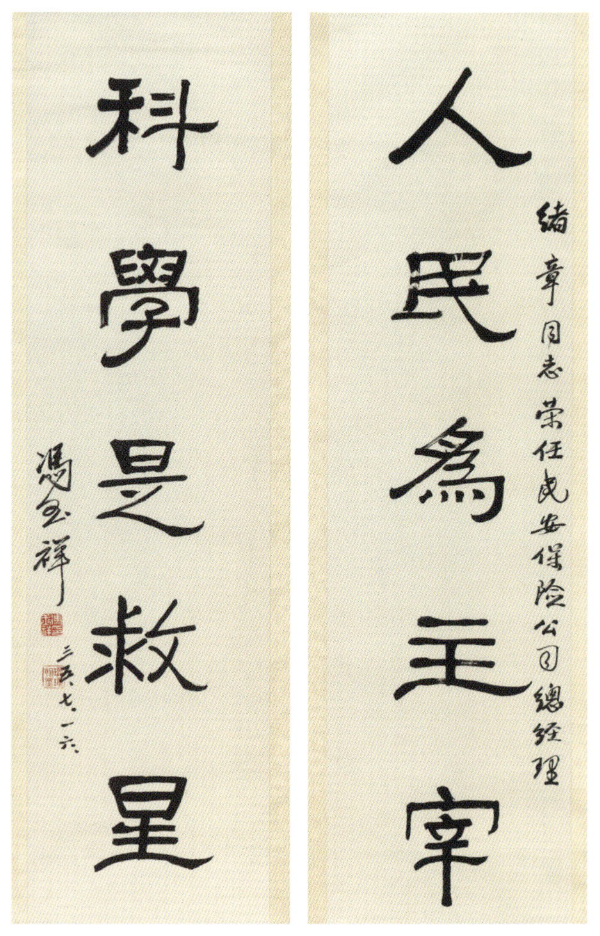

This couplet was written by Feng Yuxiang to congratulate Lu Xuzhang on his appointment as the General Manager of Min'an Insurance Company. The first line reads, “People are the masters”. The second line reads, “Science is the savior”.

Feng Yuxiang was a prominent Chinese military leader and politician in the early 20th century. Lu Xuzhang was a Chinese revolutionary and politician from Ningbo who played a significant role in early 20th century China, particularly as a financial operator for the CPC.

李善祥抄写的《实践论》手稿

Manuscript of *On Practice* Hand-copied by Li Shanxiang

1951 年

22.5 cm × 18.0 cm

李锦捐赠 Acquired from Li Jin through donation

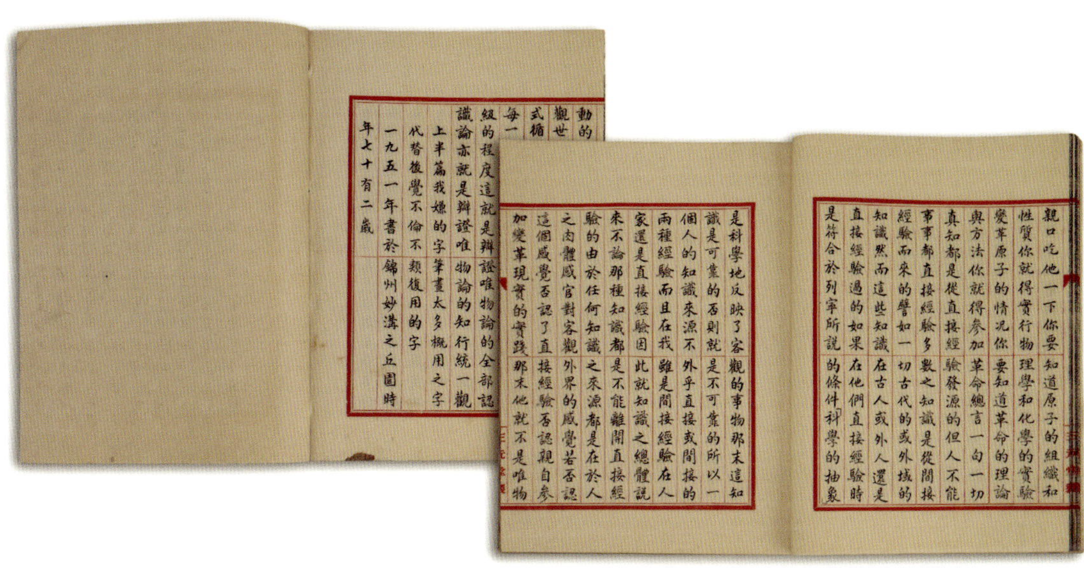
親口吃他一下你要知道原子的組織和
性質你就得實行物理學和化學的實驗
變革原子的情況你要知道革命的理論
與方法你就得參加革命總言一句一切
真知都是從直接經驗發源的但人不能
事事都直接經驗多數之知識是從間接
經驗而來的譬如一切古代的或外域的
知識然而這些知識在古人或外人還是
直接經驗過的如果在他們直接經驗時
是符合於列寧所說的條件科學的抽象

是科學地反映了客觀的事物那末這知
識是可靠的否則就是不可靠的所以一
個人的知識來源不外乎直接或間接的
兩種經驗而且在我雖是間接經驗在人
家還是直接經驗因此就知識之總體說
來不論那種知識都是不能離開直接經
驗的由於任何知識之來源都是在於人
之肉體感官對客觀外界的感覺若否認
這個感覺否認了直接經驗否認親自參
加變革現實的實踐那末他就不是唯物

動的
觀世
式循
每一
級的程度這就是辯證唯物論的全部認
識論亦就是辯證唯物論的知行統一觀
上半篇我嫌的字筆畫太多概用之字
代替後覺不倫不類復用的字
一九五一年書於錦州妙溝之丘園時
年七十有二歲

这份《实践论》手抄本为李善祥亲笔书写。李善祥（1880—1959），宁波小港李家人，著名爱国实业家。青年时代接受民主思想启蒙，1911 年被推选为首任镇海县民事长（县长）。后立志兴办实业，1912 年赴辽宁经营天一垦务公司并创立南山耕余果艺学院，被誉为“中国苹果之父”。抗日战争时期，积极投入抗日救亡运动。1940 年春夏大饥荒期间，他动员镇海富户开仓济民，抢救被日军炸伤的乡民，还开办难民收容所。中华人民共和国成立后，他把所有家产全部捐献给国家。

李善祥一生倡导“实业救国”，从身体力行办企业的实践中，对毛泽东《实践论》提出的诸多思想感同身受、十分推崇。他用隽秀的楷书工工整整地把《实践论》抄写了一遍，手抄本末页落款“一九五一年书于锦州妙沟之丘园，时年七十有二岁”。

This handwritten copy of Mao Zedong's *On Practice* was transcribed by Li Shanxiang (1880-1959) of the Li family from Xiaogang, Ningbo. Li Shanxiang was a renowned patriotic industrialist. In 1912, he went to Liaoning to operate the Tianyi Farming Company and founded the Nanshan Agricultural and Horticultural College, earning him the title of "Father of Chinese Apples". After the founding of the People's Republic of China, he generously donated all his family property to the country.

Throughout his life, Li advocated industrial development for China's national restoration. He deeply resonated with and highly admired many of the ideas put forth by Mao Zedong in *On Practice*, based on his practical experience in running businesses. He meticulously transcribed it in elegant calligraphy. The last page bears the inscription "Written in 1951 at Qiuyuan, Miaogou, Jinzhou, at the age of seventy-two".

王宽诚捐赠“维大号”战斗机的相关信函

Correspondence by Kwan-cheng Wong Regarding the Donation of the “Weida” Fighter Aircraft

1951 年

27.7 cm × 20.3 cm

王宽诚家族捐赠 Acquired from the Kwan-cheng Wong Family through donation

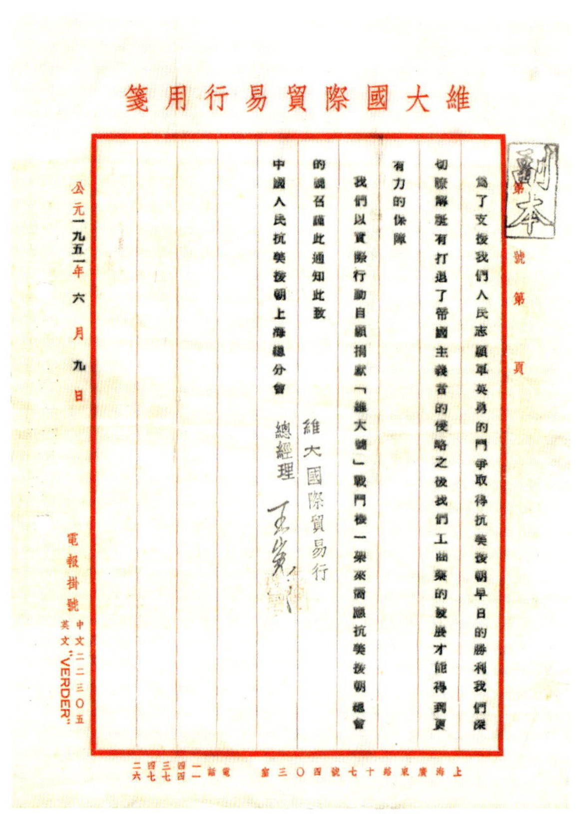

維大國際貿易行用箋

副本

第　號第　頁

為了支援我們人民志願軍英勇的鬥爭取得抗美援朝早日的勝利我們深切瞭解祇有打退了帝國主義者的侵略之後我們工商業的發展才能得到更有力的保障

我們以實際行動自願捐獻「維大號」戰鬥機一架來響應抗美援朝總會的號召謹此通知此致

中國人民抗美援朝上海總分會

維大國際貿易行
總經理 [signature: 王寬誠]

公元一九五一年六月九日

電報掛號 中文二二三〇五 英文“VERDER”

上海廣東路十七號四〇三室 電話 一四三四二 二四七七六

该信函记录了王宽诚在抗美援朝时期捐助“维大号”战斗机的事迹，上有王宽诚亲笔签名和印章。1947 年，王宽诚由上海去香港发展，设立维大洋行、幸福企业等数十家公司。到港后，王宽诚将大部分资金用于购买地皮。中华人民共和国成立后，他积极投资内地建设。抗美援朝战争爆发后，王宽诚踊跃为国家购买大量紧缺军用物资，并带头捐献战斗机一架。为筹集资金，他不惜将公司收购的香港地皮出售来应急。

This letter records Kwan-cheng Wong’s donation of a fighter plane to the Chinese military during the Korean War. It bears Wong’s handwritten signature and seal. In 1947, Wong moved from Shanghai to Hong Kong, where he established several companies. When the Korean War broke out, he purchased a significant amount of much-needed military supplies for the Chinese military.

卢绪章补发工资后补交党费明细单

Memo From Lu Xuzhang on Paying CPC Membership Dues After Receiving a Late Salary Payment

1974 年

25.4 cm × 17.5 cm

卢绪章家族捐赠 Acquired from the Lu Xuzhang Family through donation

卢绪章是中国共产党最具传奇色彩的党员之一。新中国成立前，他创办的广大华行不仅是党在秘密战线的工作机构，也是经营有方的经济实体，为中国人民解放事业筹集了宝贵资金。中华人民共和国成立后，卢绪章将圆满完成历史使命的广大华行进行了资产清理，然后把近 200 万美元上交给组织。

1974 年 1 月，卢绪章收到补发工资 7000 多元，他首先想到的就是要将耽误了几年的党费赶紧交上。这份补交党费明细单不仅记录了卢绪章严格履行党员义务的行为，更反映出他对党的忠诚。“我从 1937 年入党后，就把自己的一切献给了国家，献给了党。”正如卢绪章自己所说的那样，他始终把党和国家的发展作为奋斗终身的目标。中华人民共和国成立后，他从事外贸领导工作，在冲破帝国主义禁运封锁方面功绩显赫；改革开放后，他开拓了中国的旅游事业，为中国引进外资和宁波的发展做出了卓越贡献。

Lu Xuzhang, a remarkable member of the CPC, founded the Guangda Huahang Bank, which operated as both a covert Party organization and a successful economic entity, raising significant funds for the Chinese liberation cause before the establishment of the People's Republic of China. Afterward, Lu Xuzhang fulfilled his mission by turning in nearly 2 million dollars to the Party after asset clearance. This detailed memo on paying CPC membership dues not only highlights his commitment to his party responsibilities but also underscores his loyalty to the Party.

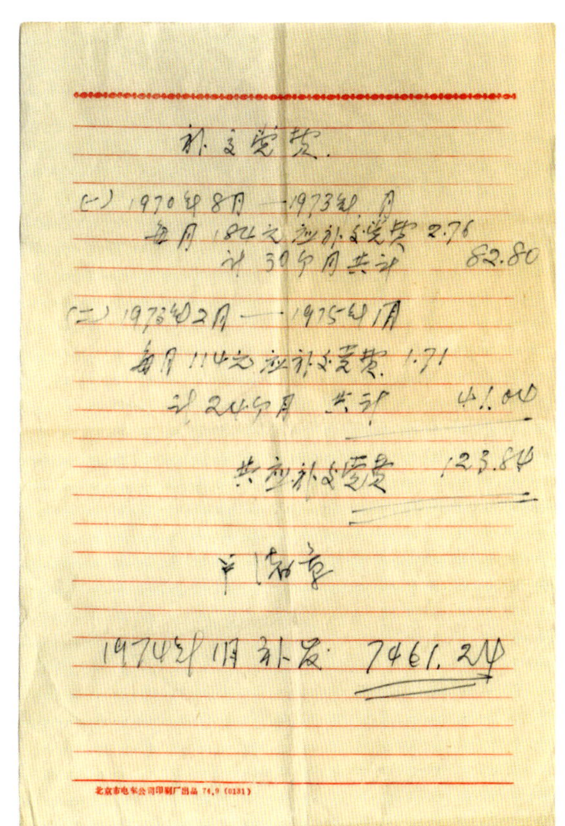

补交党费.

(一) 1970年8月—1973年1月
每月184元 应补交党费 2.76
计30个月共计 82.80

(二) 1973年2月—1975年1月
每月114元 应补交党费 1.71
计24个月 共计 41.04

共应补交党费 123.84

卢绪章

1974年1月 补发: 7461.24

北京市电车公司印刷厂出品 74.9 (0131)

苏浙公学敬赠包玉刚的热心教育奖杯

Education Philanthropy Award Trophy Presented by the Kiangsu-Chekiang College to Sir Y. K. Pao

1976 年

10.5 cm × 10.5 cm × 38.0 cm

包氏家族捐赠 Acquired from the Pao Family through donation

苏浙公学位于香港宝马山，为旅港苏浙沪商人协会（香港苏浙沪同乡会前身）于 1958 年创办，校训为“整齐严肃”。1993 年转为政府直接资助学校。

该奖杯为 1976 年 9 月 22 日苏浙公学敬赠包玉刚校董的热心教育奖杯。包玉刚曾担任苏浙公学校董，为苏浙公学的发展献计献策。包玉刚的父亲包兆龙热心公益事业，也曾资助苏浙公学扩展校舍。包兆龙、包玉刚历来重视教育，先后捐建上海交通大学包兆龙图书馆，捐资创建宁波大学，设立“包兆龙包玉刚中国留学生奖学金”等，积极助力祖国教育事业。

The Kiangsu-Chekiang College, situated on Braemar Hill in Hong Kong, was founded by the Kiangsu, Chekiang and Shanghai Residents (H.K.) Association in 1958.

The trophy, given on September 22, 1976, is a heartfelt educational award presented by the College to Sir Y.k. Pao, who once served as a board member at the school and played a significant role in its development.

黄华致卢绪章信函

Correspondence from Huang Hua to Lu Xuzhang

1981 年

19.0 cm × 13.0 cm

卢绪章家族捐赠 Acquired from the Lu Xuzhang Family through donation

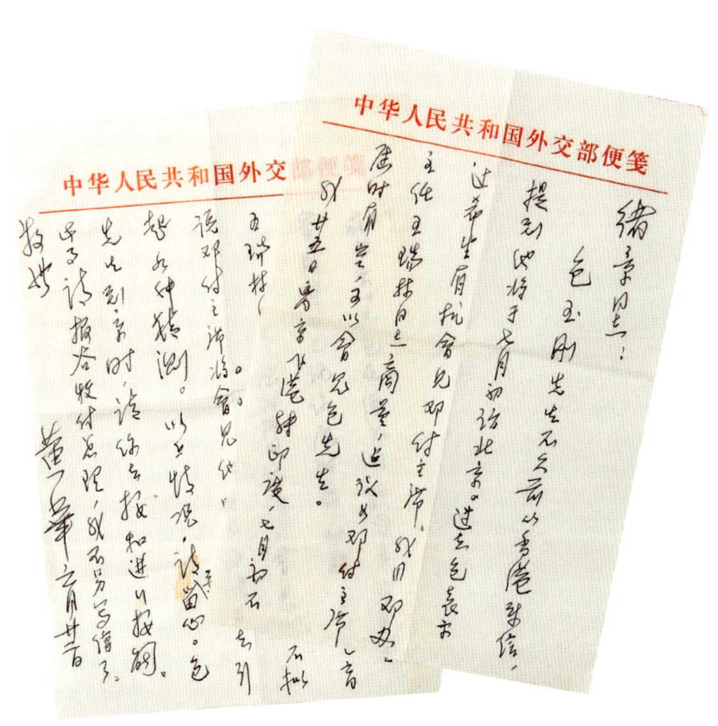
中华人民共和国外交部便笺

绪章兄：

……

黄华 六月廿二日

中华人民共和国外交部便笺

1981 年 6 月 22 日，时任外交部部长的黄华致信卢绪章，传达了包玉刚希望与邓小平见面的心愿。在卢绪章的促成下，当年 7 月 6 日，邓小平会见了包玉刚。此后，包玉刚又多次受到邓小平接见，并在香港回归过程中做出了重大贡献。1984 年，邓小平做出“把全世界的宁波帮都动员起来，建设宁波”的指示，卢绪章受中央的委托到宁波指导工作，帮助宁波制定长远发展规划，并积极发动海内外宁波帮力量共同建设宁波。

On June 22, 1981, then-Foreign Minister Huang Hua conveyed Sir Y.k. Pao's desire to meet with Deng Xiaoping in a letter to Lu Xuzhang. Thanks to Lu Xuzhang's efforts, on July 6 of the same year, Deng Xiaoping granted a meeting with Sir Y.K. Pao. Subsequently, there were several more meetings between the two. In 1984, Deng Xiaoping issued a directive to "mobilize the Ningbobang all around the world to develop Ningbo". Lu Xuzhang, acting on behalf of the central government, traveled to Ningbo to provide guidance, assist in formulating long-term development plans for Ningbo, and actively engage the Ningbobang all over the world to collectively support Ningbo's development.

宁波大学 0001 号搪瓷碗

Ningbo University Commemorative Enamel Bowl No. 0001

1986 年

底径 12.0 cm × 6.0 cm，口径 18.0 cm

朱兆祥家族捐赠 Acquired from the Zhu Zhaoxiang Family through donation

这是 1986 年宁波大学建校初期仅供教师购买的搪瓷碗，编号 0001，具有不可替代的历史价值和纪念意义，与宁波帮博物馆馆藏的宁波大学 001 号脸盆相得益彰，不但见证了宁波高等教育事业的发展历程，同时也凸显出宁波帮人士关心、支持家乡建设的桑梓情怀。

朱兆祥，1921 年生于宁波镇海，毕业于浙江大学，是著名的力学家、教育家和科技事业活动家，一生奉献科技事业，为家乡教育事业的发展做出了重要贡献。他在担任宁波大学首任校长期间，将该校建成一所初具规模的综合性大学。

This enamel bowl, bearing the number 0001, was originally offered for sale exclusively to teachers following the founding of Ningbo University in 1986. It holds unique historical significance and serves as a commemorative item.

宁波大学 001 号脸盆、首届新生纪念徽章

Ningbo University Commemorative Basin No. 001 and First-Year Student Commemorative Badge

1986 年

①直径 34.5 cm × 10.5 cm ②直径 2.5 cm × 0.5 cm

①李学兰捐赠 Acquired from Li Xuelan through donation ②徐一萍捐赠 Acquired from Xu Yiping through donation

① 脸盆

② 徽章

宁波大学创办于 1986 年，由包玉刚率先捐资倡导创办，邓小平同志题写校名。学校在创建和发展过程中，获得了众多海内外“宁波帮”和“帮宁波”人士的大力帮助和广泛支持。

001 号脸盆的主人是现宁波大学的李学兰老师，她是宁波大学正式招收的第一届学生。报到时，李学兰在学校的小卖部无意中买到这只“001 号”脸盆。对于这件具有纪念意义的物品，李学兰特别予以珍藏，希望它能够见证宁波高等教育事业的发展历程，以及宁波帮人士关心、支持家乡建设的历史。

这枚 1986 年宁波大学首届新生纪念徽章，见证了宁波大学的创办以及宁波高等教育的发展历程。徽章的主人徐一萍将这枚极具纪念意义的徽章收藏至今，并捐赠予宁波帮博物馆，希望博物馆更好地讲述徽章背后的故事。

The owner of Basin No. 001 was Professor Li Xuelan from Ningbo University. She was among the very first students officially enrolled at the university in 1986. When Li registered, she happened to purchase this “No. 001” basin from the school’s convenience store. Recognizing the significance of this memento, Li has treasured it as a symbol of the university’s journey of development.

This 1986 commemorative badge was among those given to the first cohort of students at Ningbo University. Its owner, Xu Yiping, has preserved the momento, and generously donated it to Ningbobang Museum.

马临的香港基本法起草工作纪念牌

Memorial Plaque for Ma Lin's Participation in the Drafting of the Basic Law of Hong Kong

1990 年

40.0 cm × 30.0 cm

马临捐赠 Acquired from Ma Lin through donation

马临（1924—2017），生于北京，原籍浙江鄞县。马临的家族是鄞县望族、书香门第，仅在马临父辈中，就有马裕藻、马衡、马鉴、马准、马廉五位著名教授。1957 年起，马临先后任教于香港大学病理学系、香港中文大学生物化学系。1978 年至 1987 年，马临担任香港中文大学校长，1986 年被委任为非官守太平绅士。曾任香港特别行政区基本法起草委员会委员，第八、第九届全国政协委员。

香港顺利回归，宁波帮厥功至伟。从中英关于香港问题的谈判、《中英联合声明》的签署，到《香港特别行政区基本法》的起草，马临与包玉刚、王宽诚、安子介、邬维庸等宁波帮人士，利用自己在香港的社会影响和与英国方面的良好关系，为推动香港回归进程倾尽全力。

Ma Lin (1924-2017), born in Beijing to a family who hailed from Yin County, Ningbo. Ma Lin's family was a respected and educated family in Yin County. Starting in 1957, Ma Lin taught at the University of Hong Kong in the Department of Pathology and later at the Chinese University of Hong Kong in the Department of Biochemistry. From 1978 to 1987, he served as the President of the Chinese University of Hong Kong and was appointed a non-official Justice of the Peace in 1986. He also served as a member of the Drafting Committee for *the Basic Law of the Hong Kong Special Administrative Region* and was a member of the Eighth and Ninth National Committee of the Chinese People's Political Consultative Conference.

马临的香港中文大学校长袍

Ceremonial Robe of Ma Lin, Former President of the Chinese University of Hong Kong

134.0 cm × 168.0 cm

马怡芳捐赠 Acquired from Ma Yifang through donation

作为一名科学家和教育家，马临一贯强调“人才是致富之根，科技是强国之本，国家之根本在于教育”。1978 年，马临出任香港中文大学校长，在担任校长期间对大学教育学制进行了一系列改革，不但为香港中文大学长远发展奠定基础，对香港高等教育亦贡献良多。他于 1987 年 10 月荣休，1987 至 2011 年期间担任中大逸夫书院校董会首任主席。

马临情系桑梓，长期关心宁波教育事业，先后推动邵逸夫基金会等多个教育项目落地宁波，为宁波教育事业的发展多方谋划，贡献卓著。

In 1978, Ma Lin took on the role of President at the Chinese University of Hong Kong. During his tenure as President, he implemented a series of educational reforms, not only laying the foundation for the long-term development of CUHK but also making significant contributions to higher education in Hong Kong. He retired in October 1987. Ma Lin maintained a deep connection to his hometown Ningbo and showed a long-term interest in the educational development in the city. He actively promoted several educational projects, including the Shaw Foundation, to be established in Ningbo, making remarkable contributions to the advancement of education in Ningbo.

范徐丽泰获得的金紫荆星章

Gold Bauhinia Star Medal Awarded to Rita Fan Hsu Lai-tai

1998 年

5.0 cm × 11.0 cm

范徐丽泰捐赠 Acquired from Rita Fan Hsu Lai-tai through donation

此枚星章为中华人民共和国香港特别行政区政府于 1998 年授予范徐丽泰女士，由其本人捐赠给宁波帮博物馆。

范徐丽泰，宁波镇海人。在香港积极从事社会教育事业以及公共事业。其中特别值得一提的是，她利用自己在香港的社会影响、与英国方面的良好关系，倾全力推动香港和平回归进程。香港回归后，范徐丽泰连任三届香港特别行政区立法会主席。为表彰她做出的重大贡献，特区政府特授予该星章。金紫荆星章由香港特别行政区政府自 1998 年开始颁授，对象为对社会有重大贡献或积极参与公共志愿服务而得到高度评价的人士。

This medal was awarded to Rita Fan Hsu Lai-tai by the Hong Kong Special Administrative Region Government of the People's Republic of China in 1998 and graciously donated by her to Ningbobang Museum. Originally from Zhenhai, Ningbo, Rita Fan Hsu Lai-tai has played a vital role in Hong Kong's social and public affairs. Her most notable contributions include her active involvement in promoting the peaceful return of Hong Kong, utilizing her substantial influence in Hong Kong and her strong connections with the UK to facilitate the return process. After Hong Kong's return, she served as the President of the Legislative Council of the Hong Kong Special Administrative Region for three consecutive terms. In recognition of her exceptional contributions, the SAR Government presented her with this medal.

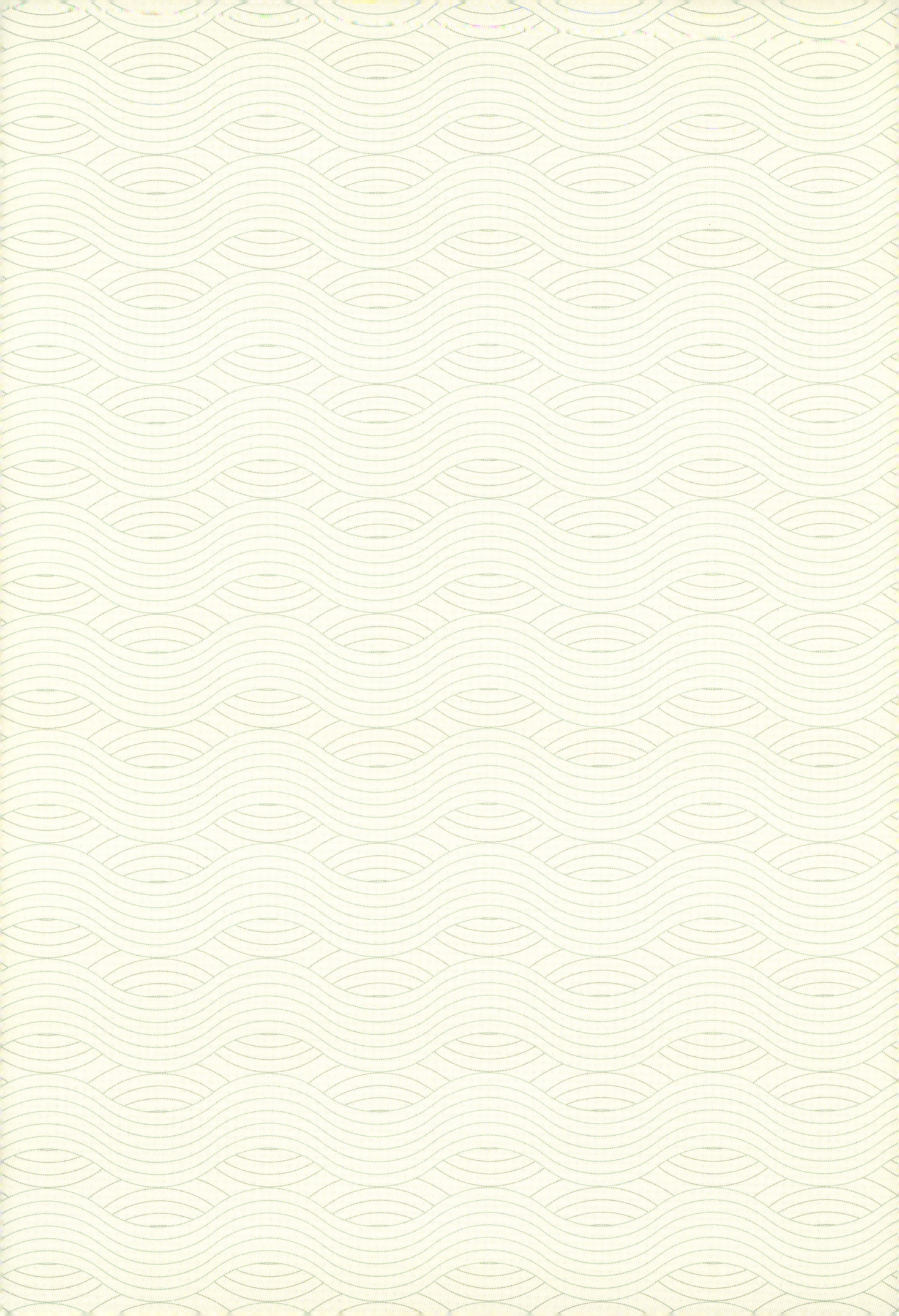

群星璀璨

Diverse Achievements

戴传曾《切尔诺贝利核电站事故后国际核安全顾问组特别会议情况汇报》手稿

Report on the Special Meeting of the International Nuclear Safety Advisory Group Following the Chernobyl Nuclear Power Plant Accident Manuscript by Dai Chuanzeng

1986 年

26.5 cm × 19.0 cm

戴依明、戴卫明、戴宏明捐赠 Acquired from Dai Yiming, Dai Weiming, and Dai Hongming through donation

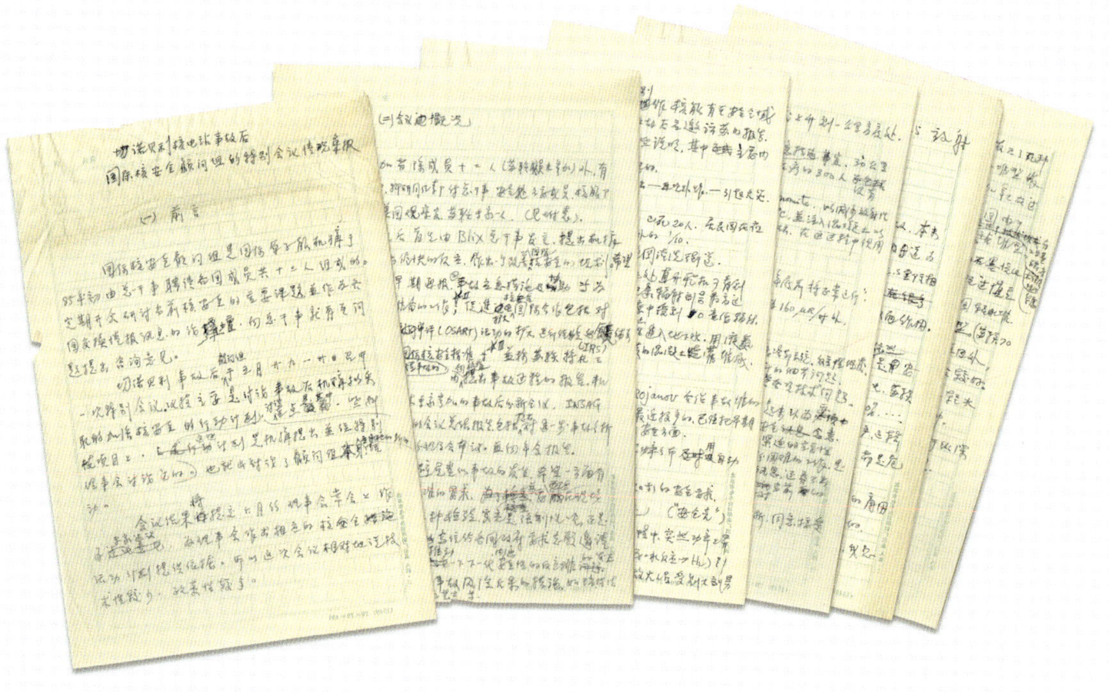
切诺贝利核电站事故后
国际核安全顾问组的特别会议情况汇报

(一) 前言

(二) 会议概况

戴传曾（1921—1990），宁波鄞县人，中国科学院院士，原子能专家，中国核能科学奠基人之一，中国核安全研究工作创始人。1942 年毕业于西南联大，后赴英国利物浦大学进修获得博士学位。1951 年回国后，进入中国科学院工作，在实验核物理、反应堆物理、反应堆工程和核安全等研究工作与组织领导方面做了大量工作，为我国核事业的发展做出了重大贡献。

20 世纪 80 年代初期，戴传曾指导开展了我国微型中子源反应堆的物理方案论证，并亲自组织和审定初步设计及施工设计方案，于 1984 年 3 月建成了全部由我国自己设计建造的微型中子源反应堆。该反应堆经济、安全，既是一种方便的中子活化分析工具，也是很好的教学培训设备，在此

戴传曾国家科学技术进步一等奖证书

National Science and Technology Progress First Prize Certificate for Dai Chuanzeng

1987 年

22.3 cm × 16.5 cm

戴依明、戴卫明、戴宏明捐赠 Acquired from Dai Yiming, Dai Weiming, and Dai Hongming through donation

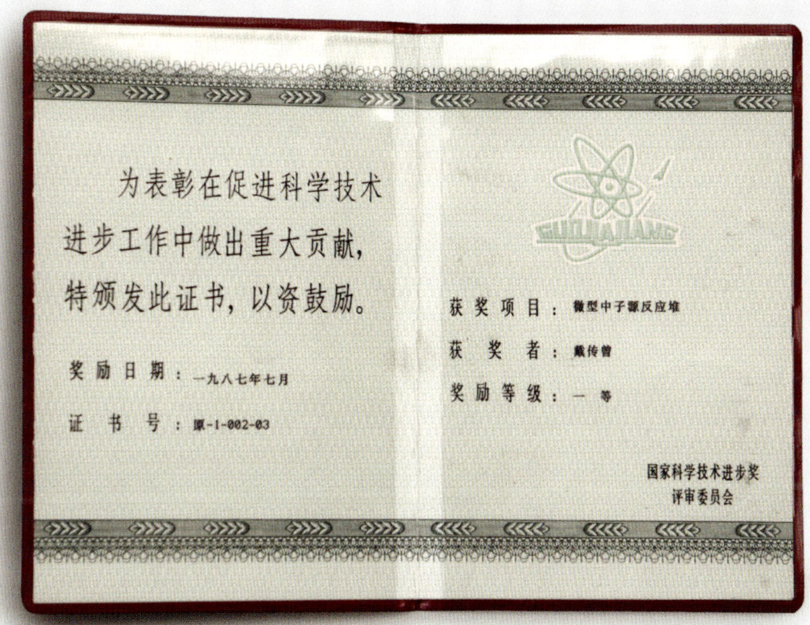

为表彰在促进科学技术进步工作中做出重大贡献，特颁发此证书，以资鼓励。

奖励日期：一九八七年七月

证书号：原-1-002-03

获奖项目：微型中子源反应堆

获奖者：戴传曾

奖励等级：一等

国家科学技术进步奖评审委员会

基础上发展的微型强中子源反应堆得到了广泛的商业推广。戴传曾凭借着这项重大成果荣获 1987 年度国家科学技术进步奖一等奖。

Dai Chuanzeng (1921-1990), originally from Yin County, Ningbo, was a Chinese Academy of Sciences academician and a pioneer in atomic energy. In the early 1980s, he played a crucial role in designing and building China's domestically developed miniature neutron source reactor. This reactor, completed in March 1984, was both cost-effective and safe. It served as a useful tool for neutron activation analysis, as well as an excellent educational and training device. Dai Chuanzeng's remarkable contributions earned him the First Prize of the 1987 National Science and Technology Progress Award.

谈家桢手稿

Tan Jiazhen's Manuscripts

27.0 cm × 19.0 cm

谈家桢家族捐赠 Acquired from the Tan Jiazhen Family through donation

谈家桢（1909—2008），宁波慈城人，国际著名遗传学家，中国现代遗传学奠基人之一，杰出的科学家和教育家。中华人民共和国成立后，他在复旦大学建立了中国第一个遗传学专业，创建了第一个遗传学研究所，组建了第一个生命科学学院。1980 年当选为中科院院士。1999 年，国际编号为 3542 号小行星被命名为“谈家桢星”。谈家桢心系家乡、关注教育，曾全力支持宁波大学筹建工作，并于 1985 年受聘担任宁波大学名誉校长，后多次到校考察、访问、授课。1989 年设立“谈家桢生命科学奖学金”，初衷即鼓励家乡学子报考生命科学领域各专业。

这两份谈家桢手稿分别是《现代生物学的特征、地位和作用》和《生物工程与世界新技术革命》，是谈家桢兢兢业业为中国遗传学事业奋斗过程的真实记录，具有重要的历史、科学价值。

Tan Jiazhen (1909-2008), a native of Cicheng, Ningbo, was an internationally renowned geneticist and a pioneer of modern genetics research in China. These two manuscripts written by Tan Jiazhen are titled *Characteristics, Status, and Role of Modern Biology* and *Biotechnology and the Global New Technological Revolution*. They represent authentic records of Tan Jiazhen's dedicated efforts in the field of genetics in China and hold significant historical and scientific value.

周永茂《燃料原件堆内考验》手稿

Manuscript of *In-Pile Testing of Fuel Components* by Zhou Yongmao

18.0 cm × 25.0 cm

周永茂捐赠 Acquired from Zhou Yongmao through donation

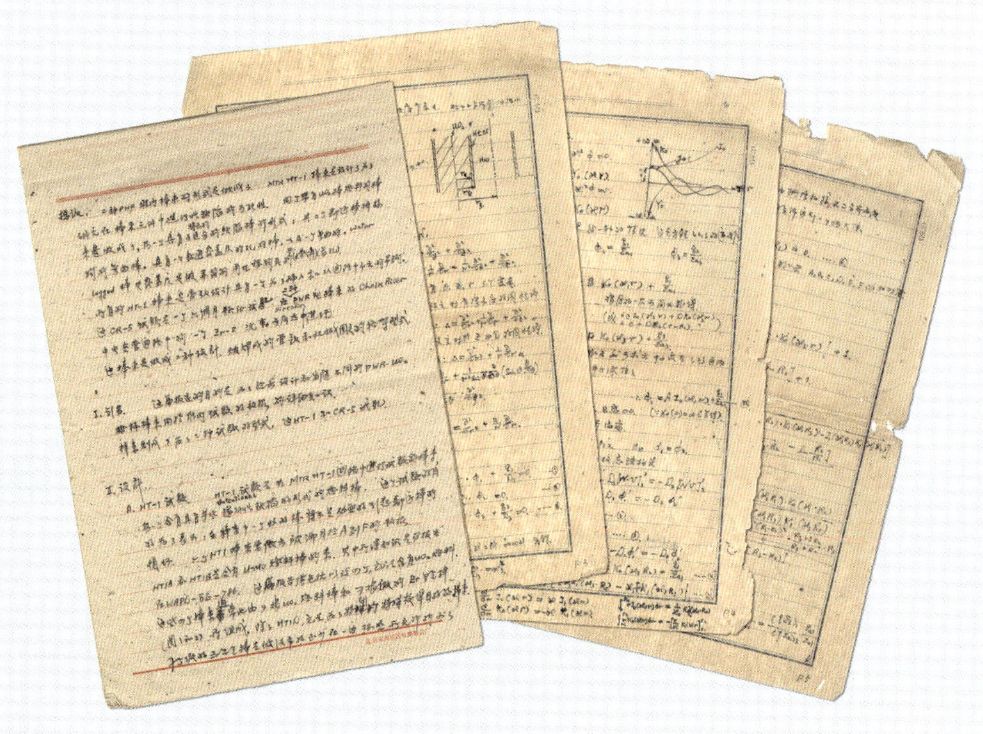

周永茂，1931 年 5 月 15 日出生于宁波镇海，核反应堆工程专家，中国工程院院士，中国中原对外工程有限公司高级工程师。

周永茂是中国核反应堆科学技术事业学科带头人、开拓者、奠基者之一。他长期在反应堆工程和科技第一线从事设计、研究和建设工作，承担并完成了国家交给的许多核科研任务：完成了“双流程堆芯”潜艇核动力堆本体的早期设计方案；主持生产堆、动力堆、游泳池堆的燃料元件与氚靶元件的首次国产工艺定型工作；参与了高通量堆设计建造和工程的重大决策，该堆的设计国外尚无先例；核工业二次创业期间，领导民用微堆的开发，该堆在国内建造 4 座、国外建造 5 座，赢得了很好的国际信誉和经济效益。先后获得国家

周永茂《原型微堆剖析与商用微堆方案思考》手稿

Zhou Yongmao's *Analysis of Prototype Microstacks and Consideration of Commercial Microstack Solutions* Manuscript

1987 年

26.0 cm × 19.0 cm

科学技术进步奖一等奖、1987 年全国科学大会奖，1995 年当选为中国工程院院士（能源与矿业工程学部），2000 年获得何梁何利基金科学与技术进步奖。

Zhou Yongmao, born on May 15, 1931, in Zhenhai, Ningbo, is a nuclear reactor engineering expert and an academician of the Chinese Academy of Engineering. Zhou is a pioneer and leading figure in the development of China's nuclear reactor science and technology, having dedicated his career to the design, research, and construction of nuclear reactors. In 1995, he was elected as an academician of the Chinese Academy of Engineering. In 2000, he was honored with the prestigious Ho Leung Ho Lee S&T Award.

杨福愉使用过的中国科学院第六次学部委员大会公文包

Briefcase Used by Yang Fuyu at the 6th Academic Committee Meeting of the Chinese Academy of Sciences

29.0 cm × 21.0 cm

杨重高捐赠 Acquired from Yang Zhonggao through donation

杨福愉（1927—2023），出生于上海，祖籍宁波镇海，生物化学专家，中国科学院院士，中国生物膜领域的主要奠基人之一。

杨福愉于 1960 年进入中国科学院生物物理研究所工作，历任研究员、副所长、生物大分子国家重点实验室学术委员会主任、名誉主任。20 世纪 60 年代起，杨福愉从事线粒体膜的结构与功能研究，做出具有特色的创新成果。20 世纪 70 年代中期以来，他致力于生物膜膜脂——膜蛋白相互作用的研究。他提出“克山病是一种心肌线粒体病”的观点，他创新地使用“匀浆互补法”，预测农作物杂种优势。杨福愉先后获得国家自然科学奖三等奖、中国科学院自然科学奖二等奖、卫生部科技进步奖等国家级奖项，1991 年当选为中国科学院学部委员（院士）。

杨福愉一生潜心科学、求实创新、奖掖后学，为生命科学领域研究和生物物理研究的发展做出了不可磨灭的杰出贡献。

Yang Fuyu (1927-2023), born in Shanghai with ancestral roots in Zhenhai, Ningbo, was a biochemist, a member of the Chinese Academy of Sciences, and one of the primary researchers in the field of biological membranes in China.

中国科学院
第六次学部委员大会

李志坚 1997 年度陈嘉庚信息科学奖奖牌

Li Zhijian's Tan Kah Kee Prize in Information Sciences (1997) Medal

32.0 cm × 25.0 cm × 1.5 cm

李志坚（1928—2011），浙江宁波人，微电子技术专家，中国科学院院士，清华大学教授、半导体教研组主任、微电子学研究所长，1991 年当选为中国科学院学部委员（院士）。

在六十年的学术生涯中，李志坚主要从事半导体和微电子科技方面的研究。20 世纪 50 年代初，在半导体薄膜光电导和光电机理研究中，提出电子晶粒间界理论，在此基础上研制成高信噪比 PbS 红外探测器。1959 年研制成高超纯多晶硅。20 世纪 60 年代从事硅器件研究，其中平面硅工艺及高反压硅高频三极管成果促进了国内有关的研究和生产。1977 年以后主要从事大规模、超大规模集成技术及器件物理的研究，领导、指导和直接参与了多种静态存储器，8 位、16 位高速微处理器、EEPROM 和 1 兆位汉字 ROM 等超大规模集成电路芯片的研制工作，并取得成功。同时开发出 3 微米和 1 微米成套工艺技术；指导并发明半导体红外高速退火

李志坚《纳电子学》手稿

Li Zhijian's *Nanoelectronics* Manuscript

29.5 cm × 21.0 cm

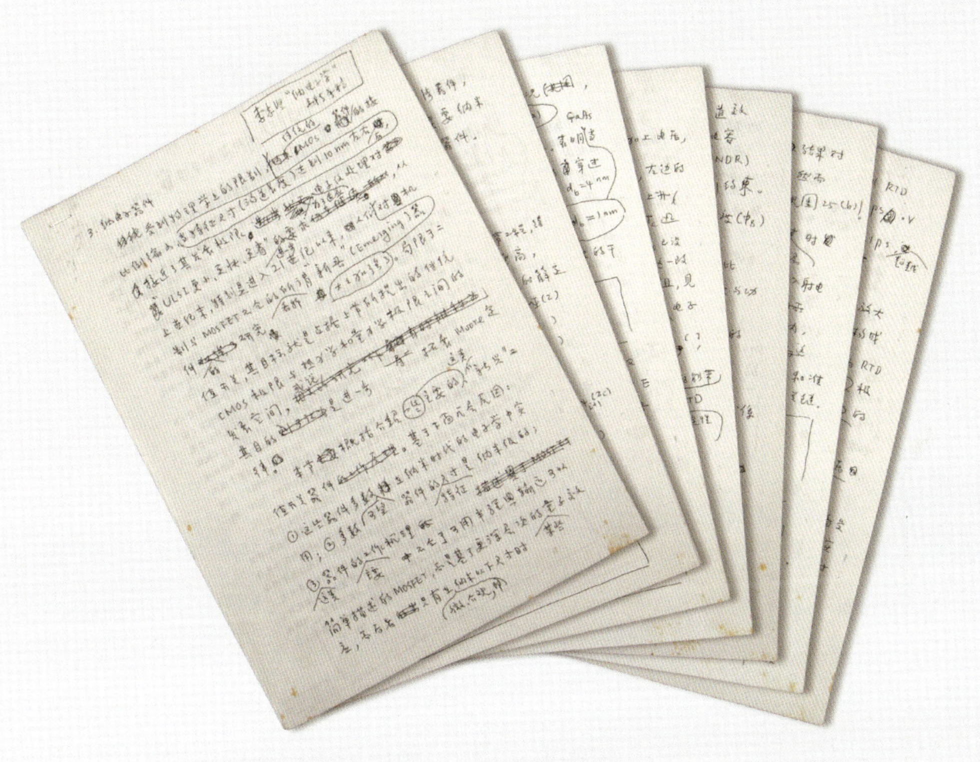

技术和设备。

作为中国硅基半导体科学研究的奠基人和开创者、中国MEMS和SOC技术研究的先驱者，李志坚先后获国家科技进步一等奖，中国专利金奖、陈嘉庚信息科学奖、何梁何利基金科学与技术进步奖等。

Li Zhijian (1928-2011), a native of Ningbo, was a professor at Tsinghua University and an expert in microelectronics technology and a member of the Chinese Academy of Sciences.

Throughout his six-decade academic career, Li focused primarily on research in the fields of semiconductors and microelectronics technology. He is recognized as a pioneer and founding figure in China's silicon-based semiconductor research and a trailblazer in the study of Micro-Electro-Mechanical Systems (MEMS) and System on a Chip (SOC) technologies. Li received several prestigious awards, including the National Science and Technology Progress First Prize and the Tan Kah Kee Prize in Information Sciences.

中国老教授协会授予翁史烈的老教授科教兴国贡献奖奖牌

Contribution to Science and Education Award Received by Weng Shilie from the China Senior Professors Association

2000 年 9 月 7 日

28.0 cm × 20.0 cm × 1.5 cm

翁史烈，1932 年 5 月 21 日出生于浙江宁波，热力机械专家，中国工程院院士，上海交通大学机械与动力工程学院教授、博士生导师。

作为科学家，翁史烈致力于热力发动机研究，是我国新一代热力涡轮机的开拓者之一。他主持承担了我国航空涡轮风扇发动机的多用途改型研制；开拓我国新一代热力发动机，提高其现代化水平；研制成我国第一台陶瓷绝热涡轮复合柴油机原理样机；完成了我国第一批增压器陶瓷涡轮转子的设计和试验台建设；率先将信息科学和计算机技术引入传统的动力机械领域。1995 年，翁史烈当选为中国工程院院士。

作为教育家，他确定了上海交通大学多学科、综合性发展的战略格局，牵头组建了中国首批热力涡轮机博士点和重点学科，建设气动力学实验室、仿真实验室、博士后流动站，培养了一支高水平的热力涡轮机学科梯队。

2000 年 9 月，中国老教授协会和中国老教授事业基金管理委员会在北京举行中国老教授协会建会 15 周年庆祝会，翁史烈等 10 位同志获“老教授科教兴国贡献奖”，以表彰他们在实施科教兴国战略中做出的显著成绩，并弘扬老教授、老专家的无私奉献精神。

Weng Shilie, born on May 21, 1932, in Ningbo, was an expert in thermal mechanics. He was a member of the Chinese Academy of Engineering and a professor at the School of Mechanical Engineering at Shanghai Jiao Tong University. In September 2000, the China Senior Professors Association held its 15th-anniversary celebration in Beijing, during which Weng and 9 other colleagues received the “Contribution to Science and Education Award”.

刘元方国家自然科学基金委员会化学科学部第一届专家咨询委员会委员聘书

Liu Yuanfang's Appointment Letter as a Member of the First Expert Advisory Committee of the Chemistry Department of the National Natural Science Foundation of China

2002 年

16.5 cm × 21.0 cm × 1.5 cm

刘元方同志：

您被聘请为国家自然科学基金委员会化学科学部第一届专家咨询委员会委员

国家自然科学基金委员会

二〇〇二年三月

中国科学院学部主席团致刘元方的感谢书

Letter of Appreciation from the Presidium of the Chinese Academy of Sciences to Liu Yuanfang

2004 年 6 月

15.0 cm × 10.5 cm × 4.0 cm

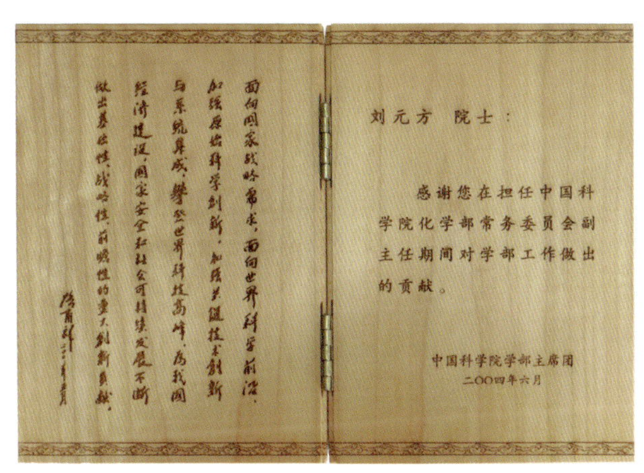
面向国家战略需求，面向世界科学前沿，加强原始科学创新，加强关键技术创新与系统集成，攀登世界科技高峰，为我国经济建设、国家安全和社会可持续发展不断做出基础性、战略性、前瞻性的重大创新贡献。

路甬祥

刘元方 院士：

感谢您在担任中国科学院化学部常务委员会副主任期间对学部工作做出的贡献。

中国科学院学部主席团

二〇〇四年六月

刘元方，生于 1931 年 2 月，宁波镇海人，核化学与放射化学专家、中国科学院院士、北京大学化学与分子工程学院教授。

刘元方主要从事核化学与放射化学领域的研究工作，做出了许多开拓性和创造性的贡献。他创立和建设了我国第一个放射化学专业。1960 年，他领导建成了我国第一台 5 万转 / 分的浓集 ^{235}U 的雏型气体离心机；1980 年，利用超铀元素重离子核反应首次直接制得 ^{251}Bk，解决了从几十种元素中快速分离纯 Bk 的难题，重制了 ^{251}Bk 的衰变纲图等；1994 年以来，在生物 – 加速器质谱学研究尼古丁的基因毒性中做出了突出成果；2001 年以来，积极从事纳米材料的生物效应研究。

1986 年，刘元方负责的“从金川矿中提取铑和铱的新方法”获国家教委科技进步一等奖。1991 年，当选为中国科学院化学部院士。

Liu Yuanfang, born in February 1931 in Zhenhai, Ningbo, is a nuclear and radiochemical scientist, a member of the Chinese Academy of Sciences, and a professor at the College of Chemistry and Molecular Engineering at Peking University. In 1986, Liu Yuanfang was responsible for the development of a “New Method for Extracting Rhodium and Iridium from Jinchuan Group's Ore”, which received the National Education Commission's First Prize for Scientific and Technological Progress. In 1991, he was elected as an academician of the Chinese Academy of Sciences in the Division of Chemistry.

贝时璋星运行轨道图铜牌

Plaque Showing the Orbit of Asteroid 31065 Bei Shizhang

38.0 cm × 27.0 cm

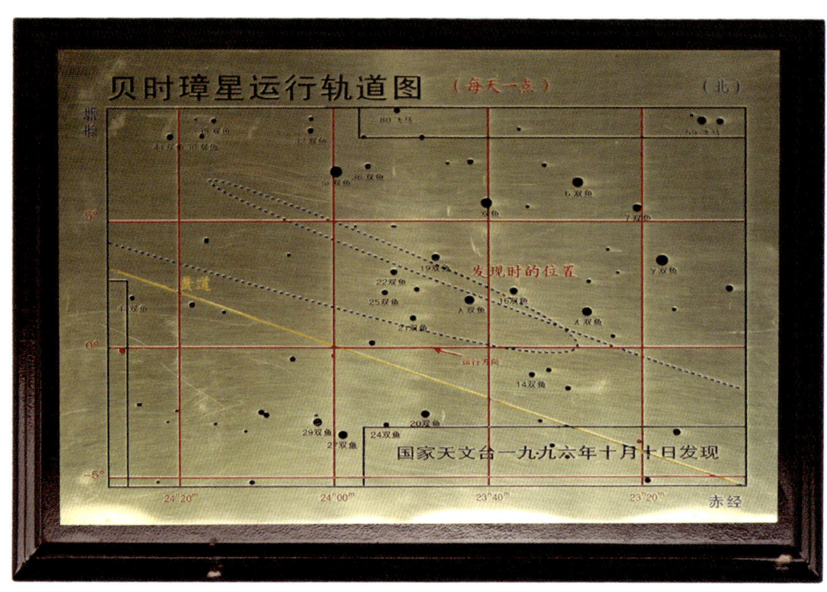

贝时璋（1903—2009），宁波镇海人，生物学家。1948 年当选为中央研究院院士，1955 年被选聘为中国科学院学部委员（院士），中国生物物理学的奠基人。

贝时璋一直从事实验生物学研究工作，主要研究包括动物个体发育、细胞常数、再生、中间生、性转变、染色体结构、细胞重建、昆虫内分泌腺、甲壳类动物眼柄激素等方面，其中尤以关于细胞重建的研究最为突出。20 世纪 30 年代初期，在丰年虫中间性的性转变过程中观察到细胞重建现象。1970 年代，先后在丰年虫、鸡胚早期发育、小鼠造血系统（骨髓）、根瘤菌和沙眼衣原体等方面进行了细胞重建的研究，首次发现细胞的繁殖增生除细胞分裂外，还存在着另外一条途径——细胞重建，创立了“细胞重建学说”。

贝时璋是中国生物物理学的拓荒者，以“学科交叉”理念创建了浙江大学生物系、中国科学院生物物理研究所和中国科学技术大学生物物理系，为中国生物物理学的发展培养了大批人才。他组织开展了“核试验放射性本底自然监测”“核爆试验对动物本身及其远后期辐射效应监测”“生物探空火箭”等研究工作，为中国生命科学和“载人航天”事业做出了杰出贡献。

2003 年，国际小行星中心和国际小行星命名委员会根据中国国家天文台的申报，正式批准将该台于 1996 年 10 月 10 日发现的国际永久编号第 36015 的小行星命名为“贝时璋星”，以表彰贝时璋在科学研究上所取得的突出成就。

Bei Shizhang (1903-2009), a native of Zhenhai, Ningbo, was a renowned biologist. In 2003, the International Astronomical Union’s Minor Planet Center officially named asteroid number 36015 “Beishizhang” in recognition of his outstanding achievements in scientific research.

柴之芳获得的 George von Hevesy 奖牌

George von Hevesy Medal Awarded to Chai Zhifang

2005 年
直径 11.5 cm × 1.0 cm
柴之芳捐赠 Acquired from Chai Zhifang through donation

柴之芳，1942 年 9 月生于上海，祖籍宁波，放射化学专家、中国科学院院士。1964 年毕业于复旦大学原子能系，同年加入中国原子能研究所，1972 年转入中科院高能物理研究所。柴之芳院士长期致力于核技术和核分析方法学的研究，2005 年获得国际放射化学最高奖 George von Hevesy 奖，是发展中国家首位获奖人，2019 年获中国科学院杰出科技成就奖。身为宁波人，柴之芳院士桑梓情深，始终心系家乡发展，于 2018 年 10 月 10 日加入中科院宁波材料所。

2022 年 9 月 20 日上午，“不老集——柴之芳院士个人书法展”开幕式在宁波帮博物馆举行。在开幕式上，柴之芳院士将该奖牌捐赠予宁波帮博物馆。

Chai Zhifang, born in September 1942 in Shanghai to a family from Ningbo, is a renowned radiochemist and a member of the Chinese Academy of Sciences. Chai dedicated his career to advancing nuclear technology and nuclear analytical methodologies. In 2005, he received the prestigious George von Hevesy Award, the highest honor in the field of radiochemistry, becoming the first recipient from a developing country.

沈自尹《补肾法调节肾 PQ 虚证 T 细胞凋亡的规律——重塑基因平衡》手稿

Manuscript of *Regulating the Balance of Kidney PQ Deficiency and T-cell Apoptosis: Reshaping Genetic Equilibrium* by Shen Ziyin

29.0 cm × 21.0 cm

沈自尹（1928—2019），浙江宁波人，中西医结合学专家，中国科学院院士，复旦大学附属华山医院教授。

沈自尹主要从事中西医结合思路和方法的开拓、肾本质的研究和传统老年医学研究。20 世纪 50 年代，他率先对被中医称为“命门之火”的肾阳进行研究。20 世纪 70 年代初，根据大量的临床实例和科学实验，沈自尹首先提出中西医结合的途径是“辨病与辨证相结合”，从而改变了中西医药简单相加的局面，之后又提出“微观辨证和辨证微观化”，对中医辨证向科学化、客观化发展起到积极推动作用。1979 年起采用同病异证组进行下丘脑—垂体—靶腺轴功能对比观察，可推论肾阳虚主要发病环节在下丘脑，这一成就的意义是首次用现代科学方法在国际上证实肾阳虚症有特定的物质基础。沈自尹先后获得卫生部全国医药卫生科学大会重大科技成果奖、卫生部乙级重大科技成果奖等 21 项国家级和上海市重大科技成果奖，2017 年获评全国中医药杰出贡献奖。

沈自尹是中西医结合学科的开拓者之一，中西医结合思路和方法、脏象学说和病证关系研究的开创者之一，为推动中医、中西医结合工作的发展做出了重大贡献。

Shen Ziyin (1928-2019), a native of Ningbo, was a scholar in the field of integrative traditional Chinese and Western medicine. He was a member of the Chinese Academy of Sciences and a professor at Huashan Hospital, Fudan University. Shen was a pioneer in the discipline of integrative medicine, contributing significantly to the development of integrative approaches that combine traditional Chinese and Western medicine, as well as the study of organ patterns and the relationships between disease and symptoms.

补肾法调节肾阳虚证T细胞凋亡的规律——重塑基因平衡

复旦大学华山医院中西医结合研究所

沈自尹

在"肾"本质的研究中，最初得到肾阳虚证具有下丘脑—垂体—肾上腺皮质轴功能紊乱的结论[1]。中医认为"肾"为先天之本，主生长、发育、衰老的过程，肾虚辨证标准如腰脊酸痛、腿软、耳鸣耳聋、齿落发脱、性功能减退等都是老年人生理机能衰退的表现，肾虚与衰老显然具有共同的外部证候，因此在观察肾阳虚证的甲状腺与性腺(男)轴的功能时，always增加了相应的老年人组[2]，结果显示老年人组的甲状腺与性腺(男)轴功能的异常值与成年人的肾阳虚组甚为类似，说明肾虚证是未老先衰，而衰老亦就是生理性肾虚证。

Basedovsky 1977年以大量实验依据提出著名的神经内分泌免疫(NEI)网络学说，他认为各司其职的神经、内分泌、免疫3个系统构成了一个完整的网络系统（为了便于实验取材，我们用外源性皮……）

1

99.3-400格 500本

……下调促凋亡基因FasL、TNFR1的表达，而且下调促凋亡基因Bcl-2的表达。

……组明显降低，上调抗凋亡基因Bcl-2的表达，无论反映肾阳虚的……，老年人，都表现……

归纳以上三项实验所见，老年大鼠、老年人，都表现……证的皮质酮大鼠或老年大鼠的凋亡级联反应，并有上调的凋亡基因低表达……有T细胞过度凋亡；抗凋亡基因高表达；上调抗……，而且促凋亡基因可以下调促凋亡基因；上调抗……。温补肾阳复方可以下调凋亡级联反应。而对照的健脾、活血复方均无此作用。显示温补肾阳复方……凋亡基因，同时下调凋亡级联反应。显示温补肾阳复方对于促、抗凋亡基因……健脾、活血复方均无此作用……是通过对于促、抗凋亡基因……方调节T细胞凋亡是通过重塑基因平衡。

……之间的协同与整合，重塑基因可遗传的主要贮存单元。

基因是生物体内信息可遗传的基本单元，只有细胞才具有全能性，但绝不是全能的基本单元，因为基因不能单独发生作用，基因的活动是涉及基因组中一群基因形成大、小网络协同活动，程序化表达，从而使细胞能处于稳态，使生命有条不紊地进行。基因群在体内存在着互相对立又互相依赖的对子，可相互制约又可相互转化，好比中医的阴阳五行中所讲的对立统一、相生相克的状况。在运用脏象学……

5

99.3-400格 500本

华山医院

“天宫一号”“神舟九号”首次载人交会对接模型

Model Commemorating the First Crewed Docking Between Tiangong 1 and Shenzhou 9

47.0 cm × 46.0 cm × 21.0 cm

庄祥昌捐赠 Acquired from Zhuang Xiangchang through donation

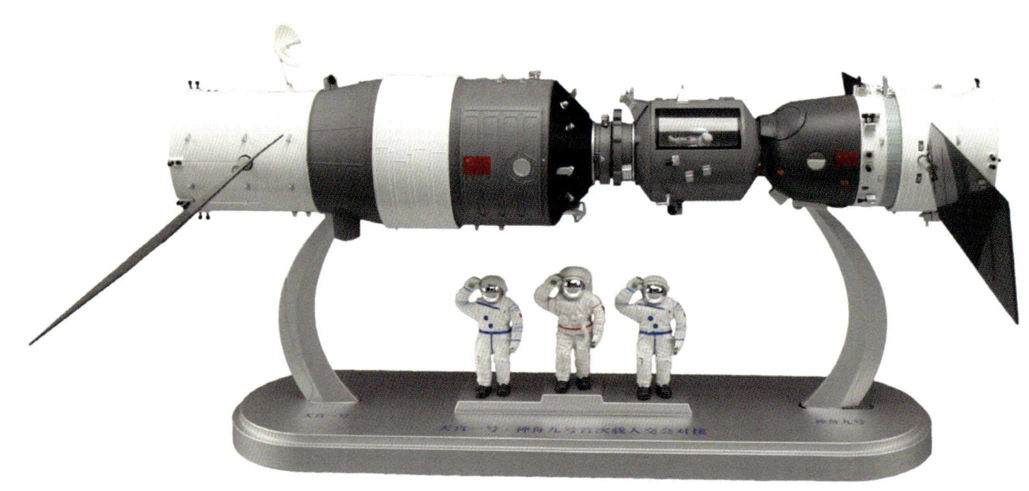

“天宫一号”是中国第一个目标飞行器和空间实验室，于 2011 年 9 月 29 日 21 时 16 分 3 秒在酒泉卫星发射中心发射，飞行器全长 10.4 米，最大直径 3.35 米，由实验舱和资源舱构成。2012 年 6 月 16 日，“神舟九号”载着景海鹏、刘旺、刘洋三名航天员发射升空，进入预定轨道。6 月 18 日，“神舟九号”与“天宫一号”对接成功，建立刚性连接，形成组合体。“天宫一号”与“神舟九号”载人交会对接任务的圆满成功，是我国空间交会对接技术的又一重大突破，标志着我国载人航天工程第二步战略目标取得了具有决定性意义的重要进展，为今后的载人航天的发展、空间站的建设奠定了良好的基础。

庄祥昌，祖籍宁波，国际宇航科学院院士，从事航空生理和航天医学的研究，涉及失重、超重、救生等领域，为中国第一代该领域专家。国际宇航科学院是非政府性的国际学术组织，由世界著名科学家冯 · 卡门倡导，于 1960 年 8 月 16 日成立于瑞典斯德哥尔摩。宇航科学院院士由在航天学的某个领域或对空间探索至关重要的某个科学分支中做出卓著贡献的个人组成。

Tiangong 1, China's inaugural space laboratory, was launched from the Jiuquan Satellite Launch Center on September 29, 2011, at 21:16:03. On June 18, it achieved a successful rendezvous and docking with the Shenzhou 9 spacecraft, marking a crucial advancement in China's space technology. This accomplishment was a pivotal step towards China's second phase of manned spaceflight, setting a strong foundation for future crewed missions and space station construction.

“神舟十号”与“天宫一号”载人飞行任务纪念模型

Shenzhou 10 and Tiangong 1 Manned Spaceflight Mission Commemorative Model

47.0 cm × 46.0 cm × 21.0 cm

包为民捐赠 Acquired from Bao Weimin through donation

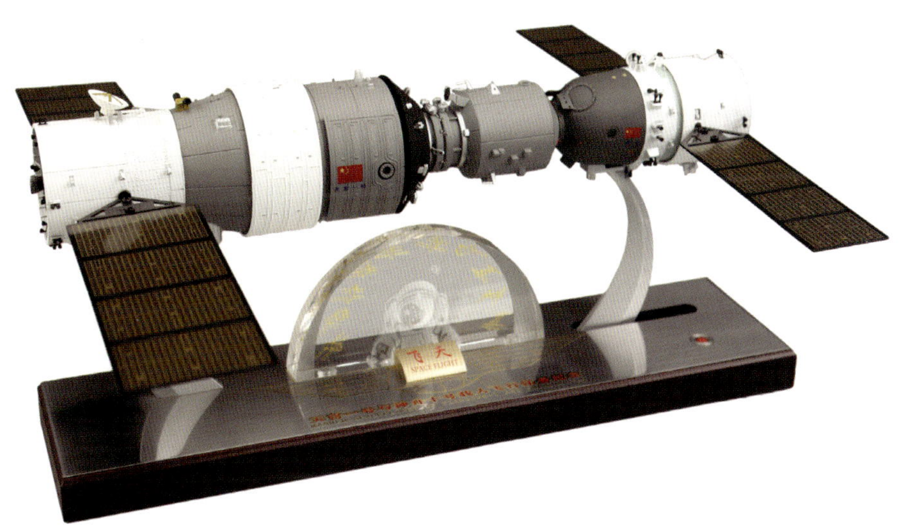

2013 年 6 月 13 日 13 时 18 分，“神舟十号”与“天宫一号”在太空中实现自动交会对接，并完成了载人天地往返运输系统的首次应用性飞行等任务，这标志着中国载人航天第二步任务第一阶段完美收工，将全面进入空间实验室和空间站研制阶段。

2016 年 6 月，宁波籍院士包为民先生回到家乡，并向宁波帮博物馆捐赠“神舟十号”与“天宫一号”载人飞行任务纪念模型。

包为民，祖籍宁波镇海，著名制导与控制专家，2005 年当选为中国科学院院士，现任西安电子科技大学空间科学与技术学院院长、中国航天科技集团公司科技委主任，是中国航天运载器及控制系统领域的学术带头人，为“神舟十号”与“天宫一号”在太空中完成自动交会对接做出了重要贡献。

On June 13, 2013, at 13:18, the Shenzhou 10 spacecraft achieved an automated rendezvous and docking with the Tiangong 1 space module in space. This achievement paved the way for further development in Chinese space laboratories and space stations.

In June 2016, Bao Weimin, an academician originally from Zhenhai, Ningbo, generously donated commemorative models of the Shenzhou 10 and Tiangong 1 missions to Ningbobang Museum. Bao, who is currently serving as the Dean of the School of Aerospace and Technology at Xidian University and the Director of the Science and Technology Committee of China Aerospace Science and Technology Corporation, is a leading figure in China's aerospace carrier and control systems field. His contributions were pivotal in the successful automated rendezvous and docking of Shenzhou 10 and Tiangong 1 in space.

葆初赠李梅塘字幅卷轴

Scroll Gifted by Baochu to Li Meitang

清代

236.6 cm × 58.6 cm

张健飞捐赠 Acquired from Zhang Jianfei through donation

卷轴正文为："吕正献公自少讲学，即以治心养性为本。寡嗜欲，薄滋味，无疾言遽色，无窘步，无惰容。凡嬉笑俚近之语，未尝出诸口。于世利纷华，声伎游宴，以至于博弈奇然玩，淡然无所好。"落款"梅塘二兄世大人雅正""辛卯中秋效先弟葆初"。钤印"葆初禧印""字效先，号冬心"二枚。

卷轴书者阿鲁特·葆初（？—1900），字效先，号冬心，满洲镶黄旗人，为清朝唯一的满族状元崇绮之子。早年善于书画，有《绘境轩读画记》留世。受赠者为小港李家坤房李梅塘（1841—1900）。民国《镇海县志》记载："李容子嘉，字梅塘，袭先人遗业，操奇制胜，家资至数百万。……卒赠荣禄大夫。"

该卷轴由鄞县学者、原上海光华大学校长、《四明丛书》编纂者张寿镛先生的曾孙张健飞捐赠。张健飞的祖母李佩芬是梅塘公的孙女。张健飞先生长年旅居美国，在得悉宁波帮博物馆有小港李家及张寿镛的相关收藏、展示之后，在甬参加"张寿镛与《四明丛书》"纪念座谈会期间，亲赴宁波帮博物馆捐献该卷轴。

The text of this scroll reads, "Lord Lu Zhengxian, from a young age, devoted himself to the pursuit of knowledge and based his principles on self-cultivation. He had few indulgences, modest tastes, and never engaged in frivolous or trivial conversations. He remained composed and never displayed arrogance. He did not participate in worldly pleasures, entertainment, or even in games, maintaining a serene detachment."

It is signed with "For the perusal of the respected Mei Tang, the second elder brother" and "By your humble brother Baochu, courtesy name Xiao Xian, during Mid-Autumn of Xinmao year."

Seals on the scroll include "Baochu's Auspicious Seal" and "Courtesy name Xiao Xian, artist name Dongxin". The scroll was transcribed by Arute Baochu (d. 1900), courtesy name Xiaoxian, artist name Dongxin. He was a Manchu from the Xianghuang Banner and the son of Chongqi, who was the only Manchu to achieve the top scholar position during the Qing Dynasty.

The scroll was donated by Zhang Jianfei, the great-grandson of Zhang Shouyong, a scholar from Yin County, Ningbo and president of the former Kwang Hua University in Shanghai.

呂正獻公自少講學即以治心養性為本寡嗜慾薄滋
味無疾言遽色無窘步無惰容凡嬉笑俚近之語未嘗
出諸口於世利紛華聲伎遊宴以至於博奕奇[illegible]玩淡
然無所好

梅塘二兄世大人雅正 辛卯中秋 敦先弟葆初

高振霄墨梅画卷

Ink Plum Painting and Calligraphy Scroll by Gao Zhenxiao

1932 年

219.0 cm × 43.2 cm

佐藤房雄捐赠 Acquired from Sato Fuyo through donation

高振霄(1877—1956),字云麓,别署闲云,又号顽头陀,著名书法家。宁波鄞县人,清末进士,官至翰林院编修。民国后寓居上海,以书自给,间画墨梅,每日读书临碑,至老不辍。其子高式熊,著名书法家、金石篆刻家、印泥制作大师,中国书协会员、西泠印社副秘书长、上海市书协顾问、上海市文史研究馆馆员。高振霄、高式熊父子并称"双美"。

1932 年,高振霄开始画梅,署名老顽、顽头陀,作画必自题一绝,久之,汇成《梅花诗五百首》。诗稿手写本 10 本,名其居室曰"云在堂"。

该画卷梅花清冷,风骨凛然,体现了绘者的高风亮节。画上题诗一首:"瘦影临风总不如,独持衰朽厌琼琚。凭谁写出清冷意,履笠青衫策短驰",款识"壬申夏日老顽",钤印"顽头陀"一枚。此外有闲章"烈晴霜""洞天真逸""绛霄云在"三枚。

此画卷由日本友人佐藤房雄于 2009 年 10 月 22 日捐赠。佐藤房雄为日本佐藤株式会社原社长,乃高振霄之子高式熊文友,听闻兴建宁波帮博物馆,专程从日本远赴宁波将收藏多年的画卷捐予馆方。

Gao Zhenxiao (1877-1956) was a renowned calligrapher from Yin County, Ningbo. He resided in Shanghai after the establishment of the Republican era and became a professor there, dedicating himself to teaching and maintaining his calligraphic practice. He persisted in his artistic pursuits until old age. In his later years, Gao created a daily ink plum blossom painting, along with a poem. In total, he produced over five hundred of these artworks. Gao's paintings are characterized by their elegant portrayal of plum blossoms. His poems on this scroll read:

In the wind, my slender shadow stands,
Yet it can't compare to nature's hands.
I hold decay, weary of gems and gold,
Who can write the frosty, quiet story untold?

With straw sandals, a green hat on my head,
I walk short steps where paths have led.

The scroll is signed "An old eccentric in the summer of Renshen year" and bears the seal "Rebel Monk". There are also three artistic seals "Bright and Sunny Frost", "Heavenly Cave True Tranquility", and "Vermilion Sky Clouds".

This scroll was donated by Sato Fuyo on October 22, 2009. Fuyo was the former president of Sato Corporation in Japan and a close friend of Gao Zhenxiao's son, Gao Shixiong. Upon hearing about the construction of Ningbobang Museum, he traveled from Japan to Ningbo to donate the scroll.

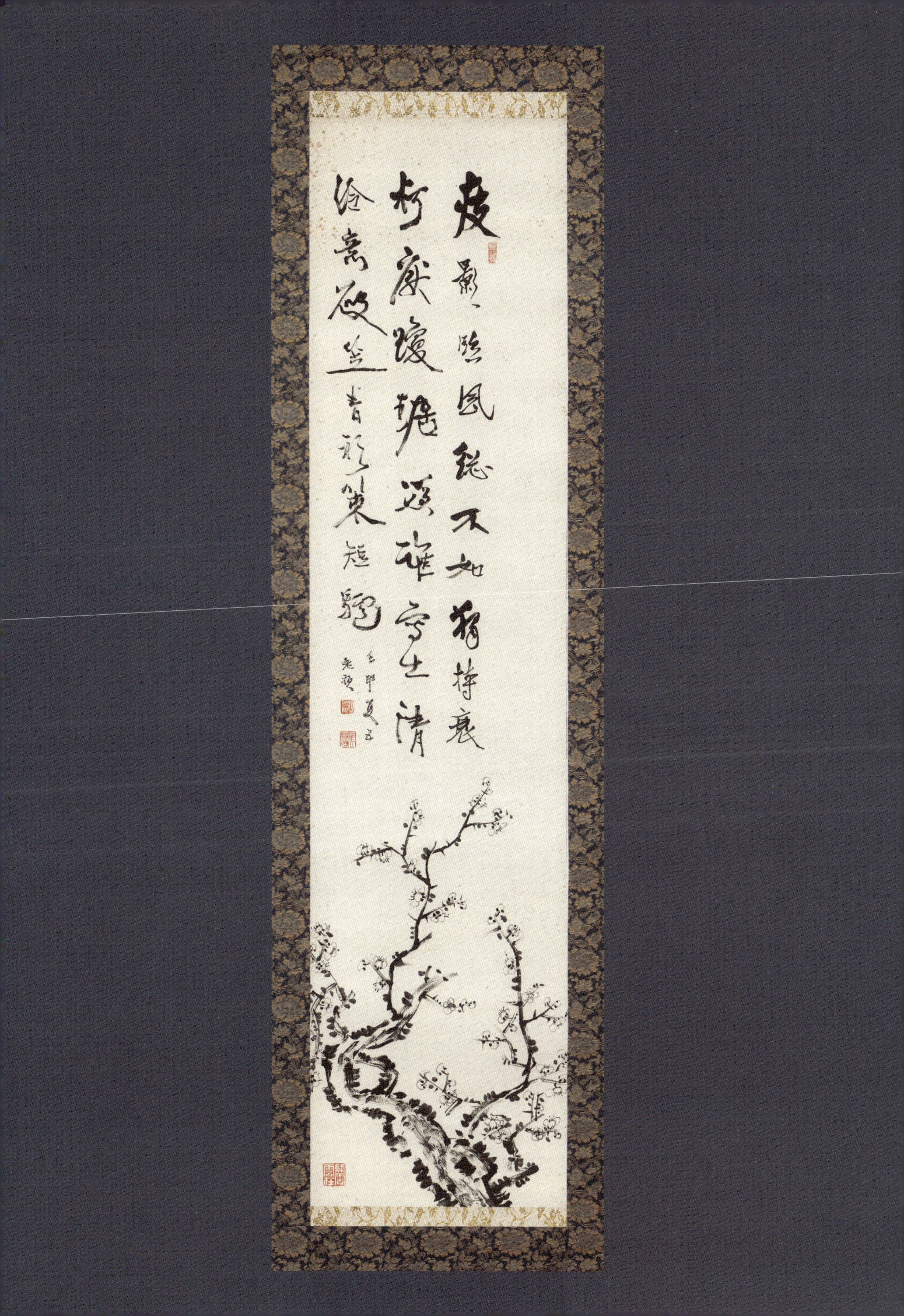

高式熊使用过的文房用具

Stationery Used by Gao Shixiong

①直径 13.0 cm × 5.0 cm ②5.0 cm × 5.0 cm × 2.5 cm ③15.5 cm × 11.0 cm × 1.5 cm ④直径 0.8 cm × 23.5 cm ⑤直径 1.5 cm × 15.0 cm ⑥直径 1.5 cm × 13.0 cm ⑦8.0 cm × 4.5 cm × 7.5 cm

高定珠捐赠 Acquired from Gao Dingzhu through donation

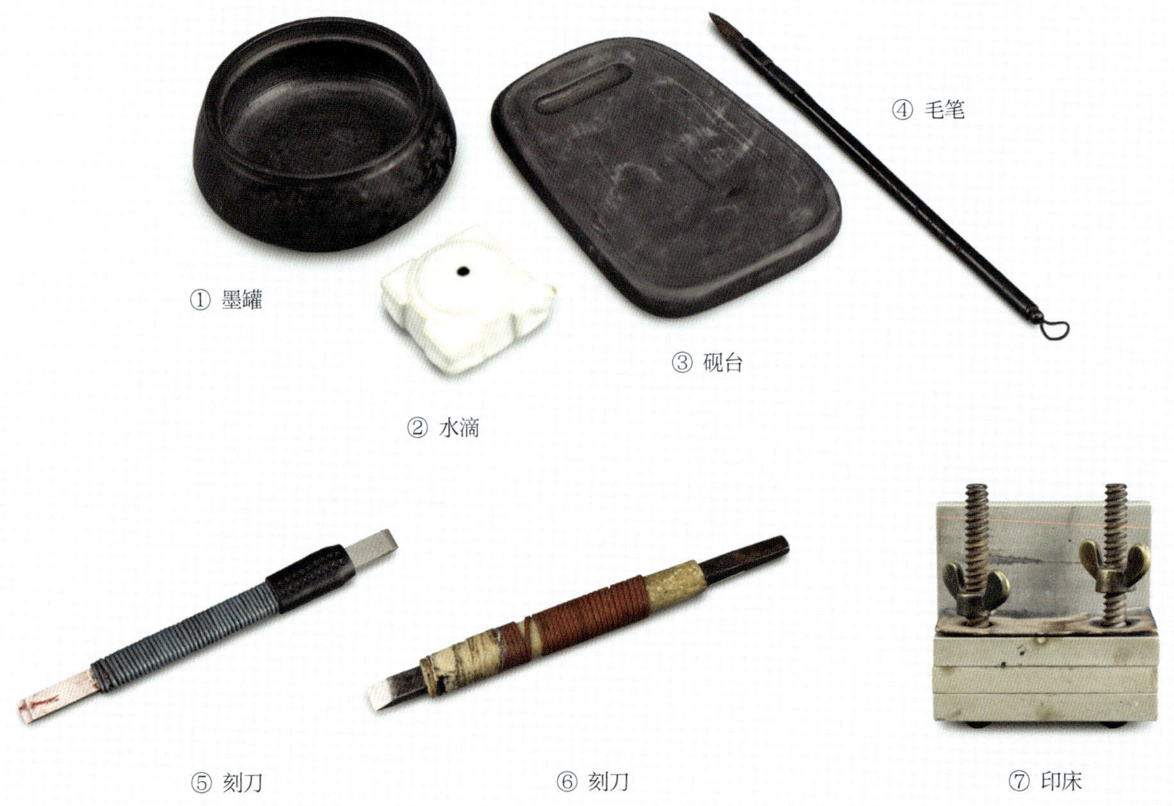

① 墨罐 ② 水滴 ③ 砚台 ④ 毛笔 ⑤ 刻刀 ⑥ 刻刀 ⑦ 印床

高式熊（1921—2019），名廷肃，字式熊，号采苓、羽弓，著名书法家和篆刻家。高振霄之仲子。高式熊书法得父亲高振霄亲授，16 岁开始自学篆刻，1947 年加入西泠印社，得名家赵叔儒、王福庵、张鲁庵等前辈指点，在书法、篆刻以及印学研究上成就斐然。

这批文房用具包括墨罐、水滴、砚台、毛笔、篆刻用具等。这些用具非常俭朴，陪伴高老度过晚年时光，展现了他对于传统文化孜孜以求的执着品质和为艺术事业奋斗一生

高式熊“四明一个古稀翁”篆章和“学老学庵”篆章

Seal with the Inscription “SimingYige Guxi Weng” (A 70-Year-Old Man of Siming) and Seal with the Inscription “Xue Lao Xue Yan” (Following Lu You’s Footsteps) Carved by Gao Shixiong

1947 年

①3.0 cm × 3.0 cm × 8.2 cm ②3.0 cm × 3.0 cm × 8.2 cm

高定珠捐赠 Acquired from Gao Dingzhu through donation

① “四明一个古稀翁”篆章

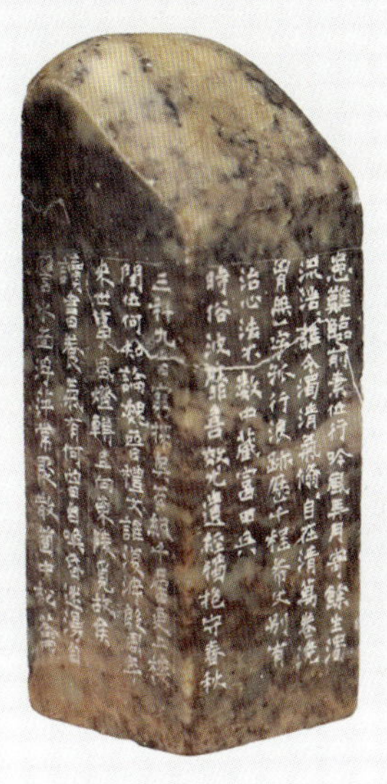

② “学老学庵”篆章

的工匠精神。

两枚篆章是高式熊初学篆刻时为父亲七十寿辰所做，边款为高振霄诗作。

Gao Shixiong (1921-2019) was a renowned calligrapher and seal engraver. This set of stationery includes an inkpot, a water basin, an inkstone, a brush, and several seal engraving tools. These simple items accompanied Gao in his later years, reflecting his unwavering dedication to traditional culture and the artisan spirit of a lifetime devoted to the art. Two of the seals were created by Gao when he first learned seal engraving, celebrating his father’s seventieth birthday, with inscriptions by Gao Zhenxiao.

葛祖兰《蟹工船》翻译手稿

Manuscript of *The Crab Cannery Ship* Translated by Ge Zulan

1955 年

20.5 cm × 16.4 cm

葛文洪捐赠 Acquired from Ge Wenhong through donation

葛祖兰（1887—1987），宁波籍翻译家、作家、著名俳句诗人，宁波庄桥人。1904 年考中秀才，翌年东渡日本留学，1909 年毕业于早稻田大学师范研究科，历任两广优级师范学校、两广高等工业学校教授，上海市澄衷中学、新陆师范校长，商务印书馆编辑等职。其以研究创作俳句闻名中日学界，著译颇丰，有《日本俳谐史》《俳句因学记》《祖兰俳存》与《祖兰俳存补遗》等。曾获日本《杜鹃》诗刊“杜鹃诗人”和最高荣誉“同人”称号及《九年田》诗刊的“九年田推荐作家”荣誉称号。译著有《第二次接吻》《蟹工船》等，编译有《自修适用日语汉译读本》《日本现代语辞典》《日本姓名辞典》等。

《蟹工船》是日本作家小林多喜二的代表作，发表于 1929 年，也是日本现代文学史上无产阶级文学的启蒙之作。葛祖兰于 1955 年开始对其进行翻译并修正多稿。

Ge Zulan (1887-1987) was a distinguished translator, writer, and a notable *haiku* poet from Zhuangqiao, Ningbo. In 1905, he set off to Japan for further studies, completing his studies at Waseda University in 1909. One of his most significant endeavors was his translation to Chinese of *Kani Kōsen* ("The Crab Cannery Ship"), a 1929 novel by Japanese author Kobayashi Takiji.

蟹工船译稿

葛祖蘭

李秋君钱塘江图轴

Qiantang River Painting Scroll by Li Qiujun

1959 年
113.0 cm × 60.0 cm
李玫捐赠 Acquired from Li Mei through donation

该作品为李秋君作于 1959 年，释文“钱塘江为浙江主流，江上竹木筏日夜顺流而下，源源不尽，支援各地加速社会主义建设”，款识“一九五九年浙人李秋君”。钤印“李秋之印”“秋君”。

李秋君(1899—1973)，名祖云，字秋君，斋名欧湘馆，宁波小港李家李薇庄之女。李秋君于 1912 年在上海务本女中毕业，初从长兄祖韩习书作画，后师从女画家吴淑娟。她以山水、仕女画见长，著有《秋君书稿》《欧湘馆诗稿》若干卷，一生与丹青结缘。1934 年，发起组织中国女子书画会，1938 年，创办上海灾童教养所。李秋君不但是一位画家，还是一位社会活动家、爱国民主人士，曾与兄祖韩等人筹备济难书画展，力助何香凝，还曾捐款慰劳八路军。上海解放后，历任上海市人民代表，担任中华人民共和国成立后初建的“民主妇联”(妇联前身)首届执委。

This artwork was created by Li Qiujun in 1959. The accompanying inscription reads: “Qiantang River, the lifeline of Zhejiang, where bamboo and timber rafts glide day and night, a ceaseless flow supporting regions far and wide, hastening the progress of socialist construction.” It is signed by “Li Qiujun of Zhejiang, 1959.” The seals on the artwork bear the name of the artist.

Li Qiujun (1899-1973) was a painter and the daughter of Li Weizhuang from the Li family in Xiaogang, Ningbo.

錢塘江為浙江主流江上
竹木筏日夜順流而下
源:不盡支援各地加速
社會主義建設
一九五九年浙人李秋君

草婴《克鲁采奏鸣曲》翻译手稿

Manuscript of The *Kreutzer Sonata* Translated by Cao Ying

36.0 cm × 26.0 cm

草婴家人捐赠 Acquired from Cao Ying's family through donation

草婴(1923—2015),原名盛峻峰,祖籍宁波镇海骆驼桥,是卓越的文学翻译家,曾获"高尔基文学奖""翻译文化终身成就奖"等。草婴几十年如一日笔耕不辍,一生全部奉献给了文学翻译事业,他饱含心血的鸿篇译著和精益求精的工作态度都是留给世人的无尽馈赠。

这份手稿的翻译内容是列夫·托尔斯泰《克鲁采奏鸣曲》中《年轻沙皇的梦》章节。从1977年到1997年,草婴完成了《托尔斯泰小说全集》12卷的翻译工作,包括《战争与和平》《安娜·卡列尼娜》《复活》3部长篇小说,60多篇中短篇小说等,总计400万字,成为目前世界上唯一一个以一己之力将托尔斯泰所有小说从俄文直接翻译成另外一种语言的人。

Cao Ying (1923-2015), born Sheng Junfeng, was an outstanding Russian literature translator from Luotuoqiao in Zhenhai, Ningbo. He holds the unique distinction of being the only person in the world to single-handedly translate all of Tolstoy's novels from Russian into another language.

The translation in this manuscript pertains to a section from Leo Tolstoy's *Kreutzer Sonata*, specifically the chapter titled *The Young Tsar*.

王范地手稿

Wang Fandi's Manuscripts

20 世纪 80 年代

28.0 cm × 21.0 cm

张先玲捐赠 Acquired from Zhang Xianling through donation

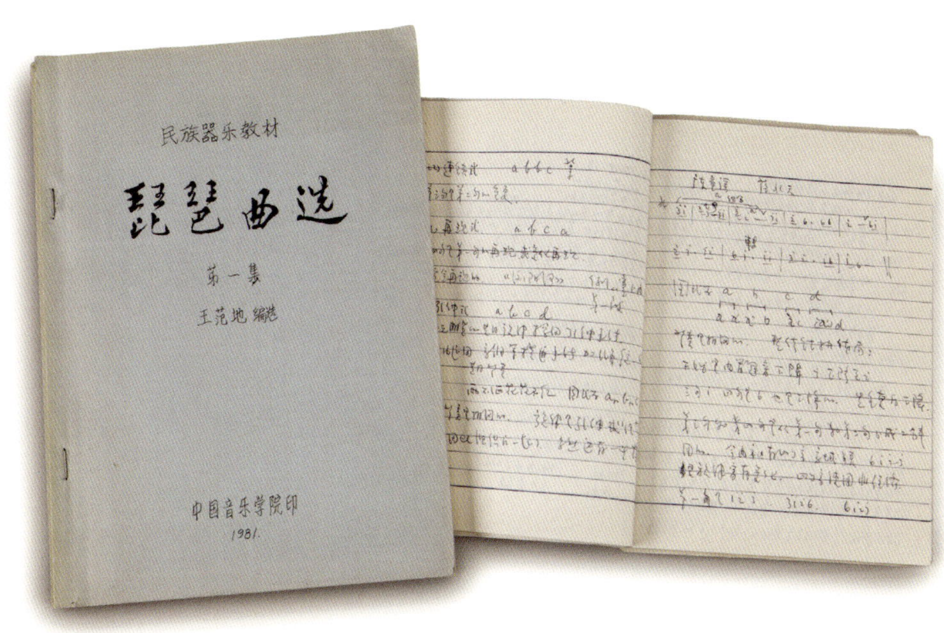

该手稿为王范地的学习笔记，记录了他在学习民族音乐时的相关知识要点。

王范地（1933—2017），宁波镇海人，中国资深琵琶演奏家、教育家、理论家，中国音乐学院教授、中国国际文化交流中心荣誉理事，中国音乐家协会会员。20 世纪 50 年代起，王范地就活跃于国内外舞台上，在 1957 年的第六届世界青年联欢节国际民间器乐比赛中荣获金质奖章。20 世纪 60 年代起，王范地开始从事琵琶专业教学和理论研究，培养了数百名琵琶演奏员和教师，他也是中国第一位琵琶硕士研究生的导师。他的教学和研究成果在国内外具有广泛的影响。

王范地集演奏、教学和理论研究于一身，曾创编《天山之春》《送我一支玫瑰花》《红色娘子军随想曲》等琵琶独奏曲，并对中国多种民族乐器有着深入的研究，在继承传统的基础上，对琵琶艺术的表演、创作、教学研究做出了贡献。

This manuscript is Wang Fandi's study notes, documenting key points of knowledge related to his study of ethnic Chinese music.

Wang Fandi (1933-2017), a native of Zhenhai, Ningbo, was a distinguished Chinese pipa player, educator, and theorist. He served as a professor at the China Conservatory of Music.

俞峰、俞极、俞潞使用过的钢琴

Piano Used by Yu Feng, Yu Ji, and Yu Lu

154.0 cm × 65.0 cm × 130.0 cm

俞峰、俞极、俞潞捐赠 Acquired from Yu Feng, Yu Ji, and Yu Lu through donation

俞峰，1964 年出生于宁波，中央音乐学院院长、教授、宁波交响乐团艺术指导兼首席指挥。2015 年底，宁波交响乐团成立，俞峰担任乐团艺术指导兼首席指挥，通过他在国际交响乐界的影响力和号召力，乐团多次与来自国内外知名音乐家合作演出，大幅提升了宁波交响乐团水平，为宁波交响乐团的建设发展起到了极大的推动作用。2017 年，俞峰文艺大师工作室成立，积极承担“音乐之城”建设重任，举办高端培训，开展大师公开课，培养城市音乐人才。2019 年，

指挥家俞峰使用过的指挥棒和指挥专用包

Conductor's Baton and Briefcase Owned by Conductor Yu Feng

①36.0 cm × 1.5 cm ②44.0 cm × 23.0 cm × 49.0 cm

俞峰捐赠 Acquired from Yu Feng through donation

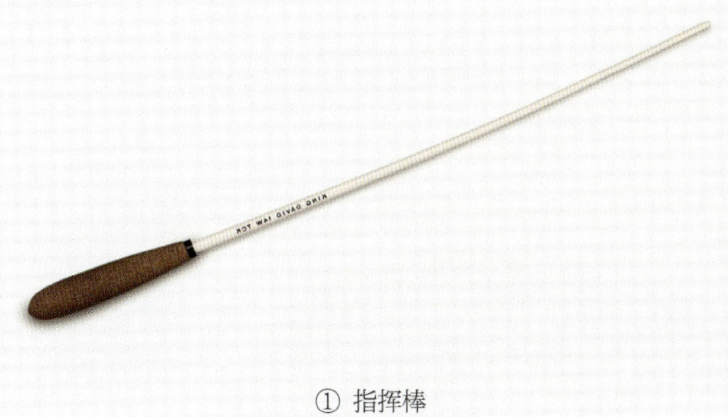

① 指挥棒

② 指挥专用包

俞峰被授予"宁波市荣誉市民"称号。

指挥棒和指挥专用包系俞峰在演出中使用，钢琴则陪伴俞峰度过了学习音乐的珍贵岁月，其子俞极、侄子俞潞都使用过。

Yu Feng, born in 1964 in Ningbo, is the President of the Central Conservatory of Music, as well as the artistic director and chief conductor of the Ningbo Symphony Orchestra. The conductor's baton and specially designed conductor's briefcase were used by Yu during performances, while the piano had been a constant companion throughout his years of studying music. His son Yu Ji and his nephew Yu Lu, also made use of the piano.

陈逸飞创作的《东方少女》雕塑和使用过的调色板

Chen Yifei's Sculpture *Eastern Girl* and Palette

① 180.0 cm × 90.0 cm × 308.0 cm　② 50.0 cm × 37.0 cm

陈逸飞家族捐赠 Acquired from the Chen Yifei Family through donation

① 雕塑

② 调色板

《东方少女》是宁波籍著名艺术家陈逸飞的作品，完成于 2000 年。在 2015 年陈逸飞逝世十周年之际，由陈逸飞夫人宋美英捐赠予宁波帮博物馆。

陈逸飞毕生追求美的事业，致力于大视觉、大美术理念的传播。他的作品不仅令西方世界体味到了恬淡而高雅的东方文化境界，更“曾以中国的美丽，感动过全世界”。

《东方少女》的创作灵感源自其夫人的鼓励，也得益于陈逸飞对东西方艺术的深入理解和独到阐释。作品中的少女手提鸟笼，轻摇折扇，从老上海的石库门弄堂款款走来，把浪漫与写实相融的创作风格，把中西艺术对美的合力阐释，分享给每一位正在欣赏她的人。

Eastern Girl is a sculpture by artist Chen Yifei, who hails from Ningbo. It was completed in the year 2000. A young girl is depicted holding a birdcage and delicately swaying a folding fan as she strolls through the lanes of old Shanghai. On the occasion of the tenth anniversary of Chen's passing in 2015, the painting was donated to Ningbobang Museum by the artist's wife, Song Meiying.

胡溧素描《外婆》

Grandmother by Hu Li

38.0 cm × 35.0 cm

李萍（胡溧夫人）捐赠 Acquired from Li Ping (Hu Li's wife) through donation

胡溧，祖籍宁波镇海，从小深受艺术的熏陶和启迪，上海大学美术学院油画系毕业后留校执教，后赴美留学获硕士学位，为威斯康星大学终身教授。胡溧被誉为“当代最有创造力和想象力的人物画家之一”，其巨幅油画《女娲留下的两只鸟》《南京大屠杀》在国际上久负盛名，彰显了强烈的爱国情感和深沉的艺术思想。

胡溧幼年跟随外婆在宁波生活，对家乡怀有深厚的感情。2014 年 10 月，胡溧将他在中国举办的第一个画展选址于家乡宁波。2016 年胡溧逝世后，夫人李萍将他创作的百余件油画作品捐赠给宁波，完成了他“把最好的作品留在家乡”的心愿。

Hu Li, originally from Ningbo's Zhenhai district, was passionate about art from a young age. After graduating from the oil painting department at Shanghai University's School of Fine Arts, he stayed on as a teacher. He later pursued further studies in the United States, earning a master's degree, and became a lifelong professor at the University of Wisconsin.

In his childhood, Hu Li lived with his grandmother in Ningbo, fostering a profound attachment to his hometown. After Hu Li's passing in 2016, his wife, Li Ping, generously donated over a hundred of his oil paintings to Ningbo.

潘公凯创作的《夏梦图》
Summer Dream by Pan Gongkai

2017 年

514.0 cm × 96.0 cm

潘公凯捐赠 Acquired from Pan Gongkai through donation

潘公凯出生于宁波宁海，是国画大师潘天寿之子。曾先后担任中国美术学院、中央美术学院院长 18 年，积极推进学科结构科学化、理念国际化，为中国美术教育的当代转型做出了重要贡献。

2016 年 11 月 2 日，由宁波帮博物馆和宁波大学共同主办的“跨界 · 实践——潘公凯水墨与建筑作品展”在宁波帮博物馆开幕。借在家乡办展的机会，潘公凯特为宁波帮博物馆创作了一幅水墨长卷《夏梦图》。该长卷以温情的夏日为背景，展现了画家对故乡荷塘景色的魂牵梦萦，寄托了游子对家乡深深的眷恋。

Pan Gongkai, born in Ninghai, Ningbo, is the son of Chinese painter Pan Tianshou. In 2016, Pan Gongkai created an ink wash painting titled *Summer Dream* for Ningbobang Museum. This painting depicts a lotus pond on a warm summer day, reflecting the artist's deep attachment to the beauty of his hometown.

（局部）

李爱维墨竹团扇面

Li Aiwei's Fan

直径 21.5 cm；折起 31 cm × 27 cm；展开 83 cm × 27 cm

李宜华捐赠 Acquired from Li Yihua through donation

李爱维（1932—　），小港李家坤房李祖熏之女，画家。初随陆抑非习画，后受教于林风眠。1958 年离沪去瑞士定居，在国外又问艺于张大千。

李爱维先后于欧洲、远东及美国多地举办超过 50 次展览，包括 1967 年于伦敦皇家美术院、1965 年于巴黎国际女性沙龙展及 1984 年于日内瓦植物博物馆等著名机构。其作品被巴黎塞鲁希尔美术馆永久典藏。日本广岛一佛寺为纪念 1945 年原子弹爆炸之受难者，选用李爱维绘画之竹树图案作为新建寺院之外墙装饰。

Li Aiwei (b.1932), is a painter born into the Li family of Xiaogang, Ningbo. In 1958, she left Shanghai and settled down in Switzerland, where she studied art under Zhang Daqian.

Li has held over 50 exhibitions around the world, including such prestigious institutions as the Royal Academy of Art in London in 1967, the Salon International de la Femme in Paris in 1965, and the Botanical Museum in Geneva in 1984. Her works are permanently housed in the Musee Cernuschi in Paris. In recent times, Li was commissioned to compose a painting of bamboo trees to adorn the exterior of a new temple in Hiroshima, Japan, a temple was constructed as a memorial to the victims of the atomic bombings in 1945.

郑介初使用过的收藏工具一组

Tools Used by Renowned Collector Zheng Jiechu

一套多件

郑介初捐赠 Acquired from Zheng Jiechu through donation

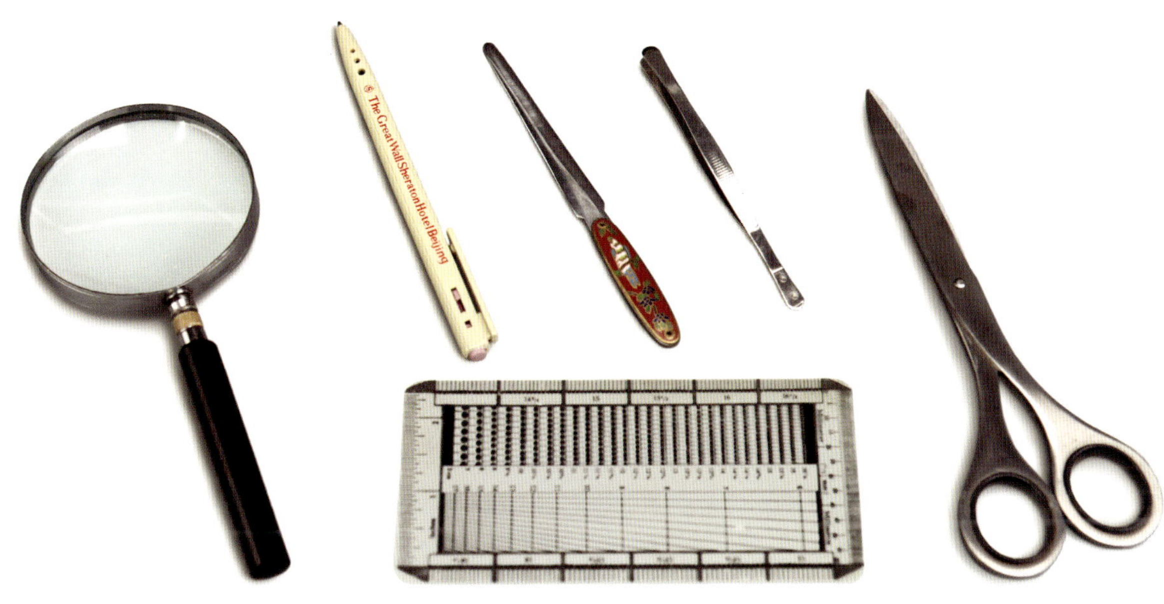

该套用具为香港收藏家郑介初的日用品。郑介初，笔名哲夫，生于 1930 年，祖籍宁波镇海。

20 世纪 90 年代初，郑介初偶然发现了一张绘制 1862 年宁波旧影的铜版画，自此开始了对相关宁波文史资料的收藏，并向宁波的多家博物馆无偿捐赠文物。郑介初毕生致力于收集遗散在海外的中国邮品、老照片和近代文献，向国内多个城市的博物馆多次捐献文物，先后编辑出版《宁波旧影》《厦门旧影》《武汉旧影》《青岛旧影》等，为保护、传播民族文化做出了贡献。

This set of items belonged to Hong Kong collector Zheng Jiechu. Zheng, born in 1930, has ancestral roots in Zhenhai, Ningbo.

In the early 1990s, Zheng stumbled upon a copperplate print from 1862 depicting Ningbo's cityscape. It sparked his passion for collecting historical materials about the city. He generously donated these artifacts to various museums in Ningbo. Throughout his life, Zheng dedicated himself to gathering Chinese philatelic items, old photographs, and historical documents from all over the world.

上海千顷堂书局出版的《中西汇通医经精义》

Essence of Integrated Chinese and Western Medical Classics Published by the Shanghai Qianqingtang Publishing House

1908 年

17.5 cm × 11.5 cm

谢文一捐赠 Acquired from Xie Wenyi through donation

上海千顷堂书局创办于 1883 年，不但是中国近代历史上最早创办的民营出版机构之一，而且是最早专业出版中医药及医学类书籍的出版机构之一。民国时期，在负责人谢祖芳的大力推动下，千顷堂书局把中医药以及医学类书籍作为出版重点，出版如《金匮要略心典》《本草问答》《近世内科国药处方集》等图书多达 17 类 500 余种，积极传播中医药文化。

1908 年，上海千顷堂书局出版发行了“中西汇通医书”系列，包括《中西汇通医经精义》《本草问答》《伤寒论浅注补正》《金匮要略浅注补正》等。

Established in 1883, the Shanghai Qianqingtang Publishing House stood out as one of the earliest private publishing houses in modern Chinese history and was among the pioneer specialists in the publication of traditional Chinese medicine and medical science texts. During the Republican era, the publishing house, under the dynamic leadership of Xie Zufang, dedicated itself to the dissemination of traditional Chinese medicine and medical sciences. It released over 500 titles in traditional Chinese medicine, spanning 17 distinct categories, including works like *Essentials of the Golden Chamber, Questions and Answers on Herbal Medicine*, and *Collection of National Medicine Prescriptions for Modern Internal Medicine*. In doing so, Qianqingtang played a crucial role in promoting the rich heritage of traditional Chinese medicine.

In 1908, Qianqingtang published the *Chinese and Western Integrated Medical* books series, including *Essence of Integrated Chinese and Western Medical Classics, Questions and Answers on Herbal Medicine, Simple Annotations and Corrections to Treatise on Febrile Diseases*, and *Simple Annotations and Corrections to Essentials of the Golden Chambei* etc.

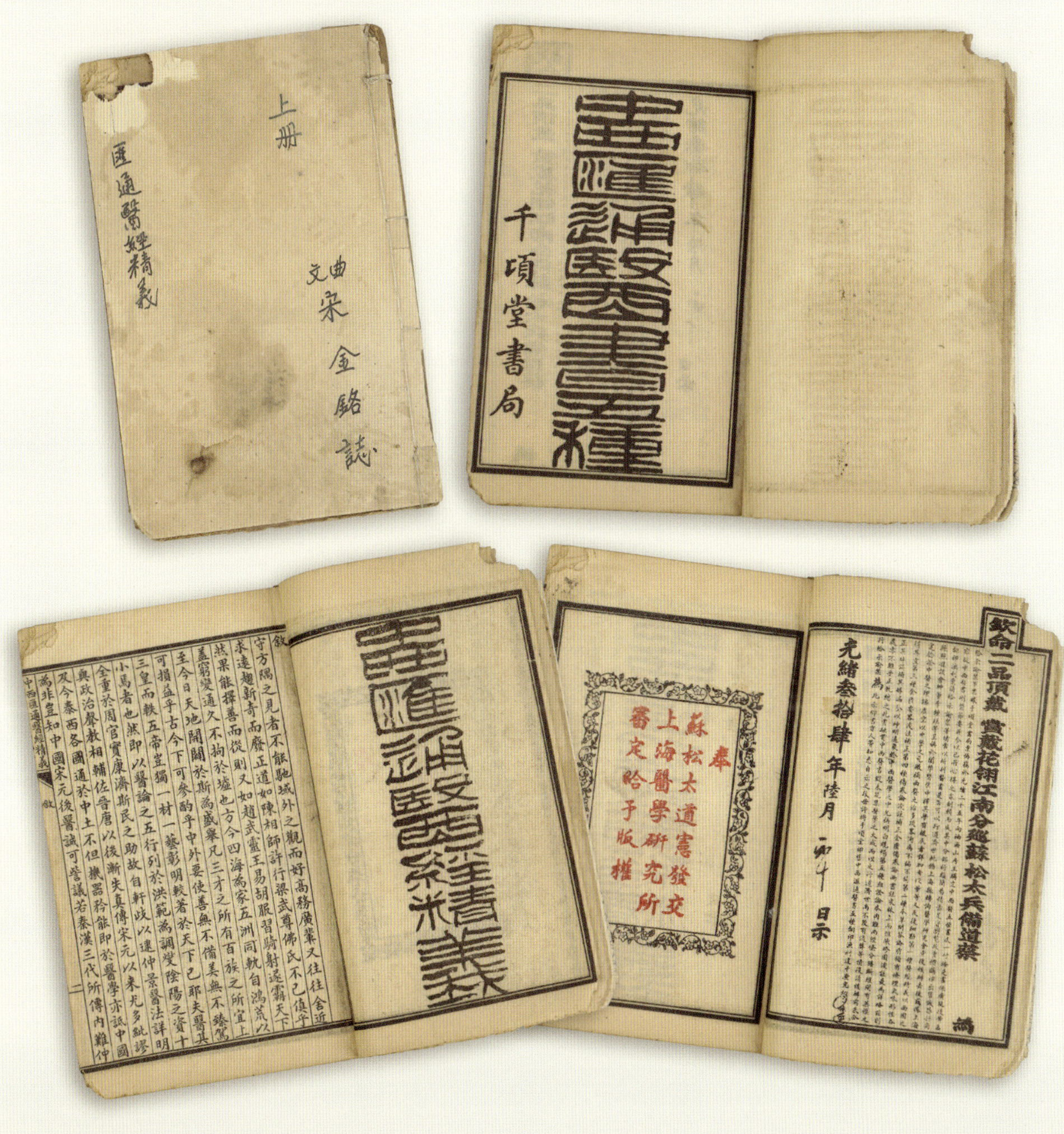

宁波帮博物馆实物、史料征集方案

宁波帮是一个与时偕行的群体，在各领域为民族、国家乃至世界做出了重要贡献。宁波帮博物馆是收藏、研究、展示、传播宁波帮历史与人文的公共文化服务机构，秉持全天下宁波人“情感地标、精神家园”的理念，长期向社会各界征集相关实物史料，征集范围包括但不局限于以下方向：

1. 反映宁波帮各个历史时期在不同地域、行业发展特点和杰出贡献的实物、史料；

2. 反映宁波帮先驱及代表人物、宁波帮家族，以及教育、文化等各领域甬籍知名专家成长历程、事业成就和社会贡献的实物、史料；

3. 反映宁波帮人士（家族）社会地位及社会交往的名家书画、艺术品，宁波帮人士个人收藏系列等；

4. 反映宁波籍科学家成长历程、学术成就、社会贡献等方面的代表性实物、资料；

5. 反映宁波市荣誉市民个人成就、社会地位，以及对宁波突出贡献的代表性实物、史料；

6. 与宁波帮历史文化以及各领域杰出宁波帮人士相关的代表性实物、史料。

征集方式以捐赠为主，辅以征购、复制。诚挚欢迎社会各界的联络支持，如有意向请联系：

浙江省宁波市镇海区思源路 255 号
宁波帮博物馆 典藏研究部 丁悠初
邮编：315201
电话：+86-574-56800632
邮箱：nbbbwg@163.net

NINGBOBANG MUSEUM
MATERIALS OBJECTS AND HISTORICAL MATERIALS COLLECTING SCHEME

The Ningbobang is a group that keeps up with the times and has made important contributions to the world in various fields. Ningbobang Museum is a public cultural service institution that collects, studies, displays, and disseminates the history and culture of the group. The museum has been collecting relevant material objects and historical materials from various sectors of society for a long time, including but not limited to the following areas:

1. Material objects and historical materials illustrating the evolving traits and remarkable contributions of the Ningbobang across various eras, regions, and sectors;

2. Material objects and historical materials showcasing the life, achievements, and social contributions of iconic figures/families of the Ningbobang, and eminent individuals in education, culture, and other domains;

3. Calligraphy works, art pieces, and the personal collection series reflecting the social status and interactions of the Ningbobang individuals or families;

4. Material objects and historical materials showcasing the life, achievements, and social contributions of Ningbo scientists;

5. Material objects and historical materials evidencing the achievements and social stature of Ningbo's honorary citizens and their distinguished contributions to Ningbo;

6. Material objects and historical materials associated with the historical culture and prominent figures of the Ningbobang.

Collection of materials is mainly done via donation, supplemented by procurement and replication. If you are interested in donating or providing relevant information, please contact:

Ding Youchu, Department of Collection and Research, Ningbobang Museum
255 Siyuan Road, Zhenhai District, Ningbo City, Zhejiang Province, China
Postal Code: 315201
Tel: +86-574-56800632
Email: nbbbwg@163.net

图书在版编目（CIP）数据

拾珍：藏品里的宁波帮 / 宁波博物院（宁波帮博物馆）编. -- 宁波：宁波出版社，2023.12
ISBN 978-7-5526-5196-6

Ⅰ.①拾… Ⅱ.①宁… Ⅲ.①博物馆－文物－介绍－宁波 Ⅳ.①K872.553

中国国家版本馆CIP数据核字（2023）第233117号

SHIZHEN CANGPIN LI DE NINGBOBANG

拾珍 藏品里的宁波帮

宁波博物院（宁波帮博物馆）编

出版发行 宁波出版社
宁波市甬江大道1号宁波书城8号楼6楼 315040
编辑部电话 0574-88396290
责任编辑 俞 琦 陈姣姣
责任校对 虞姬颖
责任印制 陈 钰
装帧设计 马 力
开 本 889mm×1194mm 1/16
印 张 15.5
字 数 500千
印 刷 浙江新华数码印务有限公司
版 次 2023年12月第1版
印 次 2023年12月第1次印刷
标准书号 ISBN 978-7-5526-5196-6
定 价 280.00元